A QUESTION OF SPORT
QUIZ BOOK

David Gymer and David Ball

Foreword by
Sue Barker

With special thanks to the *A Question of Sport* production team.
Gareth JM Edwards (Series Producer). Kieron Collins (Executive Producer).

1 3 5 7 9 10 8 6 4 2

Published in 2011 by BBC Books, an imprint of Ebury Publishing
A Random House Group company

Main text by David Gymer and David Ball
Copyright © Woodlands Books Ltd 2011

The Random House Group Limited Reg. 954009

Addresses for companies within the Random House Group can be found
at www.randomhouse.co.uk

A CIP catalogue record for this book is available from the British Library

ISBN 978 1 84 9903257

The Random House Group Limited supports the Forest Stewardship Council (FSC®),
the leading international forest certification organisation. Our books carrying the FSC
label are printed on FSC® certified paper. FSC is the only forest certification scheme
endorsed by the leading environmental organisations, including Greenpeace. Our paper
procurement policy can be found at www.randomhouse.co.uk/environment

Commissioning editor: Albert DePetrillo
In-house editor: Joe Cottington
Project editor: Steve Tribe
Production: Phil Spencer

Printed and bound by CPI Group (UK) Ltd, Croydon, CR0 4YY

To buy books by your favourite authors and register for offers,
visit www.randomhouse.co.uk

Contents

Foreword by

Sue Barker

I've been lucky enough to do many wonderful things during my career so far, but one of the things I am most proud of is *A Question of Sport*. First and foremost, just like you, I am a fan of the show. The programme has been a mainstay of BBC Television since 1970, meaning that many of us have grown up with it and we all have a special bond and relationship with QS. The fact that I have been able to be involved in the show, first as a viewer, then as a guest, and finally as the presenter has – for me – been nothing short of an honour.

Before you get down to the serious business of tackling the thousands of sporting teasers that lie ahead, I thought I should give you a bit of background on my relationship with the longest-running sports quiz in the world. I began my QS journey in quite bizarre circumstances that I'm sure not too many other people can say. It was in the early 1980s, and I was dressed in a life-size costume of a skunk or a chipmunk or some sort of rodent for the Mystery Guest round. Quite what I was meant to be doing at Earl's Court that day I'm not entirely sure. Anyway, suffice to say I was pretty well hidden and when the video ended the contestants back in the studio all seemed to have blank faces. Willie Carson's team had the first opportunity to guess and they plumped for the Middleweight Champion boxer Alan Minter. Bill Beaumont's team didn't do much better when Trevor Francis guessed it was England goalkeeper Ray Clemence. Bearing in mind that both these sportsMEN are well over six feet tall, I wasn't exactly flattered!

My next appearance on the show was slightly more conventional, as Gareth Edwards and I sat alongside captain Emlyn Hughes as we took on Bill Beaumont's team. I can remember being extremely nervous, especially for the Home or Away round. I can totally empathise with the guests these days, as you never want to get your own home question wrong. The rules of the show then, as they are now, are very strict and absolutely no one has any idea of the questions they are going to be asked, so the spotlight is well and truly on. Thankfully I got my question right that day – well, at least that's my story and I'm sticking to it.

In 1996, I was contacted by the legendary David Coleman – an institution on *A Question of Sport* since the mid 1970s – and he asked me personally if I would be interested in taking on the role as questionmaster. Naturally, my initial reaction was to jump at it, but at the same time I was filled with dread as it is a daunting task to follow such a broadcasting great. How could anybody fill those shoes? Nevertheless I took over with John Parrott and Ally McCoist in the captains' chairs and, some 450 episodes later, I am still here and enjoying it as much as, if not more than, ever. As well as JP and Ally, I have had my work cut out trying to control Frankie Dettori during his spell as a captain, and now I have the immense pleasure of keeping order as Matt Dawson and Phil Tufnell run riot. We all have such fun making the programme, but at the end of the day you can't take the competitive spirit out of the captains who, despite all the joking and banter, really want to win.

Over the years, I have been privileged to have the best seat in the house as *A Question of Sport* has welcomed some of the great names from the world of sport onto the panel. In my other job as a BBC Sports presenter, I have been fortunate to work alongside legends such as Michael Johnson, John McEnroe and Steve Redgrave, but it is still a thrill for me to get the opportunity to quiz some great names from other sports. There have been so many fantastic names to join us on the show, the majority of whom feature throughout this book, but a couple of personal highlights for me include Seve Ballesteros, a wonderful golfer and a great man who sadly passed away in 2011, and Mark Spitz, whose exploits at the 1972 Olympics were inspirational to any budding sporting youngster at the time.

Quizzing, and *A Question of Sport* in particular, is very much a sport in its own right. There are tactics, the ability to cope under pressure, teamwork and individual brilliance. The highs and lows of success and failure are present in the QS studio just as they would be at Wembley, Lord's or Wimbledon. I have seen great internationals look crestfallen as they make a mistake, and also the elation when they manage to get the answer to a really tricky question right. I can vividly remember Sam Torrance struggling over this question: 'Which American golfer won two Majors during the 1990s but never played in the Ryder Cup?' Now, Sam is a Ryder Cup legend in his own right and his knowledge of the event is verging on encyclopaedic. So every name that Ally McCoist put forward as a potential answer was knocked back by Sam with a 'no, he played in the Ryder Cup.' After many minutes of genuine pain and anguish, suddenly Sam yelled out, 'Daly, John Daly!' The expression on his face was nothing short of euphoric and rivalled his pleasure in sinking the winning putt at the Belfry in 1985. It was a magical moment, one of hundreds that I have been delighted to witness in the studio.

Everyone has their personal favourite round on *A Question of Sport* and, whether that is Mystery Guest, Home or Away or What Happened Next, this book covers all of them and more. When I travel up to Manchester to record QS, I always spend time with the production team before the show going through the questions and I play along myself with all the rounds as I test myself, but I won't say how well or badly I get on. My personal favourite is the One Minute Round as I love the time pressure and particularly enjoy trying to guess the names of the sports people who share their names with a type of hat, facial hair or sea creature. How else would we have ever heard of the fantastic names of Larry Fedora, Johnny Moustache and

Prince Octopus Dzanie? That round for me sums up everything that is great about *A Question of Sport* – a fantastic mixture of sporting facts and knowledge coupled with a lot of fun and laughter. Just like playing any sport, everyone wants to win but equally important is enjoying taking part and making some wonderful friends along the way.

Good luck with all the questions and challenges that lie ahead over the next 500 or so pages. I have tried my hand at a number of them and mark my words, it is a lot easier when you have the answers in front of you.

Game 1

On this episode of A Question of Sport are...

Michael Owen (Football)
First appeared on the show as a guest in 1998

Sean Fitzpatrick (Rugby Union)
First appeared on the show as a guest in 2005

Mark Ramprakash (Cricket)
First appeared on the show as a guest in 1991

Kelly Holmes (Track athletics)
First appeared on the show as a guest in 1994

The first ever episode of *A Question of Sport* was aired on 5 January 1970 with David Vine hosting the show. The captains were Henry Cooper and Cliff Morgan and the guests were George Best, Ray Illingworth, Lillian Board and Tom Finney.

Round 1 – Opening Rally

1. Name the 12 playing members of Europe's Ryder Cup winning team in 2010.

Round 2 – One Minute Round

1. Who captained India to victory in the 2011 Cricket World Cup final win over Sri Lanka?

2. In which sport did Stephanie Cook win Olympic gold for Britain in 2000?

3. On which day is the King George VI horse race traditionally run every year?

4. Of which Olympic sport is this an anagram? HOT CANDLE

5. David Boon scored 21 Test centuries for Australia before captaining which English county?

6. In which sport have competitors included the Dump Truck and Typhoon?

7. Which darts player is nicknamed Hawaii 501?

These sports stars all share their surnames with natural water features.

8. Tony _____ (Rallying)

9. Johan _____ (Tennis)

10. Zinzan _____ (Rugby Union)

Round 3 – Mystery Guest

1. I was born in 1981 and first tried my chosen sport at the age of three (4 points)

    Although I am claustrophobic I spend a lot of time sitting in a confined space (3 points)

    In 2005 I became my sport's youngest ever World Champion (2 points)

    I was the first Spaniard to win the World Championship in my sport (1 point)

2. I was a National Junior under 18s Champion at the age of 13 (4 points)

    In 1988 I won an Olympic gold medal but this was only a small part of my successes that year (3 points)

    I married another star from my sport and we have both won at Wimbledon (2 points)

    I partnered Gabriela Sabatini in four Grand Slam Women's Doubles finals winning one at Wimbledon (1 point)

Round 4 – Home or Away

1. *Michael Owen.* Who became the first Englishman to score in the three successive World Cup finals when he scored against Ecuador in 2006?

2. *Sean Fitzpatrick.* Who in 1980 played in England's Grand Slam

winning team and 23 years later coached them as they won the World Cup?

3. *Mark Ramprakash.* Who by scoring 221 at Lord's in 2004 posted England's highest individual Test score since Graham Gooch's triple century in 1990?

4. *Kelly Holmes.* Which athlete competed in her sixth Olympic Games in Beijing having won 800m gold in 2000 and a bronze in 1996?

Round 5 – Captain's Away

1. In which sport do women contest the Curtis Cup every two years?

2. Which famous race was first run in 1903 and was won by Maurice Garin?

3. Name the two countries beginning with the letter S that hosted a Formula One Grand Prix in 2010?

4. In which sport is the Doggett's Coat and Badge awarded?
   a) Modern Pentathlon
   b) Rowing
   c) Handball

Round 6 – What Happened Next

1. Spartak Moscow are playing FC Saturn in the Russian League and Spartak Moscow are awarded a penalty and their striker Alex steps up to take the kick, what happened next?
   a) As Spartak striker Alex takes the penalty his boot comes off and the goalkeeper saves the boot but the ball goes in.
   b) A fan runs onto the pitch and scores the penalty before

Alex can take it.

    c) Alex takes the penalty and the ball hits both posts, then the keeper, and deflects into the goal.

4. Boxers Cello Renda and Paul Samuels are in the middle of a Middleweight bout at the Fenton Manor Sports Complex in Staffordshire in 2009, what happened next?
    a) Whilst separating the boxers, the referee Tony O'Connor slips on the canvas and knocks over Samuels.
    b) Renda and Samuels hit each other at the same time and knock each other out.
    c) Renda ducks a right hook from Samuels which causes Samuels to fall through the ropes and onto the floor below.

Round 7 – On the Buzzer

This buzzer round is all about Australia.

1. Which scrum half won 139 caps for Australia between 1994 and 2007 to become Rugby Union's most capped player?

2. Who became the first football player to score for Australia at the World Cup when he scored against Japan in 2006?

3. Which famous horse race is held at Flemington Park every year in November and was won three times in a row by Makybe Diva in the 2000s?

4. In 1990 which BBC commentator became only the second ever Australian to win the USPGA Championship?

5. In 1975 which Australian snooker player lost his third World Championship final having previously finished runner up in 1968 and 1973?

6. Which Australian Formula One driver won the World Championship in 1980?

7. Which city was the first to host the Summer Olympics in Australia?

8. In which motor sport did Australian Jason Crump become a World Champion for the third time in 2009?

9. Who replaced Ricky Ponting as the Test captain of Australia in 2011 following the Cricket World Cup?

10. In which sport did Tony David become the first Australian World Champion by defeating Mervyn King in the final?

11. Which Australian rider won the 500cc World Championship in five consecutive years between 1994 and 1998?

12. Which country beat Australia 34 – 20 in the 2008 Rugby League World Cup final?

13. Which sport do the Geelong Cats, the St Kilda Saints and the Sydney Swans play?

14. In 2000 which female athlete won the Olympic 400m on home soil in Sydney?

15. Which Australian played in two Champions League finals with Liverpool in the 2000s?

16. In which sport did Australian Anna Meares win three World Championship gold medals in 2011?

17. Who defeated Andy Murray in the Men's Singles final at the Australian Open in 2011 to win his second Grand Slam title?

18. In which field event did Steve Hooker win Olympic gold for Australia in Beijing?

19. Which Australian won three gold and two silver medals at the Sydney Olympics to become the most successful swimmer at the Games?

20. In which sport did Australian Stephanie Gilmore win four successive World Championships between 2007 and 2010?

Game 2

On this episode of A Question of Sport are…

John Terry (Football)
First appeared on the show as a guest in 2005

Will Carling (Rugby Union)
First appeared on the show as a guest in 1988

Sean Kerly (Field Hockey)
First appeared on the show as a guest in 1986

Jessica Ennis (Track and field athletics)
First appeared on the show as a guest in 2008

Round 1 – Opening Rally

1. Name the first 10 bowlers to take 400 wickets in Test cricket.

Round 2 – One Minute Round

1. For which country did British born Fiona May win a World Championship Long Jump title?

2. In which sport do the winners of a major final receive the Vince Lombardi Trophy?

3. Which jockey's name is this an anagram of? BURLY WASH

4. Who scored both goals for AC Milan as they beat Liverpool in the 2007 Champions League Cup final?

5. In which sport did 'the Albatross' Michael Gross win Olympic, World and European gold medals?

6. In which position did Matt Dawson play for England in the 2003 World Cup final?

7. Which British tennis player won her only tennis Grand Slam at the French Open in 1976?

These sports stars all share their surnames with jobs.

8. Dennis _____ (Snooker)

9. Roger _____ (Football)

10. Wendell _____ (Rugby League)

Round 3 – Mystery Guest

1. I competed for Great Britain at the Olympics and Wales at the Commonwealth Games (4 points)

    I was born in 1967 and retired in 2003 but unfortunately I never fulfilled my ambition of winning Olympic gold (3 points)

    I faced many hurdles in my career but I overcame them to win World Championship gold and become a world record holder (2 points)

    I am now a sports pundit on television and starred on Strictly Come Dancing (1 point)

2. My father was an Australian Rules Footballer and I played the sport myself (4 points)

    In 2002 I became only the 4th man in my sport to be ranked number one in the world for every week in the calendar year (3 points)

    In 2001 I won the US Open the year before I conquered Wimbledon (2 points)

    I won the Davis Cup with Australia in 1999 and 2003 (1 point)

Round 4 – Home or Away

1. *John Terry.* Who left Manchester United in 2008 and the following year won the Champions League with Barcelona?

2. *Will Carling.* Which English forward toured with the British and Irish Lions in 1997 and 2005 but didn't make his Test debut for the team until his third tour in 2009?

3. *Sean Kerly.* In 2009 England won the European Men's Hockey Championship by beating the Olympic Champions – who are they?

4. *Jessica Ennis.* Which Olympic Champion is the only Heptathlete to win the World Championships on three successive occasions?

Round 5 – Captain's Away

1. Dating back to 1839 the Grand Challenge Cup is the oldest of all races at which annual event?

2. At the 2011 US Masters which country had three of their golfers finish in the top 6?

3. Name the two Rugby League teams that won the Challenge Cup in the 2000s whose names begin with the letter W?

4. Which of the following is the only driver to win the Formula One World Title, the Indianapolis 500 and Le Mans?
    a) Jackie Ickx
    b) Graham Hill
    c) Jackie Stewart

Round 6 – Great Sporting Moments

1. With seconds left of the 1968 Challenge Cup Ken Hirst slid through the muddy turf and brought Wakefield to within one point of Leeds' score. All it needed now was for one of the best kickers in Rugby League to send the conversion through the posts to win the game. Who famously missed the kick?

2. The semi-final had got off to a clean start and the British athlete was running smoothly until, 150m into the race, he heard a pop

and pulled up injured and saw Steve Lewis cruise into the 400m Olympic final. From the stands his father Jim ran onto the track and helped him across the line in tears to sympathetic applause from the crowd. Which British athlete's Olympic experience in 1992 ended this way?

Round 7 – On the Buzzer

Every question in this buzzer round is about the year 1997.

1. On which day of the week did Lord Gyllene win the Grand National at Aintree?

2. Captained by Matthew Maynard which cricket team won their first County Championship since 1949?

3. Which American won the World Championship 110m hurdles final to retain his title?

4. Which team reached the finals of the FA Cup and the League Cup yet were still relegated from the Premier League?

5. Britain's Herbie Hide and Henry Akinwande both held versions of boxing World Titles during 1997, but at which weight?

6. Who became the first Canadian to win the Formula One World Championship?

7. In which sport did Jansher Khan win a sixth successive British Open beating Peter Nicol in the final?

8. Which biennial competition was staged at Valderrama in October?

9. Which Australian beat Greg Rusedski in the US Open final?

10. Which famous BBC commentator retired after his 50th Grand National?

11. In which sport did Britain's James Hickman earn a gold medal in a World Championship in Gothenburg?

12. Who hit a five minutes and 20 seconds 147 maximum break at the Crucible Theatre?

13. Which club retained the Rugby League Challenge Cup by beating the Bradford Bulls for a second successive season?

14. Wilson Kipketer broke a Briton's world record and retained his World Championship Title in which event?

15. Which French club beat Leicester Tigers to lift the Heineken Cup for the first time?

16. At the age of 44 which Essex and England batsman retired from county cricket?

17. Who was the 'Swiss Miss' who won three of the tennis Grand Slam Singles Titles in 1997?

18. With which team did Scotland's Paul Lambert win the Champions League by beating Juventus in the final?

19. Which American golfer won his first Major by triumphing at the US Masters by 12 shots?

20. Which Cuban won his second high jump World Championship gold medal four years after winning his first?

Game 3

On this episode of A Question of Sport are...

Ally McCoist (Football)
First appeared on the show as a guest in 1988

Gavin Henson (Rugby Union)
First appeared on the show as a guest in 2005

Annabel Croft (Tennis)
First appeared on the show as a guest in 1985

Luke Donald (Golf)
First appeared on the show as a guest in 2005

David Vine was the first host of *A Question of Sport* and took charge of the programme for the first five series.

Round 1 – Opening Rally

1. Other than goalkeeper Peter Shilton name the 10 players that started the 1990 Football World Cup semi-final for England.

Round 2 – One Minute Round

1. Which Spaniard won the World Matchplay Championship at Wentworth on four occasions in the 1980s?

2. In which athletics event did Françoise Mbango Etone win Cameroon's only gold medal of the 2008 Summer Olympics?

3. Which racecourse hosts the Scottish Grand National every year?

4. Which British Olympian is this an anagram of? A SLIM GEM

5. In which city has Snooker's World Championships been held since 1977?

6. Which Scottish Football League team play their home games at the Tynecastle Stadium?

7. Which team won the 2011 University Boat Race?

These sports stars all share their surnames with jobs.

8. Jason _____ (Athletics)

9. Michael _____ (Snooker)

10. Alastair _____ (Cricket)

Round 3 – Mystery Guest

1. I was born in September 1961 in Pittsburgh and played for my team from 1983 until 1999 (4 points)

   I was the first rookie to start as a quarterback in the Superbowl (3 points)

   I was the first quarterback to reach 60,000 passing yards in a career, a feat which was surpassed by Brett Favre (2 points)

   In 2005 I was inducted into the American Football Hall of Fame for my career with the Miami Dolphins (1 point)

2. Although I was born in Europe I represented the USA throughout my career (4 points)

   I am a product of Stanford University and my brother was also a tennis player (3 points)

   Between 1978 and 1984 I partnered Peter Fleming to 10 Grand Slam Doubles finals (2 points)

   As a professional I won the Wimbledon Men's Singles Title on three occasions although I didn't always endear myself to umpires or my opponents (1 point)

Round 4 – Home or Away

1. *Ally McCoist.* Which England midfielder won League Championships with Everton, Rangers and Marseilles between 1984 and 1996?

2. *Gavin Henson.* In 2007 which South African equalled Jonah Lomu's record of scoring 8 tries in a World Cup?

3. *Annabel Croft.* Who in 2008 became the first British player to win a Junior Title at Wimbledon in 24 years?

4. *Luke Donald.* Who narrowly missed out on his sixth Open Championship win by losing in a playoff to Stewart Cink in 2009?

Round 5 – Captain's Away

1. In which sport might you high five a setter after a successful smash?

2. David Weir of Great Britain won which race for an unprecedented fifth time in April 2011?

3. Name the two Scotsmen who held a version of the World Lightweight Title in the 1970s?

4. Who is the only man to win a Formula One World Championship and a World Motor Cycling World Title?
    a) Mike Hailwood
    b) Jim Clark
    c) John Surtees

Round 6 – What Happened Next

1. Golfer Andrew McLardy is in action at the Houston Open and is on the 17th tee, what happened next?
    a) As McLardy starts his backswing, he is put off by a car alarm and completely misses the ball.
    b) McLardy hits his drive left of the fairway and it flies straight into a litter bin.

c) McLardy loses grip of his club after hitting his tee shot, and his ball flies away behind him and lands amongst the watching spectators.

2. Melaine Walker has just won the 400m Hurdles at the 2009 World Championships in Berlin. The tournament mascot Berlino the Bear is helping her celebrate and gives her a piggy back but what happened next?
   a) Walker's shorts rip and an official takes her flag from her to cover her modesty.
   b) The mascot keeps running and interrupts the Women's Discus final that is currently taking place.
   c) The mascot runs straight into some stacked hurdles and he ends up on his back dropping Walker in the process.

Round 7 – On the Buzzer

All the answers to this buzzer round begin with the letter A, in the case of a person it's the surname that must start with that letter.

1. Who captained the USA at the 2008 Ryder Cup, 17 years after winning the USPGA Championship?

2. Which country won the Netball World Championship three times during the 1990s?

3. Which country finished third at the 2007 Rugby Union World Cup beating France in the 3rd place playoff?

4. Which English team beat Bayern Munich 1-0 in the 1982 European Cup final?

5. At which racecourse did Frankie Dettori win all seven races in the same day in 1996?

6. Which Darts player won his second BDO World Championship by beating Dave Chisnall in 2010?

7. Who took over from Andy Robinson as the England Rugby Union coach in 2006?

8. Which American city is home to a Major League Baseball team called the Braves, an NBA team called the Hawks and an American Football team called the Falcons?

9. Which England player went 54 Test innings without being dismissed for a duck before Ben Hilfenhaus dismissed him at the Oval in 2009?

10. In which sport do the Richmond Tigers, West Coast Eagles and the Western Bulldogs compete?

11. How are the 11th, the 12th and the 13th holes at Augusta collectively known?

12. What nationality is three time Formula One World Champion Niki Lauda?

13. In which sport did Alberto Tomba win a gold medal at the Winter Olympics in 1992?

14. Who became the first American to win the Indianapolis 500 and the Formula One World Championship?

15. Which horse won the 2004 Grand National to give trainer Ginger McCain his fourth victory in the famous race?

16. Which British sailor won Olympic gold in the Finn Class at the 2008 games?

17. In which sport did England's Duncan Busby win two gold medals at the Commonwealth Games?

18. Which city hosted the first Summer Olympic Games and hosted the competition again 108 years later in 2004?

19. Which British boxer fought Lennox Lewis for the WBC Heavyweight Title in 1997?

20. In the 2000s which female skier won seven gold medals in the Giant Slalom at the British National Alpine Ski Championships?

Game 4

On this episode of A Question of Sport are...

Steven Gerrard (Football)
First appeared on the show as a guest in 2002

Ben Ainslie (Sailing)
First appeared on the show as a guest in 1997

George Foreman (Boxing)
First appeared on the show as a guest in 2004

Sally Gunnell (Track athletics)
First appeared on the show as a guest in 1989

Round 1 – Opening Rally

1. Name the first ten British Drivers to win the Formula One World Championship.

Round 2 – One Minute Round

1. Which Spanish football team play their home games at the Bernabeu?

2. Which famous race did Bjarne Riis win in 1996 and Jan Ullrich win in 1997?

3. Which country beat Cuba to win the gold medal in baseball at the 2008 Summer Olympics?

4. In which sport do women compete internationally for the Fed Cup?

5. Which English football club is this an anagram of? VITAL LOANS

6. In which event did Kelly Sotherton win an Olympic medal in Athens?

7. Which American city's NFL American Football team are called the Seahawks?

These sports stars all share their surnames with jobs.

8. Eunice _____ (Athletics)

9. Peter _____ (Golf)

10. Mark _____ (Cricket)

Round 3 – Mystery Guest

1. I was born in 1966 and won the British Amateur Championship at the age of 18 (4 points)

   I have famously partnered two of my compatriots in the Ryder Cup with great success (3 points)

   I became only the second Spaniard in history to win a Major when I won the US Masters Title in 1994, a feat I repeated again in 1999 (2 points)

   I was honoured to be named as Europe's captain for 2012 Ryder Cup (1 point)

2. I won for the first time in 1983 at the age of 19 as an amateur (4 points)

   My father and grandfather were trainers in Northern Ireland where I was born (3 points)

   Since retiring I have literally gone to the ends of the Earth as I have skied to the North Pole and trekked to the South Pole (2 points)

   I won the Grand National in 1986 and 1994 and I competed alongside Lilia Kopylova on Strictly Come Dancing (1 point)

Round 4 – Home or Away

1. *Steven Gerrard.* Who in 2007 became the first Reading player to win an England cap since Herbert Smith over 100 years before?

2. *Ben Ainslie.* In which class did Sarah Ayton, Sarah Webb and Pippa Wilson win Olympic gold for Great Britain in Beijing?

3. *George Foreman.* Which American born boxer retired undefeated in his 49 fights having held the World Heavyweight Title between 1952 and 1956?

4. *Sally Gunnell.* Between 2002 and 2007 which athlete won the Women's 400m hurdles at both the World Championships and the Commonwealth Games on two occasions?

Round 5 – Captain's Away

1. Which country did England cricket coach Duncan Fletcher once captain?

2. Which modern day Olympic event did the Greek legend of Pheidippides inspire?

3. Name the two horses that won the Cheltenham Gold Cup in the 2000s whose names begin with the letter K?

4. Which Welshman was Cliff Thorburn playing when he scored his maximum 147 break at the 1983 World Championships?
   a) Doug Mountjoy
   b) Ray Reardon
   c) Terry Griffiths

Round 6 – Great Sporting Moments

1. At the age of 32 the courageous jockey had conquered everything life had thrown at him. Less than two years earlier he had been diagnosed with testicular cancer but now he found

himself leading the Grand National at Aintree. After jumping the final fence his horse Aldaniti made a dash for the finishing line. Which Grand National winning jockey is this?

2. Sensing the chance to emulate the great Jesse Owens' Olympic achievement the American took the baton from Calvin Smith and sprinted for the line to win his 4th gold medal of the Games. Who completed his medal haul in the 100m relay?

Round 7 – On the Buzzer

Everything in this buzzer round took place in the year 2009.

1. Who scored four goals for Arsenal in their 4-4 draw with Liverpool at Anfield?

2. Which city staged the first Test of the 2009 Ashes series?

3. Which Irishman captained the British and Irish Lions in the their three Test tour of South Africa?

4. Who won the USPGA Championship to become the first Asian golfer to win a Major?

5. Which horse won the Cheltenham Gold Cup for the second time having previously won the race two years earlier?

6. Who at the 130th attempt won his first Formula One race by winning the German Grand Prix?

7. Which player beat Andy Murray in the Wimbledon Singles semi-final before losing to Roger Federer in the final?

8. In the World Athletics Championship in Berlin Greg Rutherford broke Chris Tomlinson's British Record in which event?

9. Who made the first defence of his World Super Middleweight Title by defeating Jermain Taylor?

10. Which Warrington Wolves player scored a drop goal in the Challenge Cup quarter-final, semi-final and the final itself?

11. In which sport did Britain's Gemma Spofforth win a World Championship gold medal?

12. Which horse did Michael Kinane ride to victory in the 2000 Guineas, the Epsom Derby and the Prix de l'Arc de Triomphe in 2009?

13. In 2009 which city was named as the hosts of the Summer Olympics in 2016?

14. In which sport did Sinead and John Kerr win a record 7th British Championship?

15. Which English golfer won the 2009 Race to Dubai?

16. Which England batsman scored a century on his debut for England at the Oval against Australia in 2009?

17. Which country won their first Grand Slam in the Six Nations Championship since 1948?

18. In which sport did Lizzie Armitstead, Joanna Rowsell and Wendy Houvenhagel win World Championship gold for Britain?

19. Who besides Lionel Messi scored for Barcelona in their 2-0 defeat of Manchester United in the 2009 Champions League final?

20. Who by winning a field event was the only man to win a gold medal for Britain at the 2009 World Championships?

Game 5

On this episode of A Question of Sport are...

Franz Klammer (Skiing)
First appeared on the show as a guest in 2002

Matthew Hoggard (Cricket)
First appeared on the show as a guest in 2004

Jim Courier (Tennis)
First appeared on the show as a guest in 2005

Rory Underwood (Rugby Union)
First appeared on the show as a guest in 1986

David Coleman chaired the programme in the 1970s, the 1980s and the 1990s. His final show as host of the programme was on 30 May 1997, having taken charge of the show over 350 times.

Round 1 – Opening Rally

1. Name the top 10 countries in the medal list for the 2008 Summer Olympics in Beijing.

Round 2 – One Minute Round

1. Which country hosted the 1999 Cricket World Cup?

2. With which sport do you associate with the Jules Rimet Trophy?

3. Born in Slovakia but representing Switzerland which tennis player won the Australian Open Ladies Singles Title?

4. Which Manchester United player is this an anagram of?
   CANINE ACTOR

5. In Olympic boxing which weight comes between Bantamweight and Lightweight?

6. Which Rugby League team played their 2011 home games at the Jungle?

7. How many players are there in a netball team?

These sports stars all share their surnames with flowers.

8. Dennis _____ (Football)

9. Justin _____ (Golf)

10. Dennis _____ (Cricket)

Round 3 – Mystery Guest

1. I was born in 1946 and won 32 caps for my country (4 points)

   I am now known as a coach having won League Titles in Italy and Spain (3 points)

   I succeeded Arrigo Sacchi as manager of AC Milan and helped them to four Serie A titles in the 1990s (2 points)

   I was appointed England manager in December 2007 (1 point)

2. I am considered by many to be the best player in modern times in my sport (4 points)

   I made my international debut in 1989 and am a true icon in my country (3 points)

   I made my first Test century at the age of 17 against England (2 points)

   I scored my 99th international century during the 2011 Cricket World Cup which my country went on to win (1 point)

Round 4 – Home or Away

1. *Franz Klammer.* At the 2010 Winter Olympics which American skier won gold, silver and bronze medals?

2. *Matthew Hoggard.* In the 1st innings of the 1st Test at Brisbane in November 2010 which England bowler recorded figures of 6 for 125 on his Ashes debut?

3. *Jim Courier.* By beating France which European country won the 2010 Davis Cup for the first time in their history?

4. *Rory Underwood.* Who scored England's only try in their 2007 World Cup semi-final win but missed the final due to injury?

Round 5 – Captain's Away

1. Against which club did John Arne Riise score a League Cup final goal in just 45 seconds in 2005?

2. Cumberland and Cornish are variations of which sport?

3. Name the two Irishman who won the Snooker World Championship between 1985 and 2011?

4. In which Olympic sport is the Val Barker trophy awarded?
   a) Boxing
   b) Field Hockey
   c) Water Polo

Round 6 – What Happened Next

1. During a game from the 3rd Division of Spanish football, what happened next?
   a) There is a tannoy announcement telling supporters of a car break-in in the car park. The car belongs to the referee who temporarily halts the game to go and assess the damage.
   b) A swarm of bees surrounds the players and the referee is forced to halt the game whilst the players take cover.
   c) The ball is kicked over the stand but as it's the last ball his teammate who is warming up as a substitute on the sideline is forced to leave the stadium to go and find the ball.

4. The 2009 125cc Grand Prix from Catalunya is in its closing stages, what happened next?
    a) Leader Julian Simon turns his head to see where his rival Andrea Lannone is and loses his balance, resulting in him crashing out.
    b) Julian Simon crosses the finish line and starts celebrating even though there is still one lap to go, costing him first place.
    c) A flock of birds lands on the track and both riders fall whilst trying to slalom their way through them.

Round 7 – On the Buzzer

This buzzer round is all about the south of England.

1. Which club ended Spurs' Champions League campaign in 2011 by defeating them 5-0 on aggregate?

2. Which Somerset player opened England's batting in the 2005 Ashes?

3. Born in Hammersmith which boxer fought Tim Witherspoon and Oliver McCall in World Heavyweight Title fights?

4. Which circuit has staged the British Formula One Grand Prix on over 40 occasions?

5. Exeter born Liam Tancock is a World Champion in which sport?

6. Located in Berkshire which racecourse stages the King George V and the Queen Elizabeth Stakes?

7. John Barnes played in FA Cup finals for Liverpool, Newcastle United and which Hertfordshire based team?

8. Which Open Championship golf course is situated in Kent?

9. With which club were the Armitage brothers playing when they played in England's Rugby Union side?

10. In which English athletics stadium did Yelena Isinbayeva become the first woman to clear 5 metres in the pole vault?

11. At which venue does the AEGON Championship take place in London a couple of weeks before Wimbledon?

12. In which sport have Guildford Heat been British Champions?

13. Which snooker tournament did Stephen Hendry win at Wembley Arena for five years running between 1989 and 1993?

14. For which team did Shane Warne play County Championship cricket in the 2000s?

15. With Shaun Edwards and Martin Offiah in their side which club reached their only Challenge Cup final in 1999?

16. Where is the Royal Regatta held on the River Thames every year?

17. Which Londoner known as the King of the Bling, lost in World Championship finals to Eric Bristow and John Part?

18. In 1998 which West Country side became the first English team to win Rugby Union's Heineken Cup?

19. When Spurs beat Wigan 9-1 in the Premier League in 2009 which southerner scored 5 goals in the first half?

20. Which Essex born athlete won Commonwealth gold for England in the Decathlon in 2006?

Game 6

On this episode of A Question of Sport are…

Matt Le Tissier (Football)
First appeared on the show as a guest in 1995

Shaun Pollock (Cricket)
First appeared on the show as a guest in 2008

James Toseland (Motorcycle racing)
First appeared on the show as a guest in 2008

Ruby Walsh (National Hunt racing)
First appeared on the show as a guest in 2005

Round 1 – Opening Rally

1. Name the ten different teams to have won the Champions League between 1996 and 2010.

Round 2 – One Minute Round

1. Which Scottish club did Alex Ferguson manage between 1978 and 1986?

2. Which American city's NFL American Football team are called the Bengals?

3. Which country hosted a Moto GP race in 2010 at Estoril?

4. Who captained Australia in the final Ashes Test of the 2011 series?

5. Which cricket team is this an anagram of? RISKY HERO

6. In which sport did Britain's Kristina Cook win an Olympic bronze medal at the 2008 Games?

7. In which sport do the winners receive the Stanley Cup?

These sports stars all share their surnames with birds.

8. Jason _____ (Rugby League)

9. Chris _____ (Football)

10. Jeff _____ (Cricket)

Round 3 – Mystery Guest

1. I became my country's youngest player when I made my debut at the age of 18 (4 points)

    I am one of only a few players in my sport that wear spectacles whilst playing (3 points)

    In 2011 I stepped down as the captain of my country having led them on numerous occasions (2 points)

    I became only the 2nd New Zealand cricketer to take over 300 Test wickets (1 point)

2. I enjoy motor racing but I have been a professional in my chosen sport since 1992 (4 points)

    I was born in 1975 and can play my sport right-handed or left-handed (3 points)

    I won the UK Championship aged 17 and was crowned World Champion in 2001 (2 points)

    I am known for my speed around the table and in 1997 I scored a maximum 147 break in under 5 minutes and 30 seconds (1 point)

Round 4 – Home or Away

1. *Matt Le Tissier.* Who in 2011 became the first player from his club to score a hat trick against Manchester United since 1990?

2. *Shaun Pollock.* In the 1996 World Cup final who scored 107 not out and took 3 for 42 to win the Man of the Match award as his side became the World Champions for the first time?

3. *James Toseland.* Which rider won the 125cc in 1997, the 250cc in 1999 and the first of five successive 500cc/Moto GP titles in 2001?

4. *Ruby Walsh.* On which horse did Jim Culloty become the first jockey to win three successive Cheltenham Gold Cups in nearly 40 years?

Round 5 – Captain's Away

1. What trophy did Pickles the dog find in 1966?

2. A regulation game of Ice Hockey is separated into how many periods of play?

3. Name the two countries that won the Davis Cup between 2000 and 2010 that begin with the letter S?

4. In which sport is the Louis Vuitton Cup awarded?
   a) Bobsleigh
   b) Curling
   c) Sailing

Round 6 – What Happened Next

1. Snooker player Peter Ebdon is competing at the Royal London Watches Grand Prix, what happened next?
   a) Peter Ebdon fouls in the middle of a break because he is colour-blind and pots the brown instead of a red.
   b) One of the lights falls from the canopy above the table and smashes forcing the frame to be restarted.
   c) After Ebdon plays his shot, the fire alarm goes off and the auditorium has to be evacuated.

2. In the Hungarian league Debrecen VSC have just won a penalty, what happened next?
    a) The keeper saves the penalty only to see the ball smashed into the top corner by his own teammate attempting to clear the ball.
    b) The ball rebounds off the bar, hits the referee and goes into the net.
    c) The striker's boot comes off as he hits the penalty. The boot ends up in the net but the ball goes wide.

Round 7 – On the Buzzer

This buzzer round is all about World Champions.

1. Who coached Chelsea in 2008, 6 years after coaching Brazil to their World Cup final success?

2. Which country has won cricket's World Cup on three successive occasions?

3. In which event did Allen Johnson win 4 World Championship track gold medals between 1995 and 2003?

4. Who was the first boxer to win the World Heavyweight Title for a third time?

5. Which British rider became the 500cc World Champion in 1976 and 1977?

6. In which sport did the Manly Warringah Sea Eagles become World Champions in 2009?

7. Which driver from Argentina won 5 Formula One World Championships in the 1950s?

8. Which of England's 2003 Rugby Union World Cup winning side captained them in the 2007 World Cup final?

9. Which country won all 5 of the available gold medals at the 2010 Badminton World Championships?

10. In which field event did Christian Olsson succeed a Briton as World Champion in 2003?

11. Which former snooker World Champion is known as 'Dracula'?

12. In which sport have Britain's Paul Manning and Ed Clancy been World Champions?

13. Who in 2006 partnered Toytown to become Eventing World Champion?

14. For which country did Stephen Dodd and Bradley Dredge win the golf World Cup in 2005?

15. Which European city hosted the first World Athletics Championships in 1983 and again in 2005?

16. Who in 1978 became only the second American to win the Formula One Championship?

17. In which sport did Dutchman Jelle Klaasen become a World Champion in 2006?

18. Which country hosted and won the first football World Cup in 1930?

19. Which American female skier won two gold medals at the Alpine World Championships in 2009 before winning Winter Olympic gold in the Downhill the following year?

20. Which snooker player knocked the reigning World Champion out of the 2011 Championships in the first round?

Game 7

On this episode of A Question of Sport are...

Frank Lampard (Football)
First appeared on the show as a guest in 2000

Gavin Hastings (Rugby Union)
First appeared on the show as a guest in 1989

Bob Willis (Cricket)
First appeared on the show as a guest in 1981

Paula Radcliffe (Long-distance running)
First appeared on the show as a guest in 2002

Sue Barker became the third official host of *A Question of Sport* in 1997, and her first show in charge featured John Parrott and Ally McCoist as captains, with Tim Henman, Jonah Lomu, Trish Johnson and Peter Ebdon featuring as guests.

Round 1 – Opening Rally

1. Up to 2010 name the ten teams to have won Rugby League's Challenge Cup on four or more occasions.

Round 2 – One Minute Round

1. Desmond Haynes and Gordon Greenidge opened the batting together for which Test team?

2. Which American state's NBA basketball team are called the Timberwolves?

3. Which Welshman won the World Snooker Championship on two occasions in the 2000s?

4. Which tennis term is this an anagram of? DOUBTFUL ALE

5. In which sport might a competitor use an Eskimo roll?

6. Which Rugby Union club played in the Premiership for the first time in 2011 and play their home games at Sandy Park?

7. Which racecourse stages the King George VI and the Queen Elizabeth Stakes?

These sports stars all share their surnames with rooms in a house.

8. Mevyn _____ (Cricket)

9. Ray _____ (Football)

10. Gary _____ (Swimming)

Round 3 – Mystery Guest

1. In 2010 I turned 50 and have had a career fraught with controversy (4 points)

   My talent has never been in doubt and I won trophies in South America as well as in Spain and Italy (3 points)

   My greatest moment internationally was giving my country a helping hand to win the World Cup in Mexico in 1986 (2 points)

   I managed my country Argentina at the 2010 World Cup in South Africa (1 point)

2. In 2009 I celebrated my 40th birthday and I first burst onto the scene in 1993 (4 points)

   I was voted as one of the five greatest players in my sport of the 20th century (3 points)

   I dismissed Mike Gatting with my first ball in the Ashes later described as the ball of the century (2 points)

   I have played for Australia, Hampshire, Victoria and the Rajasthan Royals (1 point)

Round 4 – Home or Away

1. *Frank Lampard.* Who became the first player to score 70 goals in the Champions League, doing so against Inter Milan in 2011?

2. *Gavin Hastings.* During the 2011 Six Nations Championship who became only the 5th player to reach 1000 points in Tests?

3. *Bob Willis.* Who against the West Indies in 1995 became the first Englishman to take a Test hat trick in England since 1957?

4. *Paula Radcliffe.* Which Irish athlete won a World Title in 1995 five years before winning an Olympic silver medal in the Women's 5000m?

Round 5 – Captain's Away

1. In Darts what is the lowest number you can't score with a single throw of a dart?

2. In the 1980s which player became Northern Ireland's first 100 cap international footballer?

3. Name the two Formula One World Champions in the 1990s whose surnames begin with the letter H?

4. What was the result of the Ryder Cup in 1969?
   a) US won by the largest ever margin.
   b) Great Britain and Ireland won by the largest ever margin.
   c) The match was tied for the first time.

Round 6 – What Happened Next

1. It is a penalty shoot-out in the 2010 Balliemore Cup final between Kinlochshiel and Lochaber Camanachd, what happened next?
   a) As the striker goes to take the penalty he loses grip of his 'caman' stick, and it flies past the goalkeeper and into the net along with the ball.
   b) Keeper Graham Kennedy uses his head to save the ball despite it being as hard as a cricket ball.

c) The penalty hits the crossbar and the entire frame of the goal collapses on top of the goalkeeper.

2. During the cycling World Cup Classics series at the Manchester Velodrome in a race between Great Britain's Jason Kenny and Australian Shane Perkins, what happened next?
   a) Other cyclists have joined the track to warm up for the next race and as Jason Kenny and Shane Perkins cross the line they are involved in a pile up with the five other cyclists.
   b) Shane Perkins tries to overtake Jason Kenny but falls into him sending both flying and Kenny wins the gold sliding across the line on his back.
   c) A photographer is trackside but gets too close to the cyclists and Jason Kenny knocks his camera clean out of his hands.

Round 7 – On the Buzzer

Everything in this buzzer round took place in the year 1985.

1. In his first season as Barcelona coach which future England manager led them to their first Spanish title in 11 years?

2. Said Aouita broke British athlete David Moorcroft's world record in which event?

3. Which left handed batsman captained England to their Ashes win scoring 732 runs in the process?

4. After winning the World Featherweight Title which Irishman defended it successfully three months later against Bernard Taylor?

5. In one of the great Rugby League Challenge Cup finals which team did Wigan beat 28-24?

6. Which centre scored 47 points on the way to Ireland winning Rugby Union's Triple Crown?

7. Which English club won the League and European Cup Winners' Cup but lost to Manchester United in the FA Cup final?

8. Which British athlete broke three world records in 19 days, the 1500m, 2000m and the mile?

9. Who beat South African Kevin Curren to win the Men's Singles Title at Wimbledon at the age of 17?

10. In December, which Indian opening batsman became the first player to score 9000 runs in Test history?

11. London Marathon winner Ingrid Krisitansen became the second woman from which country to win the event?

12. Which Juventus and France player won the Ballon D'Or for the third successive year?

13. Who became the first British golfer to win the Open Championship since Tony Jacklin triumphed in 1969?

14. Which German figure skater won her second World Championship in this year?

15. Which famous race did Frenchman Bernard Hinault win for the fifth and final time in his career?

16. Which Welsh stand off scored a try and a drop goal in a winning debut against England?

17. Which American jockey won both the 1000 Guineas and the Oaks in 1985?

18. Known as Supermex, which two-time Open Championship winner captained the USA team in their Ryder Cup loss?

19. Which snooker player beat Steve Davis in the World Championship final in a thrilling final frame?

20. Which Frenchman won the first of his Formula One World Championship Titles beating Michele Alboreto into second place?

Game 8

On this episode of A Question of Sport are...

Sharron Davies (Swimming)
First appeared on the show as a guest in 1979

Darren Gough (Cricket)
First appeared on the show as a guest in 1995

Sebastian Coe (Track athletics)
First appeared on the show as a guest in 1979

Frank Bruno (Boxing)
First appeared on the show as a guest in 1986

Round 1 – Opening Rally

1. Other than England name the 12 European countries to compete in the 2010 Football World Cup finals.

Round 2 – One Minute Round

1. Who scored over 40 FA Cup career goals with Chester City, Liverpool and Newcastle United?

2. Which international cricket team are also known as the Proteas?

3. With which type of motor racing would you associate World Champions Yvan Muller, Gabriele Tarquini and Andy Priaulx?

4. Which Rugby Union stadium is this an anagram of? MY RUDE FLAIR

5. Which American city's NHL Ice Hockey team are called the Penguins?

6. Which Swedish tennis player won both the Junior Boys' Championship and the Men's Singles Championship at Wimbledon in the 1980s?

7. What is the Women's equivalent of the Ryder Cup?

These sports stars all share their surnames with names for money.

8. Pat _____ (Australian Tennis Player)

9. Raheem _____ (English Footballer)

10. William _____ (American Baseball Player)

Round 3 – Mystery Guest

1. I retired in 2011 at the age of just 34 but I'm considered one of my sport's all time greats (4 points)

    Besides playing in my home country I also played in the Netherlands, Spain and Italy (3 points)

    I scored twice to help my country win the World Cup final (2 points)

    I have scored more goals in the World Cup than any other player (1 point)

2. I started playing my chosen sport at the age of 9 and by the time I was 16 I had represented my country (4 points)

    At 19 I led my country to victory in the Davis Cup (3 points)

    I won my first Wimbledon Singles Title in 1976 by beating Ille Nastase (2 points)

    My record of winning Wimbledon 5 years in succession was equalled by Roger Federer in 2007 (1 point)

Round 4 – Home or Away

1. *Sharron Davies.* Which swimmer was the only Briton to win Olympic medals in 2004 and 2008?

2. *Darren Gough.* Which England bowler won the County Championship with Yorkshire in 2001 and Nottinghamshire in 2005 and 2010?

3. *Sebastian Coe.* What nationality is the multiple World 10,000m champion Haile Gebrselassie?

4. *Frank Bruno.* In 1971 which Olympic gold medallist became the first person to defeat Muhammad Ali in a professional bout?

Round 5 – Captain's Away

1. Who has played for Jose Mourinho at Porto, Chelsea and Real Madrid between 2004 and 2010?

2. With two reds and all the colours left on the table in snooker what would be the maximum number of points you could score if you cleared them all?

3. Name the two winners of BBC Sports Personality of the Year Award in the 1990s whose surnames begin with the letter M?

4. How did Bob Charles create Open Championship history by winning it in 1963?
   a) Won in a record 6 man playoff
   b) Won with the highest aggregate score
   c) First left handed player to win it

Round 6 – Great Sporting Moments

1. Esha Ness the 50/1 outsider trained by Jenny Pitman and ridden by John White crossed the line first in the Grand National at Aintree but why did this race win leave a bitter taste for White?

2. In 1979 the Lytham crowds witnessed another sensational golfing moment. The 22 year old sprayed his drive on the

16th into the car park forcing him to take a drop on the dusty ground; he lofted a wedge to within 15 feet and kept his cool to sink the birdie. Who went on to win the Open Championship two holes later following that great escape?

Round 7 – On the Buzzer

All the questions in this buzzer round have an English connection.

1. Who in 1988 partnered Andrew Holmes to an Olympic Title?

2. Mike Gatting, Mike Brearley and Mark Ramprakash have all captained which English county?

3. In which sport did Englishman Nick Gillingham win medals for Britain at the Summer Olympics?

4. Which English team played Champions League football for the first time when they qualified for the group stages of the 2010 tournament?

5. In which event did Lisa Dobriskey win her Commonwealth Games gold medal for England in 2006?

6. Whose first fight as a Heavyweight saw him beat Monte Barrett in November 2008?

7. In 2010 which Englishman became the first player to become the number one ranked golfer in the world without having won a Major?

8. In which sport did Gary and Phil Neville's sister represent England?

9. Born in Sheffield which boxer fought Roy Jones Jr, Glen Johnson and Antonio Tarver in World Light Heavyweight Title bouts?

10. On which English racecourse is the Oaks run?

11. By what name were Rugby League team the Bradford Bulls previously known?

12. In which sport did Andrew Triggs Hodge win an Olympic gold in Beijing?

13. Which goalkeeper denied John Aldridge to become the first man to save a penalty at Wembley in the FA Cup final?

14. In 1977 which Yorkshire batsman scored his 100th First Class century, doing so in a Test match for England?

15. In which sport did John Amaechi help England to a Commonwealth Games bronze medal in 2006?

16. Which player scored 6 tries for England to help them win the 2011 Six Nations?

17. Which Englishman did Jo Durie partner to win the Wimbledon Mixed Doubles final in 1987?

18. In which sport has Englishman Jamie Staff won Olympic and World Sprint gold medals?

19. Which Englishman won the 2002 Snooker World Championship by beating Stephen Hendry in the final?

20. In 2011 who became the first Englishman to win the Football Writers' Player of the Year Award whilst playing for West Ham United in nearly 50 years?

Game 9

On this episode of A Question of Sport are...

Teddy Sheringham (Football)
First appeared on the show as a guest in 1993

Mark Spitz (Swimming)
First appeared on the show as a guest in 2004

Steve Davis (Snooker)
First appeared on the show as a guest in 1981

Amir Khan (Boxing)
First appeared on the show as a guest in 2004

Former Welsh Rugby Union star Cliff Morgan was a captain on the first ever episode of *A Question of Sport*. He was a captain on the show for five years, starring across from opposing captain Henry Cooper. Cliff's final appearance as captain featured Brendan Foster, Dennis Amiss, Debbie Johnsey and Willie Carson.

Round 1 – Opening Rally

1. Name the 10 host cities of the Summer Olympic Games between 1972 and 2008.

Round 2 – One Minute Round

1. With which swimming stroke did Britain's Liam Tancock win a 50m World Championship gold medal?

2. Which country finished third at the 2007 Rugby Union World Cup?

3. What nationality is golfer Camilo Villegas?

4. Which Rugby Union position is this an anagram of? FLU CHARMS

5. Which Football League team play their home games at Selhurst Park?

6. Which team won the first two Cricket World Cups?

7. Which Canadian father and son have both won Formula One Grand Prix races?

These sports stars all share their surnames with alcoholic drinks.

8. Stanley _____ (Athletics)

9. Drew _____ (Rowing)

10. Febian _____ (Football)

Round 3 – Mystery Guest

1. Like Kevin Keegan and Ray Clemence I played for Scunthorpe (4 points)

   My son played professionally as a cricketer and in both codes of rugby (3 points)

   I once held the world record for most Test wickets with 383 that I captured with England (2 points)

   I captained *A Question of Sport* opposite Bill Beaumont for years (1 point)

2. I was born in 1979 and was only an 18 year old when I made my international debut (4 points)

   I have scored in two World Cup finals (3 points)

   I have played at club level in England and France but my finest moment came in Australia in 2003 (2 points)

   Thanks to my World Cup winning drop goal I won the BBC Sports Personality of the Year Award in the same year (1 point)

Round 4 – Home or Away

1. *Teddy Sheringham.* Who in 2010 became only the third player to score a hat trick in the Newcastle United – Sunderland league derby?

2. *Mark Spitz.* Which British swimmer won the Men's 100m Breaststroke at the 1988 Olympic Games?

3. *Steve Davis.* In 2000 two Welshman contested the World Championship final for the first time. Which of his compatriots did Mark Williams beat in the final?

4. *Amir Khan.* Who by beating Antonio Margarita in November 2010 won a World Title at his eighth different weight division?

Round 5 – Captain's Away

1. Prior to his move to Hampshire, which county did Kevin Pietersen play for between 2001 and 2005?

2. Which Englishman tied for third place at the US Masters in 2005 and tied fourth in 2011?

3. Besides Rangers and Celtic which other two teams have won the Scottish Premiership between 1975 and 2011?

4. In what sport might you move the pile, flood the zone or throw a Hail Mary?
   a) Baseball
   b) American Football
   c) Basketball

Round 6 – What Happened Next

1. Warwickshire are playing Sussex in the County Championship, Ed Joyce is on strike for Sussex as Ant Botha is about to bowl, what happened next?
   a) Ed Joyce drives the ball straight back down the pitch, it hits non-striker Michael Yardy and rebounds to bowler Ant Botha who takes the catch.
   b) Joyce sweeps the ball and fielder Jonathan Trott

inadvertently catches the ball in his pocket and Joyce is dismissed.

c) Joyce hits the ball and is caught in the deep, and begins to walk off without realising a no-ball has been called and quick thinking Ian Bell runs him out.

2. Ken Doherty is in action at snooker's Grand Prix. Doherty is at the table, what happened next?

a) Doherty pots the blue but the white ball then knocks the yellow into the top corner pocket before going in the opposite pocket itself for an incredible triple pot foul.

b) As Doherty goes to take his shot he puts too much pressure on his cue as he leans on it and it snaps.

c) Just as Doherty is about to hit the cue ball a mobile phone goes off in the crowd and Doherty completely miss hits the cue ball into the middle pocket.

Round 7 – On the Buzzer

This buzzer round is all about great captains, coaches and managers.

1. Whose last game as Arsenal captain saw him score a winning penalty in the FA Cup final in 2005?

2. Which country did Rugby Union's David Sole captain a record 25 times?

3. Which Leeds Rhinos player captained them to three successive Super League Grand Final victories in the 2000s?

4. Which captain scored 91 not out for India to help his team win the 2011 Cricket World Cup final?

5. In which sport was Vincent Lombardi an incredibly successful coach?

6. In which sport has coach and performance director Dave Brailsford played an integral part in British success at the Olympics?

7. Which great boxing coach trained Muhammad Ali and also worked with Sugar Ray Leonard and George Foreman?

8. Who became the first non-British golfer to captain Europe in the Ryder Cup?

9. Which team did Chris Read captain to the County Championship Title in 2010?

10. Who in 2011 followed in his father's footsteps by training the winner of the Grand National at Aintree?

11. Who captained Italy to victory in the 2006 Football World Cup final?

12. Which country did Yannick Noah captain to victory in the Davis Cup in 1996?

13. Sean O'Loughlin captained which club to their 2010 Super League Grand Final win?

14. In Roy Keane's absence, who captained Manchester United to their 1999 Champions League final win?

15. Who captained Europe in 4 successive Ryder Cups between 1983 and 1989?

16. Which trainer completed a 1, 2, 3 finish at the Cheltenham Gold Cup in 2008?

17. Which American Football team did Bill Belichick coach to three Superbowl victories in the 2000s?

18. Who captained Great Britain's women's athletic team at the 1992 Summer Olympics and led by example winning gold?

19. Who captained the British and Irish Lions on the 2009 tour of South Africa?

20. Who was the Team Principal for Red Bull as they won both the Formula One Drivers' and Constructors' Championships in 2010?

Game 10

On this episode of A Question of Sport are...

Steve Backley (Field athletics)
First appeared on the show as a guest in 1990

Beth Tweddle (Gymnastics)
First appeared on the show as a guest in 2007

Michael Holding (Cricket)
First appeared on the show as a guest in 2001

Tim Henman (Tennis)
First appeared on the show as a guest in 1996

Round 1 – Opening Rally

1. Between 1966 and 2010 name the 10 different hosts of the Football World Cup.

Round 2 – One Minute Round

1. Which American city's NFL American Football team are called the Dolphins?

2. Which British boxer won the Super Heavyweight gold medal at the 2000 Olympics?

3. Which Welsh footballer won the BBC Sports Personality of the Year Award in 2009?

4. Which Open Championship golf course is this an anagram of? RETRY BURN

5. Which English figure skater won gold at the 1980 Winter Olympics?

6. What nationality is 1978 World Snooker finalist Perrie Mans?

7. Which famous race is 4 miles and 374 yards long and starts in Putney and ends in Mortlake?

These sports stars all share their surnames with non-alcoholic drinks.

8. Frank _____ (Boxing)

9. Giles _____ (Football)

10. Damien _____ (Golf)

Round 3 – Mystery Guest

1. I was born in 1983 and was the Player of the Year in my sport in 2007 (4 points)

    I have been timed at 10.2 seconds for the 100m, which helps me greatly in my sport (3 points)

    I scored 8 tries at the 2007 Rugby Union World Cup (2 points)

    Famously I raced a cheetah in 2007 but despite my impressive speed I was no match for the animal (1 point)

2. I was a child prodigy competing for England before I was a teenager and I went to the 1976 Olympics at the age of 13 (4 points)

    In 1978 I became a household name by winning two gold medals at the Commonwealth Games in swimming events (3 points)

    I won Olympic silver in 1980 in the 400m individual medley setting a British Record that stood for over 25 years (2 points)

    Since retiring I am now a reporter and pundit for the BBC at swimming events around the world (1 point)

Round 4 – Home or Away

1. *Steve Backley.* Between 1983 and 1997 which European athlete won six consecutive gold medals at the World Championships?

2. *Beth Tweddle.* Which Russian gymnast won Women's All Round World Championship gold in 1997, 2001 and 2003?

3. *Michael Holding.* Which fast bowler made his England Test debut in 1997 following both his father and his grandfather as Test players, although they both represented the West Indies?

4. *Tim Henman.* Which Australian won his fourth Queen's Club Championship by beating James Blake in 2006?

Round 5 – Captain's Away

1. How did Darlington's elimination by Aston Villa in the 2000 FA Cup create history?

2. England substitute fielder Gary Pratt sensationally ran out which Australian batsman in 2005?

3. Name the two countries beginning with A that competed in the 2007 Rugby Union World Cup?

4. In what sport might you hit a bleeder, throw a duster or have a rhubarb?
    a) Baseball
    b) Ice Hockey
    c) Basketball

Round 6 – Great Sporting Moments

1. Having been 2-0 down the scores were now level 2-2 and extra time seemed imminent. Liam Brady picked the ball up inside his own half and ran straight at the heart of the Manchester United defence. He found Graham Rix on the left wing who sent over a cross for which player to win the FA Cup for Arsenal?

2. After winning silver in Atlanta the British athlete's main rivals this time round at the Olympics were Denis Kapustin, Yoel

Garcia and Larry Achike. In the third round a jump of 17.71 metres secured Olympic gold for which man?

Round 7 – On the Buzzer

This buzzer round is all about the year 2004.

1. Who was 'the Viking' who won a World Darts Championship in January 2004?

2. Michael Sprott beat Danny Williams to win a British and Commonwealth Title in which sport?

3. When Great Britain won the 100m relay gold at the Olympics who ran the final leg pipping Maurice Greene on the line?

4. Which country shocked the rest of Europe by winning the 2004 European Championships by beating the hosts Portugal in the final?

5. Who was the 14 year old golfing sensation selected by the USA for the Curtis Cup team against Great Britain and Ireland?

6. Jurgen Grobler was the national coach for which successful British Olympics squad?

7. Who in March 2004 became the first spinner to take 500 Test wickets?

8. Which British athlete won a Heptathlon Olympic bronze medal in 2004?

9. Who broke Ieuan Evans' Welsh try scoring record with his 34th try for his country?

10. Which American won his first Major by winning the US Masters at Augusta in 2004?

11. Who trained his fourth Grand National winner when Amberleigh House won the race in 2004?

12. In which sport did Jamie Staff win a World Championship gold medal in Melbourne?

13. Which city staged the Olympics nearly 100 years after it hosted the first Modern Olympic Games?

14. Stephen Fleming became which country's leading scorer in Test cricket?

15. In which event did Welshman David Davies win an Olympic swimming medal?

16. Ernie Els recorded a hole in one at the Postage Stamp during the Open Championship, on which course is it?

17. Which North African country won the African Cup of Nations for the first time in their history?

18. Who in 2004 became the first Russian to win the Women's Singles Title at Wimbledon?

19. During the 2004 Summer Olympics two British cyclists won gold medals. Chris Hoy won one, who won the other in the Individual Pursuit?

20. Which Major League Baseball team beat the St Louis Cardinals to win the World Series for the first time in 86 years?

Game 11

On this episode of A Question of Sport are...

Glenn Hoddle (Football)
First appeared on the show as a guest in 1980

Mark Webber (Motor racing)
First appeared on the show as a guest in 2005

Oscar Pistorius (Paralympics track)
First appeared on the show as a guest in 2005

Pat Cash (Tennis)
First appeared on the show as a guest in 1989

British Boxer Henry Cooper was a captain on *A Question of Sport* between 1970 and 1977. His final appearance as captain of the show featured Brendan Foster, Graham Fletcher, Hilary Peacock, Clive Lloyd and Keith Fielding.

Round 1 – Opening Rally

1. Name the ten countries to win more than 10 medals at the 2010 Winter Olympics.

Round 2 – One Minute Round

1. Which Football League team play their home games at Carrow Road?

2. Which American won the Light Heavyweight boxing gold medal at the 1960 Olympics?

3. Which winner of football's World Cup is this an anagram of? MY ANGER

4. With which sport would you associate the Yokohoma Bay Stars, the Orix Buffaloes and the Chiba Lotte Marines?

5. Which European country made their Cricket World Cup debut in 1996?

6. Which country hosted a Moto GP race in 2010 at Phillip Island?

7. Which New Zealand rider won his fourth Badminton Horse Trials Title in 2011, 31 years after his first win in the event?

These sports stars all share their surnames with things you would find on a chess board.

8. Andrew _____ (Tennis)

9. Steve _____ (Horse Racing)

10. Ian _____ (Cricket)

Round 3 – Mystery Guest

1. I celebrated my 60th birthday in 2009 and was still making the headlines in my chosen sport (4 points)

   I was once involved in the so-called 'Duel in the Sun' with one of my great rivals at Turnberry (3 points)

   The only Major I failed to win in my career is the USPGA Championship (2 points)

   In 1983 I won my 5th Open Championship Title taking victory at Birkdale (1 point)

2. I was born in Bedfordshire but spend a lot of my time training in Manchester (4 points)

   In 2005 I became the first British woman to win a World Championship Title in my sport for 40 years (3 points)

   I have won gold medals at the Commonwealth Games and World Championships but my greatest success came at the 2008 Summer Olympics (2 points)

   I helped the likes of Chris Hoy and Bradley Wiggins make my sport a real success story for Britain at the Beijing Olympics (1 point)

Round 4 – Home or Away

1. *Glenn Hoddle.* Who came on as a substitute for West Ham United in the 2006 FA Cup final, seven years after having done so for Manchester United?

2. *Mark Webber.* Who is the only driver to have competed in every Formula One Championship between 1993 and 2011?

3. *Oscar Pistorius.* Which British athlete won gold at the 2004 Paralympic Games in the T46 800m?

4. *Pat Cash.* Which player reached a Wimbledon semi-final in 2009, a year after her brother did likewise?

Round 5 – Captain's Away

1. On the field of play you'd find 12 pieces of wood and under certain circumstances a maximum of 15 players – what is the sport?

2. In which sport did actor Hugh Laurie compete in an annual University race whilst his father won an Olympic gold medal in the same sport in 1948?

3. Name the two cities that have hosted the Summer Olympics which begin with the letter A since 1960?

4. With which sport would you associate a con rod, a crankcase and venturi ducts?
   a) Canoeing
   b) Motor Racing
   c) Yachting

Round 6 – What Happened Next

1. During the American Le Mans Series Antonio Garcia of the Corvette team is in the pits, what happened next?
    a) Garcia drives off with the fuel hose still connected to the car, but continues and finishes the race with it still attached.
    b) Garcia's Corvette teammate Jan Magnussen also comes into the pits and the two cars crash into each other.
    c) Garcia winds his window down to tell them to hurry up, but one mechanic takes exception and drags him out of the car telling him to change the tyre himself.

2. American Leif Olson is about to tee off at the Canadian Open's par three 15th hole. What happened next?
    a) Just as the ball lands on the green, a peregrine falcon swoops and catches the ball.
    b) The ball lands on the green, spins back and goes in the hole after ricocheting off his playing partners' ball for a remarkable hole in one.
    c) Olson over hits his tee shot and his ball lands straight into a spectator's drink at the back of the green.

Round 7 – On the Buzzer

This buzzer round is all about 1995.

1. Who captained Wigan to victory in the Challenge Cup final before going on to coach Wasps and Wales later in his career?

2. Which female trainer had her second success in the Grand National with Royal Athlete winning the race in 1995?

3. Which Scottish driver in 1995 became Britain's first ever World Rally Champion?

4. In front of their own supporters which country won Rugby Union's World Cup?

5. Which club won the top flight of English Football for the first time in 81 years?

6. Who defeated Oliver McCall to win the WBA World Heavyweight Championship in September?

7. Which British man broke a World Athletics Record in Salamanca which had belonged to Willie Banks for 10 years?

8. Who scored a drop goal for England in extra time to earn England victory over Australia to reach the World Cup semi-finals?

9. Who won her sixth Wimbledon Singles Title by beating Arantxa Sanchez Vicario to claim her 17th Grand Slam Singles victory?

10. In which sport did Carl Ripken Jr complete his 2131st consecutive game for the Baltimore Orioles?

11. Which British driver won his first Formula One Grand Prix with victory at Estoril in Portugal?

12. Which South African fast bowler helped Warwickshire to victory in the County Championship and the NatWest Trophy?

13. Which team did Paul Rideout score the winner for in the FA Cup final?

14. Which American won the 1995 US Open before going on to captain the USA in the Ryder Cup in 2010?

15. Which side did Richie Richardson captain in the Test series against England?

16. Which British driver recorded the first of his 3 Formula One Grand Prix wins by winning the British Grand Prix at Silverstone?

17. During the World Snooker Championship who fired a 147 maximum break on his way to defeating Jimmy White in the semi-finals?

18. Which future European Ryder Cup player became Spain's first winner of the European Amateur Championship?

19. Which footballer moved from Newcastle United to Manchester United for a then British Transfer Record?

20. With which basketball team did Michael Jordan make his NBA comeback with in 1995?

Game 12

On this episode of A Question of Sport are...

Alan Hansen (Football)
First appeared on the show as a guest in 1986

Paul Lawrie (Golf)
First appeared on the show as a guest in 1999

Rob Andrew (Rugby Union)
First appeared on the show as a guest in 1985

Virginia Wade (Tennis)
First appeared on the show as a guest in 2004

Round 1 – Opening Rally

1. Name the ten sports that feature in the Olympic Decathlon.

Round 2 – One Minute Round

1. Which Scottish Football League team play their home games at the Pittodrie Stadium?

2. With which sport would you associate the clean, the snatch and the jerk?

3. In which athletics event did Tia Hellebaut win Belgium's only gold medal of the 2008 Summer Olympics?

4. Who scored the most runs for Australia in the 2010/2011 Ashes series?

5. Which Olympic sport is this an anagram of? WHIMSY MINDS CENSORING

6. Which city's Rugby Union side were once called the Tykes but are now linked to the city's Carnegie College?

7. Which Spaniard won the French Open Men's Singles Title four years in a row between 2004 and 2008?

These sports stars all share their surnames with vegetables you would chop.

8. Graham _____ (Cricket)

9. Dottie _____ (Golf)

10. Eugene _____ (Baseball)

Round 3 – Mystery Guest

1. I was born in Cardiff in July 1969 and graduated from Loughborough University with a degree in Politics and Social Administration (4 points)

    I was christened Carys Davina Grey but my sister called me tiny due to my size and that led to the name I'm known as today (3 points)

    I represented Wales at the age of 15 in the Junior National Championships and won many gold medals (2 points)

    I won 11 gold medals for Britain at the Paralympic Games and won the London Marathon Wheelchair Race on six occasions (1 point)

2. I was born in Hammersmith, London in March 1972 (4 points)

    I was raised in Newbridge, South Wales by my Welsh mother and my Italian father (3 points)

    My dad won 'Coach of the Year' at the BBC Sports Personality of the Year Awards (2 points)

    In 2009 I announced my retirement finishing undefeated in 46 professional fights (1 point)

Round 4 – Home or Away

1. *Alan Hansen.* Who was the top scorer at the European Championships in 1988 scoring five goals which included a hat trick against England?

2. *Paul Lawrie.* Who in 2010 became the first European to win the US Open for 40 years?

3. *Rob Andrew.* In 2007 against England which Welshman scored a full house of try, conversion, penalty and a drop goal?

4. *Virginia Wade.* In 1988 which woman won all four Grand Slam Singles Titles as well as an Olympic gold medal?

Round 5 – Captain's Away

1. Who was the first female gymnast to gain a perfect score of 10 in an Olympic competition?

2. Name the two disciplines involved in the Winter Olympic sport Biathlon?

3. Name the two sides that play in the County Championship whose names begin with G?

4. With which sport do you associate Zandvoort, Kyalami and Watkins Glen?
    a) Motor Racing
    b) Baseball
    c) Ice Hockey

Round 6 – Great Sporting Moments

1. Now on his own and with just over 200 yards left to go the medical student summoned up all his energy to break the seemingly impossible 4 minute barrier. Which athlete became the first man to run a four-minute mile?

2. His round went from bad to worse. From six shots ahead things began to get steadily worse. On the par three 16th he yanked his tee shot into one of Augusta's lakes and his shoulders slumped, Greg Norman's Masters was lost, thanks to a flawless final round from which man?

Round 7 – On the Buzzer

This buzzer round has an American connection.

1. Which team won the 2009 Superbowl to win the competition for a record 6th time?

2. Which American city hosted the Summer Olympics in 1904?

3. Which American sprinter won World Championship gold medals in both the men's 100m and the 200m in 2007?

4. Which Major winning golfer's first name is Eldrick?

5. In which sport did Mary Lou Retton win an Olympic gold medal in 1984?

6. In which city are the American Football team the Seahawks and the Major League Baseball team the Mariners based?

7. Which American played in goal for Manchester United in the FA Cup final in 2004 and for Everton five years later?

8. Which basketball team won their first NBA Championship in 2006 thanks to Dwayne Wade and Shaquille O'Neal?

9. In which sport was Mario Andretti a World Champion in 1978?

10. Which tennis player won his first Wimbledon Singles Title in 1974 and his second eight years later?

11. Which famous horse race held at Churchill Downs was won by Calvin Borel on Super Saver in 2010?

12. Who scored for the USA in their 1-1 draw with England at the 2010 Football World Cup?

13. In which American city were the 2002 Winter Olympic Games held?

14. Which two time US Masters winner captained America to victory at the 1999 Ryder Cup at Brookline?

15. With which sport do you associate with the Florida Marlins?

16. Other than Pete Sampras who was the only American to reach the Men's Wimbledon Singles final between 2000 and 2010?

17. Which team beat the Pittsburgh Penguins in 2008 to win their 11th Stanley Cup?

18. Which American athlete won the men's 400m at both the 1996 and 2000 Summer Olympics?

19. Which American cyclist won the Tour de France on seven occasions between 1999 and 2005?

20. Which famous race did Scotsman Dario Franchitti win at the Brickyard in 2007 and 2010?

Game 13

On this episode of A Question of Sport are...

John Barnes (Football)
First appeared on the show as a guest in 1985

Gareth Edwards (Rugby Union)
First appeared on the show as a guest in 1979

Michael Stich (Tennis)
First appeared on the show as a guest in 2007

Evander Holyfield (Boxing)
First appeared on the show as a guest in 2000

Ally McCoist was a captain on the programme between 1996 and 2007. He sat in the chair opposite three regular captains and has appeared on the show a record 363 times.

Round 1 – Opening Rally

1. Name the 10 First Class cricket counties whose names end with shire.

Round 2 – One Minute Round

1. How many reds are on the table at the start of a frame of snooker?

2. Which substitute scored Birmingham City's winning goal in the 2011 League Cup final?

3. In which sport do the Detroit Redwings and the Columbus Blue Jackets play?

4. Which Australian fast bowler is nicknamed 'Dizzy'?

5. Which sport is this an anagram of? QUEER SAINT

6. Which team played their 2010/2011 Rugby Union Premiership home games at Franklin's Gardens?

7. Which team did Sebastien Buemi and Jaime Alguersuari drive for in the 2010 Formula One Championship?

These sports stars all share their surnames with parts of the body.

8. Joe _____ (Football)

9. Tony _____ (Ice Hockey)

10. Joe _____ (Boxing)

Round 3 – Mystery Guest

1. I turned 40 in 2008 and am an Olympic Champion (4 points)

   I came to prominence by winning Britain's first gold medal in my sport at the Olympics since 1920 (3 points)

   I held a track world record for the 4km individual pursuit but Australian Jack Bobridge beat the record in 2011 (2 points)

   I won gold at the Olympics before turning professional and wore the yellow jersey at the Tour de France on a number of occasions (1 point)

2. I was born in Launceston in 1974 was still playing internationally 37 years later (4 points)

   I was an international at the age of 20 and I have captained my country many times (3 points)

   When I was 8 my grandmother gave me a T-shirt which read 'under this shirt is a Test player' and it turned out to be accurate as I played for Australia in over 150 Tests (2 points)

   Unfortunately I was on the losing side in the Ashes on three occasions as captain (1 point)

Round 4 – Home or Away

1. *John Barnes.* Which Frenchman scored two late goals against England in their first game of the 2004 European Championships?

2. *Gareth Edwards.* Who won a record 17 caps for the British and Irish Lions on his five tours, which included winning a series in South Africa?

3. *Michael Stich.* Who partnered Martina Navratilova to 20 Grand Slam Women's Doubles Titles, all in the 1980s?

4. *Evander Holyfield.* Who having won his first World Title in 1993 at Middleweight won the WBA Heavyweight Title 10 years later by beating John Ruiz?

Round 5 – Captain's Away

1. Which country won the rugby Olympic gold medal in 1924, the last time the sport featured in a Summer Games?

2. Which England cricket captain's brother played in an FA Cup final for Brighton in the 1980s?

3. Name the two countries beginning with the letter C that hosted a Formula One Grand Prix in 2010?

4. With which sport do you associate Firestone, Eldorado and Winged Foot?
    a) Motor Racing
    b) Golf
    c) Boxing

Round 6 – What Happened Next

1. Real Madrid have just defeated Barcelona in the final of the 2011 Copa del Rey. The victorious Spanish side is on the team bus celebrating with their fans in Madrid, what happened next?

a) The bus driver gets lost in all the excitement and drives to city rivals Atletico Madrid's ground the Vicente Calderon instead of Real's home the Bernabeu.

b) Real Madrid defender Sergio Ramos drops the trophy off the front of the bus and the bus drives over it ruining the trophy.

c) Real manager Jose Mourinho decides to let his players enjoy the celebrations on their own and gets the bus driver to pull over so he can walk home.

2. Rossharisham Roslom is about to dive for Malaysia at the 2002 Commonwealth Games, what happened next?

a) Roslom slips whilst getting into position and falls off the platform into the water.

b) Roslom makes a mess of his jump and ends up belly flopping into the pool.

c) Roslom panics on the diving platform and has to be carried down by his trainer.

Round 7 – On the Buzzer

All the answers to this buzzer round begin with the letter S. In the case of a person it's the surname that must start with that letter.

1. Which South African won the 2011 US Masters by two strokes to claim his first victory in a Major?

2. In which city did Torvill and Dean win Winter Olympic gold?

3. Which team were beaten by Arsenal in the finals of both the FA Cup and League Cup in 1993?

4. Which Russian tennis player won the 2004 Women's Singles Title at Wimbledon?

5. Which American Football team play their home games at Candlestick Park?

6. With which basketball team did Tim Duncan win 4 NBA Championships between 1999 and 2007?

7. What is the name of the tournament that women golfers from Europe and USA compete against each other in every two years?

8. In which sport have Jason Crump, Nicki Pedersen and Tony Rickardsson all been World Champions?

9. Which country won the Rugby Union World Cup in 2007 by beating England?

10. Which country won the 1996 Cricket World Cup and lost to India in the final of the 2011 tournament?

11. Which Welsh snooker player finished runner up in both the 2000 and the 2005 World Championship?

12. Which Spanish team beat Middlesbrough 4-0 in the UEFA Cup final in 2006?

13. Which Rugby League team won the Super League Grand Final three times in the 2000s?

14. In which European country were the 1912 Summer Olympics held?

15. Which team did Leicester Tigers beat in the 2010 Guinness Premiership final?

16. Which British athlete won Olympic and Commonwealth gold medals in the Javelin?

17. Which country hosted the first ever Formula One Grand Prix to be held at night time?

18. Which county finished as runner up in all three domestic cricket competitions in 2010?

19. Which country won the Davis Cup on four occasions in the 2000s?

20. In which Winter Olympic sport did Britain's Nicky Gooch win an Olympic bronze medal in 1994?

Game 14

On this episode of A Question of Sport are...

Ossie Ardiles (Football)
First appeared on the show as a guest in 2006

Ian Thorpe (Swimming)
First appeared on the show as a guest in 2002

Darren Clarke (Golf)
First appeared on the show as a guest in 1997

Aranxta Sanchez Vicario (Tennis)
First appeared on the show as a guest in 1991

Round 1 – Opening Rally

1. Matthew Hayden became the 11th cricketer to play in 100 Tests for Australia, who are the ten players that reached the landmark before him.

Round 2 – One Minute Round

1. What nickname is English snooker player Ronnie O'Sullivan commonly known by?

2. Which Scottish Football League team play their home games at the Ibrox Stadium?

3. Which English cricketer won the BBC Sports Personality of the Year Award in 2005?

4. Which country hosts the Formula One Grand Prix which is held at the Hockenheimring?

5. Which British tennis player is this an anagram of? SURE BREAK

6. Which American city's MLB baseball team are called the Astros?

7. What nationality is 2008 French Open Women's Singles Title Champion Ana Ivanovic?

These sports stars all share their surnames with countries of the world.

8. Rob _____ (Athletics)

9. Stephen _____ (Football)

10. Michael _____ (Basketball)

Round 3 – Mystery Guest

1. I turned professional at the age of 16 having started playing my chosen sport 4 years earlier (4 points)

    I was a National Under 16 Champion in 1983 and in 1986 I became the youngest winner of a professional event in my sport (3 points)

    I always performed well in a theatre and I won my first World Championship Title in 1990 (2 points)

    I'm known as the 'King of the Crucible' having won seven World Championships there between 1990 and 1999 (1 point)

2. I was born in Milan in 1968 and I based myself there for my entire domestic career (4 points)

    My father played professionally and later went onto coach me in the national team (3 points)

    I played over 100 times for my country but missed out on the greatest achievement of all with them when we finished runners up in the 1994 World Cup (2 points)

    I won 7 League Championship Titles during my career and 5 Champions League winners' medals (1 point)

Round 4 – Home or Away

1. *Ossie Ardiles.* Who in 1998 became the first country in 20 years to win the Football World Cup as hosts?

2. *Ian Thorpe.* Which American swimmer won seven medals at the 1988 Summer Olympics, five gold, a silver and a bronze?

3. *Darren Clarke.* Who in 2010 became only the second German to win a major championship, 25 years after his compatriot Bernhard Langer won his first?

4. *Aranxta Sanchez Vicario.* Who in 2006 became the first French woman in over 80 years to win the Wimbledon Singles Title?

Round 5 – Captain's Away

1. Who are the only side in cricket's County Championship that begins with a vowel?

2. In 1983 which European city hosted the first World Athletics Championship?

3. Name the two European countries that played in the 2010 Football World Cup that begin with the letter G?

4. With which sport do you associate travelling, alley oops and three in the key?
   a) Ice Hockey
   b) American Football
   c) Basketball

Round 6 – Great Sporting Moments

1. Having birdied the 17th to get back to all square the Scot was relieved to see Andy North's drive hit the water. All the Scot had to do now was sink his putt to win the Ryder Cup. Which golfer secured the crucial point for Europe?

2. It had been an incredible game, Liverpool had been 3-0 down at half time only to score 3 themselves in 6 second half minutes. It had come down to penalties, Serginho, Pirlo and Riise had all missed, Smicer scored for Liverpool. Up stepped Andrei Shevchenko, the AC Milan striker knowing he needed to score to keep his side in the game. Who was the keeper that saved his penalty and won the Champions League for the Reds?

Round 7 – On the Buzzer

This buzzer round is all about 1992.

1. Which Manchester United goalkeeper played for Denmark as they won the European Championship in Sweden?

2. Who became the first British sprinter in 12 years to win the Olympic 100m final?

3. Which famous jockey rode his 30th and final English Classic winner at the age of 56?

4. In 1992 which country hosted the Summer Olympics for the first time?

5. What was the nickname of the USA Olympic Men's Basketball gold medal winning team?

6. Which all-rounder captained Pakistan to victory over England in the Cricket World Cup final?

7. Who was the only British woman to win a track and field gold medal at the Summer Olympics?

8. Derek Pringle, Mark Waugh and Graham Gooch helped which county to retain the County Championship?

9. Which future six weight World Boxing Champion won the Olympic Lightweight gold medal?

10. Which country won successive Grand Slams in the Five Nations Championship?

11. At which Premier League football ground did Wigan set a record by scoring 48 points in the Premiership final against St Helens?

12. Which British driver won his only Formula One World Championship Title in 1992?

13. Which three time Wimbledon Singles Champion partnered Michael Stich to the Wimbledon Men's Doubles Title?

14. Which British cyclist won an Olympic gold medal in the 4000m Individual Pursuit?

15. Who became the first British boxer to win a World Boxing title at three different weights?

16. Nick Price became the first golfer from which country to win a Major by winning the USPGA Championship?

17. In which French city were the 1992 Winter Olympics held?

18. Who did Liverpool beat 2-0 to win the FA Cup final thanks to goals from Ian Rush and Michael Thomas?

19. With the general election only a few weeks away which aptly named horse won the Grand National in April?

20. Which English snooker player recorded a 147 maximum break at the World Championship?

Game 15

On this episode of A Question of Sport are...

Geoff Hurst (Football)
First appeared on the show as a guest in 1999

Amy Williams (Skeleton racing)
First appeared on the show as a guest in 2010

Jeremy Bates (Jeremy Bates)
First appeared on the show as a guest in 1986

Philippe Saint André (Rugby Union)
First appeared on the show as a guest in 2006

On Ally McCoist's final show as captain he was joined by Matt Dawson, Gary McAllister, Peter Reid, Sam Torrance and Jonathan Davies. Ally failed to identify his Rangers boss, Walter Smith, as a mystery guest on his last appearance on the show.

Round 1 – Opening Rally

1. Name the 10 British Track and Field athletes to win an individual Olympic gold medal between 1980 and 2004.

Round 2 – One Minute Round

1. Which Football League team play their home games at Bramall Lane?

2. Which horse race is run over 1 mile and 2 furlongs at Churchill Downs, Louisville?

3. Which former England Rugby Union international is nicknamed 'Billy Whizz'?

4. Which cricket county is this an anagram of? NOTHING HAS MERIT

5. What colour does the greyhound in trap one wear?

6. With which sport would you associate the Ipswich Witches and the Coventry Bees?

7. Which city hosted the 2006 Commonwealth Games?

These sports stars all share their surnames with European capital cities.

8. Bubba _____ (American Football)

9. Brian _____ (Boxing)

10. Dion _____ (Football)

Round 3 – Mystery Guest

1. I was born near Birmingham in 1953 and early in my career was a Special Constable in the Isle of Man (4 points)

   In 1992 I became only the 2nd person to win BBC Sports Personality of the Year twice (3 points)

   I became World Champion in 1992 and the following year won the CART IndyCar World Championship (2 points)

   Red 5 is synonymous with my career in racing (1 point)

2. I was born in California in 1970 and learned my trade watching my father's technique (4 points)

   Unlike the majority of my fellow competitors I play my chosen sport left handed (3 points)

   I made my Ryder Cup debut in 1995 and was part of the America's controversial win at Brookline in 1999 (2 points)

   My first major victory came at the US Masters in 2004 a tournament I have won again on more than one occasion (1 point)

Round 4 – Home or Away

1. *Geoff Hurst.* Who played in Arsenal's double winning side in 1971 and later managed them to all three domestic competition successes?

2. *Amy Williams.* By winning silver in the Skeleton Bobsleigh which woman won Britain's only Winter Olympic medal in 2006?

3. *Jeremy Bates.* Which Australian won the US Open in 1997 and 1998 before losing in successive Wimbledon finals to Pete Sampras and Goran Ivanisevic?

4. *Philippe Saint André.* Who, in 1999, captained France in their second World Cup final before scoring a try for Wasps in their Heineken Cup win in 2007?

Round 5 – Captain's Away

1. Which surname is shared by an Open Championship winning golfer from 2004 and a Formula One World Champion from the 2000s?

2. Between 2004 and 2011 which manager led four different sides into the Champions League semi-finals?

3. Name the two teams that competed in American Football's Superbowl in 2011?

4. With which sport would you associate pinkies, squats and terminal tackle?
   a) Angling
   b) Wrestling
   c) Three Day Eventing

Round 6 – What Happened Next

1. England and New Zealand are playing each other in a Test match and Phil Tufnell is about to bowl, what happened next?
   a) Tufnell trips over his own feet and ends up flat on his face half way down the wicket.
   b) Tufnell releases the ball too early and it flies up in the air,

lands by the square leg umpire and is hit for four by the batsman.

c) Tufnell bowls a beamer, the batsman and wicket keeper duck and the ball hits a spare helmet on the pitch resulting in five runs being awarded to New Zealand.

2. During a football game in the Israeli Second Division the goalkeeper has rushed out to clear the ball, what happened next?

a) The goalkeeper heads the ball out of play and a ball boy throws a replacement to the opposition who quickly take the throw resulting in a goal.

b) The goalkeeper controls the ball, beats the attacker and dribbles up the pitch to set up a goal for his team.

c) The goalkeeper goes to clear the ball but his trousers fall down and he trips over.

Round 7 – On the Buzzer

This buzzer round is all about teams and individuals winning on home soil.

1. Which country won football's World Cup in front of their home supporters in 1998?

2. England reached the first two Cricket World Cup finals, they were both held at which English Test ground?

3. Which country was the first to win the Rugby World Cup on home soil?

4. At which tournament did Mary Pierce win her second Grand Slam Singles Title?

5. Which Manchester born athlete won Commonwealth Games Men's 200m bronze in his home city?

6. Which British boxer won a World Title in front of his home fans in Nottingham by beating Jean Pascal in 2008?

7. On which circuit did Ayrton Senna record six Formula One pole positions in his home country between 1986 and 1994?

8. In the 2010 Champions League which player scored all four of his team's goals as they beat Arsenal in the quarter-finals at the Nou Camp?

9. In December 2010 which South African won his home Open Golf Tournament for the 5th time?

10. Which Rugby League team lost the 2011 World Club Challenge against the St George Illawarra Dragons at their home ground?

11. Athletes from the host nation won all three medals in the 2010 Commonwealth Games in the Women's Discus, which country did they represent?

12. Trained on Merseyside, Amberleigh House gave which trainer a 4th Grand National win?

13. At Headingley which Yorkshireman scored 103 for England against the West Indies in 2007?

14. In which sport did Australian Leisel Jones win three individual gold medals at the 2006 Commonwealth Games in Melbourne?

15. Which major race did Frenchman Bernard Hinault win on 5 occasions between 1978 and 1985?

16. Which host country failed to win a gold medal at the 1976 Summer Olympics?

17. Which Brazilian Formula One driver won his home Grand Prix in 2006 and 2008?

18. Which English athlete won the Women's 5000m at the 2002 Commonwealth Games in Manchester?

19. In 1999 Wales were forced to play their home Five Nations fixture with England at which English ground due to the Millennium Stadium being built?

20. Manchester United won their first European Cup final in 1968 by beating which club at Wembley?

Game 16

On this episode of A Question of Sport are...

Denise Lewis (Heptathlon)
First appeared on the show as a guest in 1995

Andrew Flintoff (Cricket)
First appeared on the show as a guest in 2001

Henry Cooper (Boxer)
First appeared on the show as a guest in 1970

Jonathan Davies (Rugby)
First appeared on the show as a guest in 1987

Round 1 – Opening Rally

1. Name the ten English football teams that have reached the final of one of the three European competitions between 1981 and 2011.

Round 2 – One Minute Round

1. Which country won the 2009 Twenty20 Cricket World Cup in England?

2. Which member of the British Monarchy won the BBC Sports Personality of the Year Award in 1971?

3. Which team did Timo Glock and Lucas Di Grassi drive for in the 2010 Formula One Championship?

4. What nationality is 1973 and 1975 World Snooker finalist Eddie Charlton?

5. Which Rugby Union World Cup winner is this an anagram of? NINTH MAJOR SON

6. In which year did the USA play against Europe in the Ryder Cup for the first time?

7. Which Football League team play their home games at Spotland?

These sports stars all share their surnames with big cats.

8. Emmanuel _____ (Football)

9. Dick _____ (Boxing)

10. Jamie _____ (Rugby League)

Round 3 – Mystery Guest

1. I was born in Belfast in 1946 (4 points)

   I made my name playing in the UK but towards the end of my
   career I had spells in South Africa, America and Australia (3 points)

   I won the European Cup in 1968 and was named the European
   Footballer of the Year as well (2 points)

   I'm best known for my dazzling skills Manchester United and
   Northern Ireland (1 point)

2. I was the world number one player in my sport for seven years
   and have reached numerous World Championship finals (4
   points)

   I still play at the top level now even though I'm past 50 (3 points)

   Nowadays though I usually end up commentating on World
   Championship finals rather than appearing in them (2 points)

   I am affectionately known as the 'Nugget' (1 point)

Round 4 – Home or Away

1. *Denise Lewis.* Which American woman won the Olympic
   100m on two occasions and the 100m Hurdles at the World
   Championships three times?

2. *Andrew Flintoff.* Which batsman scored two centuries in the 2011 World Cup helping him to become the top run scorer in the tournament with 500 runs?

3. *Henry Cooper.* Which British boxer twice went the distance with Muhammad Ali and once with Joe Frazier during the 1970s?

4. *Jonathan Davies.* Who played against Australia in both the 1995 Rugby League World Cup final and the 2003 Rugby Union World Cup final?

Round 5 – Captain's Away

1. Who came on as a substitute for Chelsea in the 1998 UEFA Cup Winners' Cup final and scored within 19 seconds?

2. Between 2005 and 2007 Andy Priaulx won three consecutive World Championships in which category of motor sport?

3. Name the two Germans to win a men's golf Major between 1980 and 2010?

4. In 1995 which man appeared in his 7th Wimbledon Singles final?
   a) Pete Sampras
   b) Stefan Edberg
   c) Boris Becker

Round 6 – Great Sporting Moments

1. After an unusually slow time of 54.3 seconds for the first 400m, Dave Warren jumped into the lead before Nikolai Kirov burst past and took the lead. Suddenly the British athlete raced to

the front just 70 metres from the line and managed to hold his competitors off to win Olympic gold in 1980. Who is this victorious British Olympian?

2. Coming into the fight as a 42-1 outsider the challenger out-boxed the slugging champion Mike Tyson in the early exchanges. The power of the champion was apparent in the eighth round however when he floored his American challenger with a right uppercut. However the challenger was not to be denied and knocked Tyson out in the 10th round. Which American shocked the boxing world with this victory?

Round 7 – On the Buzzer

This buzzer round is all about the year 1988.

1. Who scored the winning goal for Wimbledon in their FA Cup final victory over Liverpool?

2. In which field event did Dalton Grant break a British Record?

3. Which British ski jumper finished last in both the 70m and 90m events at the Winter Olympics?

4. Which American athlete won both the women's 100m and 200m at the Olympic Games?

5. In which discipline did Greg Louganis retain his two gold medals at the Olympic Games?

6. Against which country in the summer Tests did England famously appoint four different captains?

7. Which city hosted the 1988 Summer Olympics Games?

8. For which country did Rugby Union player Chris Oti score a hat trick of tries against Ireland?

9. Who beat Martina Navratilova to win the first of her seven Wimbledon Singles finals?

10. Which English striker scored a hat trick at the age of 17 for Southampton against Arsenal in the League Championship?

11. On which course did Seve Ballesteros win his third and final Open Championship Title?

12. Which Rugby League team did Joe Lydon and Andy Gregory both score points for in the Challenge Cup final?

13. In which sport did Germany's Kristin Otto win six Summer Olympic gold medals?

14. Who fought Mike Tyson for the World Heavyweight Title, 10 years after his brother held the title?

15. Which country beat the hosts of the 1988 European Championships in the semi-final before beating the Soviet Union in the final?

16. Which Brazilian athlete won a 800m Olympic silver medal 4 years after he won gold in the same event at the Los Angeles Games?

17. In which sport did American Eddie Lawson win his third World Championship title in five years?

18. Pirmin Zurbriggen won a gold medal at the Winter Olympic Games in the Downhill Skiing, what nationality is he?

19. Which British golfer won his first US Masters title, his second Major of the decade, by one shot?

20. Who scored 8 times for Great Britain as the Men's Field Hockey team won gold at the 1988 Summer Olympics?

Game 17

On this episode of A Question of Sport are...

Bobby Moore (Football)
First appeared on the show as a guest in 1972

Sam Torrance (Golf)
First appeared on the show as a guest in 1983

Peter Nicol (Squash)
First appeared on the show as a guest in 2001

Clive Lloyd (Cricket)
First appeared on the show as a guest in 1977

Matt Dawson took over
as a regular captain on the
programme in 2004 following
his Rugby Union World Cup
winning exploits with England.

Round 1 – Opening Rally

1. Up until the end of the 2010 season 12 teams have played in the top flight of English Rugby Union for at least ten seasons. Name them.

Round 2 – One Minute Round

1. Which NBA basketball team play their home games at Madison Square Garden?

2. Which Rugby League team play their Super League home games at Stade Gilbert Brutus?

3. Which England striker is this an anagram of? SNARLED FIEND

4. In 1996 on which horse did Mick Fitzgerald win his only Grand National at Aintree?

5. Which Danish tennis player topped the Women's World Rankings for the first time in October 2010?

6. Which cricketer took a record 383 Test wickets for England in his career?

7. With which sport would you associate Melbourne Heart and the Newcastle Jets?

These sports stars all share their surnames with royal titles.

8. Mervyn _____ (Darts)

9. Ashwell _____ (Cricket)

10. Gerry _____ (Football)

Round 3 – Mystery Guest

1. Although I retired in 2001 I am still heavily involved in my sport as a pundit (4 points)

   I'm regarded as one of the greatest competitors of all time in my sport having dominated my two events throughout the 1990s (3 points)

   I ran to victory in two events at the Atlanta Olympics to become the only man to win these two events in Olympic history (2 points)

   Usain Bolt broke my 12 year old world record in the 200m at the 2008 Summer Olympics (1 point)

2. My mother was born in Dewsbury but I was born overseas (4 points)

   I turned professional in 1991 and reached number four in the World Rankings in 1997 (3 points)

   In the same year I reached the US Open Singles final but was defeated by an Australian (2 points)

   Despite being born in Canada I represented Britain in the Davis Cup (1 point)

Round 4 – Home or Away

1. *Bobby Moore.* Who missed out on equalling Bobby Charlton's goal scoring record in England internationals by one goal, finishing on 48 goals in his 80 appearances?

2. *Sam Torrance.* Between 1996 and 2007 which Fijian was the only non-American to win the USPGA Championship, doing so in both 1998 and 2004?

3. *Peter Nicol.* Which Pakistani squash player won the World Open on six occasions during the 1980s?

4. *Clive Lloyd.* Who between 1978 and 1994 played in over 150 Test matches and won 32 of the 93 games in which he captained his country?

Round 5 – Captain's Away

1. Between 1993 and 2000 who was the only player to beat Pete Sampras in a Singles match at Wimbledon?

2. Which country won 11 medals at the Summer Olympics in Beijing, all coming in athletics events?

3. Name the two drivers who won the Formula One World Championship whilst driving for Ferrari in the 2000s?

4. With which sport would you associate reverse swing and pen holder grip?
    a) Bowls
    b) Table Tennis
    c) Badminton

Round 6 – What Happened Next

1. At the Wimbledon Championships in 1995, Steffi Graf is just about to serve, what happened next?
    a) Graf slices her serve and it knocks the umpire off his chair.

b) Graf throws the ball up in the air but is distracted by an insect and the ball hits her in the face.

c) A fan in the crowd shouts out to Graf 'Steffi will you marry me?'

2. Newcastle United goalkeeper Shay Given has the ball in his hands and is about to clear it up field into the Coventry City half, what happened next?

a) Given rolls the ball out in front of him but before he can kick it clear Dion Dublin surprises him by running from off the pitch behind him and puts it into the net.

b) Given throws the ball against the back of his teammate John Beresford's head and the ball loops into the air over the stranded keep into the goal.

c) Given launches the ball up field and it sails well into the Coventry City half and bounces over the head of their goalie Steve Ogrizovic and into the net.

Round 7 – On the Buzzer

All the answers to this buzzer round begin with the letter D. In the case of a person it's the surname that must start with that letter.

1. Which country won the 1992 European Championship by beating Germany 2-0 in the final?

2. At which English racecourse is the English Classic the St Leger run?

3. Which golfer won his first Major in 2001 by claiming victory at the Open Championship?

4. Which Russian tennis player won the end of season ATP World Tour Title in 2009, the first time it was held in London?

5. Which Irishman won snooker's World Championship in 1997?

6. Which famous grey won the 1989 Cheltenham Gold Cup?

7. Which Indian all rounder scored over 5000 runs and took over 400 wickets in his 131 Tests between 1978 and 1994?

8. Which American Football team won the Superbowl three times in five years between 1992 and 1996?

9. Which 400m hurdler won bronze at the 2008 Olympics to become the first British woman to win an Olympic medal in the event since Sally Gunnell?

10. Which 2008 Olympic Middleweight Champion beat Paul Smith in 2010 to become the British Super Middleweight Champion?

11. Which team did Brian Clough lead to League Championship victory in 1972?

12. In which athletics event did Estonian Gerd Kanter win Olympic gold in 2008?

13. Which South African took 330 Test wickets in his international career between 1992 and 2002?

14. Which NHL Ice Hockey team have won the Stanley Cup 11 times between 1935 and 2008?

15. Which flamboyant American golfer won the USPGA Championship in 1991 and the Open Championship in 1995?

16. In which sport have Les Wallace, Steve Beaton and John Walton been World Champions?

17. Which Eastern European team won the UEFA Cup Winners' Cup for the first time in 1975?

18. In which discipline did Canadian Alexandre Despatie win three Commonwealth gold medals at the 2010 Games?

19. Which American athletics star won Olympic gold medals in the women's 100m in 1992 and 1996?

20. Which city hosted the 2010 Commonwealth Games?

Game 18

On this episode of A Question of Sport are...

Maurice Greene (Athletics)
First appeared on the show as a guest in 2000

Richard Hadlee (Cricket)
First appeared on the show as a guest in 1984

Laura Davies (Golf)
First appeared on the show as a guest in 1989

Martin Offiah (Rugby)
First appeared on the show as a guest in 1989

Round 1 – Opening Rally

1. Other than goalkeeper Gordon Banks name the ten England players that started the 1966 World Cup final.

Round 2 – One Minute Round

1. Which country hosted a Moto GP race in 2010 at Mugello?

2. With which sport do you associate the women's sports teams Chicago Sky, New York Liberty and the Minnesota Lynx?

3. What nationality is 1995 French Open Men's Singles Title Champion Thomas Muster?

4. Which team play their Rugby Union Premiership home games at Kingston Park?

5. Which Olympic host city is this an anagram of? SELLS AN EGO

6. In which sport might a competitor perform a salchow?

7. Which country did the West Indies bowl out for 58 in the 2011 Cricket World Cup?

These sports stars all share parts of their names with English counties.

8. _____ Anderson (Baseball)

9. _____ Malcolm (Cricket)

10. Johnny _____ (Boxing)

Round 3 – Mystery Guest

1. I am the son of a former Champion and in February 2009 I turned 30 (4 points)

   I myself have been a World Champion in three different classes (3 points)

   I have won over 100 races and only my compatriot Giacomo Agostini had achieved that before me (2 points)

   I won the World Championship Title five years in succession in the 2000s wearing the number 46 (1 point)

2. I was born in Volgograd and tried gymnastics when I was five years old but was considered too tall to make a career out of that sport (4 points)

   The gymnastics certainly helped me when I started my chosen sport and I dominated my field throughout the 2000s (3 points)

   I won Olympic gold in 2004 and 2008 as well as World Championship gold medals in Helsinki and Osaka (2 points)

   I have broken the world record on over 25 occasions and in London I became the first woman to clear 5 metres in my sport (1 point)

Round 4 – Home or Away

1. *Maurice Greene.* Which Namibian athlete won successive Olympic silver medals in the 200m in 1992 and 1996?

2. *Richard Hadlee.* Which Middlesex player captained England in the 1979 World Cup final at Lord's?

3. *Laura Davies.* Which Swedish woman finished runner up in the du Maurier Classic in 1998 before going on to win all four majors in the 2000s?

4. *Martin Offiah.* Who captained Leeds Rhinos to three successive Super League Grand Final victories between 2007 and 2009?

Round 5 – Captain's Away

1. 32 years separated which woman's first and last tennis Grand Slam wins?

2. Who in May 2000 became the first England international footballer to score in a winning European Cup final side whilst at a foreign club?

3. Name the two Rugby League teams that played in the 2011 Super League season beginning with the letter S?

4. Which event did Scotland's Yvonne Murray win a European Title in 1990?
    a) 3000m
    b) Long Jump
    c) 100m Hurdles

Round 6 – Great Sporting Moments

1. With seconds left and the Republic of Ireland a goal down, Steve Finnan sent in a long ball from the right back position. Niall Quinn managed to flick the ball on with the back of his head and the striker managed to chest the ball beyond Christian

Ramelow and strike the ball into the back of the net. Who was the forward scoring this World Cup goal?

2. Following his loss at the 1992 Summer Olympics, Mike Powell had won 34 straight competitions including the 1993 World Championships. In the 3rd round of the Long Jump at the Atlanta Olympics Frenchman Emmanuel Bangue and Powell were in the lead. Which American jumped 8.50 metres to win his 4th successive Olympic gold medal?

Round 7 – On the Buzzer

This buzzer round is all about the year 1999.

1. Who on January 2nd took the first Ashes hat trick by an Englishman in the 20th century?

2. Which British decathlete won World Championship silver behind Tomas Dvorak in Seville?

3. In March Lennox Lewis drew in a World Heavyweight showdown with which American boxer?

4. Which jockey broke Peter Scudamore's record for the most National Hunt winners in a career?

5. Whose wonderful goal helped Manchester United to an extra time FA Cup semi-final win over Arsenal?

6. Which country did Australia famously defeat on net run-rate in cricket's World Cup semi-final?

7. Which Scotsman won his first Major after a three way playoff at Carnoustie?

8. Which American returned to cycling after a battle with cancer and won his first Tour de France?

9. Which country won the last ever Five Nations Championships on points difference from England?

10. Which American won her first Wimbledon Singles Title by beating Steffi Graf in the German's last career Grand Slam match?

11. In which sport did Olympic medallist Paul Palmer win European gold in Istanbul?

12. Which British rider won his fourth and final World Superbike Championship?

13. Which British golfer clinched his seventh consecutive European Order of Merit Title?

14. Which boxer was named the BBC Sports Personality of the 20th Century?

15. Which club were beaten in the Champions League final by conceding two goals in injury time?

16. Which Frenchwoman beat Denise Lewis to Heptathlon gold at the 1999 World Championships?

17. Which pair of brothers scored all of Bradford Bulls' points as they won the Super League Grand Final?

18. Which Russian tennis player won the Australian Open by beating Sweden's Thomas Enqvist?

19. Which British driver finished two points behind Mika Hakkinen in the Formula One World Championship?

20. Which former Ballon d'Or winner managed Newcastle United to the FA Cup final?

Game 19

On this episode of A Question of Sport are...

Kenny Dalglish (Football)
First appeared on the show as a guest in 1979

Lucinda Green (Equestrianism)
First appeared on the show as a guest in 1983

Bernhard Langer (Golf)
First appeared on the show as a guest in 1982

Frankie Dettori (Horse racing)
First appeared on the show as a guest in 1991

Italian Frankie Dettori became the first non-British regular captain of the programme in 2002 and captained the show opposite Ally for two years.

Round 1 – Opening Rally

1. Name the ten men to reach a Wimbledon Singles final between 2000 and 2010.

Round 2 – One Minute Round

1. In which sport did Joe Davis win the first 15 World Championships?

2. Which Fijian golfer won the 1998 USPGA Championship to claim his first Major?

3. Which English football team play their home games at Vicarage Road and once had Elton John as their chairman?

4. Which NHL Ice Hockey team is this an anagram of? WINTERS ODD TIGER

5. In what capacity were John Williams and Len Ganley renowned in an indoor sport?

6. In which English city would you find the Phoenix playing their Ice Hockey home games?

7. Which team play their Rugby Union Premiership home games at Welford Road?

These sports stars all share their surnames with types of fruit.

8. Trevor _____ (Football)

9. Daryl _____ (Baseball)

10. David _____ (Rugby Union)

Round 3 – Mystery Guest

1. I won the USA's only gold medal in my sport at the 1992 Summer Olympics (4 points)

   I won my first World Title within two years of claiming Olympic gold and I went onto gain titles in other weights (3 points)

   In my last couple of fights I lost to Floyd Mayweather Jr and Manny Pacquiao (2 points)

   Since retiring I have become a promoter setting up the company Golden Boy Promotions (1 point)

2. I was born in Yorkshire in 1974 and I was tipped for stardom as a teenager (4 points)

   I made my debut for Great Britain in 1993 whilst playing for Wigan (3 points)

   I scored a try in the first Super League Grand Final in 1998 to help my team win the trophy and in 2000 I crossed codes and joined the Sale Sharks (2 points)

   My try helped England win the 2003 Rugby Union World Cup final (1 point)

Round 4 – Home or Away

1. *Kenny Dalglish.* Which player scored over 50 goals for Celtic during the 2000/2001 season?

2. *Lucinda Green.* Which British rider won the horse trials at Burghley four times and Badminton once in the 2000s?

3. *Bernhard Langer.* In 1999 at the age of 19 which Spaniard became the youngest player in Ryder Cup history winning 3 and a half points in the process?

4. *Frankie Dettori.* Between 2000 and 2005 which jockey rode Sinndar, High Chapparal and Motivator to victory in the Epsom Derby?

Round 5 – Captain's Away

1. In the 1981 Ashes Test at Headingley which English bowler took 8 for 43 to bowl Australia out for 111?

2. In 2010 which country provided World Champions in Moto GP, Moto 2 and the 125cc Motor Racing Championships?

3. Name the two American Football teams that played in the 2010 NFL season that are based in the state of Texas?

4. Which Frenchman appeared in a Wimbledon Singles final in 1997?
   a) Guy Forget
   b) Fabrice Santoro
   c) Cedric Pioline

Round 6 – What Happened Next

1. The Rajasthan Royals are in action in the Indian Premier League Twenty20 competition. Shane Watson is at the crease, what happened next?

a) The power cuts out temporarily and when the lights come back on Shane Watson has been bowled.
b) Watson's bat breaks in half but he still manages to hit the ball for six.
c) The game is interrupted by a swarm of bees forcing the players to run for cover.

2. Spurs goalkeeper Paul Robinson is about to take a free kick just outside his penalty area, what happened next?
   a) Robinson's kick sails over everyone's heads, takes an awkward bounce over Watford keeper Ben Foster and goes into the net.
   b) As Robinson goes to kick the ball he slips and scuffs the ball straight into the path of Watford striker Tommy Smith who has the simple task of rolling the ball into the empty net.
   c) Robinson slices his kick into the stands and the ball hits Watford manager Aidy Boothroyd on the touchline, knocking him over.

Round 7 – On the Buzzer

This buzzer round is all about New Zealand.

1. Which Premier League team did New Zealand footballer Ryan Nelsen join in January 2005?

2. Who scored a 2011 Cricket World Cup century for New Zealand against Pakistan on his birthday?

3. Which man became the first golfer from New Zealand in over 40 years to win a Major when he won the US Open in 2005?

4. Which former World Cup winners did New Zealand draw 1-1 with at the 2010 Football World Cup?

5. In 1967 in which sport did Denny Hulme become the first World Champion from New Zealand?

6. Which New Zealand athlete won Olympic gold in the 800m in 1960 and won both the 800m and 1500m at the 1964 Olympics?

7. Which New Zealand city hosted the Commonwealth Games in 1950 and 40 years later in 1990?

8. Who in 1987 captained New Zealand to victory in the first Rugby Union World Cup final?

9. Which New Zealand tennis player lost in straight sets to John McEnroe in the 1983 Wimbledon final?

10. Which World Championships were held near Hamilton in New Zealand on two occasions, once in 1978 and again in 2010?

11. Who by scoring a try against Scotland at the World Cup in 2007 overtook Christian Cullen to become New Zealand's record try scorer?

12. In which sport did Sarah Ulmer win an individual gold at the 2004 Olympics in Athens?

13. Which famous sailing race did Team New Zealand win in 2000 beating Luna Rossa?

14. For which Super League team did New Zealand Rugby League star Stacey Jones play in 2006 and 2007?

15. In which sport are the New Zealand women's national team known as the Silver Ferns?

16. Which New Zealand wicket keeper scored the fastest half century in World Cup cricket in 2007 coming off just 20 balls?

17. Between 1980 and 2000 which New Zealand rider won the Badminton Horse trials on three occasions and the Burghley Horse Trials five times?

18. In which sport has Bevan Docherty and Erin Baker been World Champions?

19. In which Canadian city did New Zealand win Men's Field Hockey Olympic gold at the 1976 Olympics?

20. Which New Zealand bowler became the first man to take 400 Test wickets?

Game 20

On this episode of A Question of Sport are...

Ray Clemence (Football)
First appeared on the show as a guest in 1984

Robin Cousins (Figure skating)
First appeared on the show as a guest in 1984

Richard Krajicek (Tennis)
First appeared on the show as a guest in 2004

Colin Montgomerie (Golf)
First appeared on the show as a guest in 1992

After Ally McCoist's departure from the show, *A Question of Sport* had a brief spell of guest captains sitting in the chair opposite Matt Dawson. These included Phil Tufnell, Shane Warne, Jamie Redknapp, Darren Gough, Gary Speed and Ricky Hatton.

Round 1 – Opening Rally

1. Name the ten Major League Baseball teams that won the World Series between 1995 and 2010.

Round 2 – One Minute Round

1. How was the Olympic Athletics Stadium in Beiijng more commonly known?

2. Which County Championship team play their home games at Edgbaston?

3. Which Italian team known as 'the Old Lady' won the 1996 Champions League?

4. Which English father and son have both won Formula One Grand Prix races?

5. Which English football team is this an anagram of? SWEAT IN THE MUD

6. Which men's golf Grand Slam is the last to be played in the calendar year?

7. In which sport did Amy Williams win a gold medal for Britain at the 2010 Winter Olympics?

These sports stars all share their surnames with types of fish.

8. Jamie _____ (Rugby Union)

9. Shaun _____ (Cricket)

10. James _____ (Football)

Round 3 – Mystery Guest

1. Although I made my international debut in 2001 my career has been interrupted due to injury on several occasions (4 points)

   I played for the British and Irish Lions in 2005 but another injury kept me out of the tour to South Africa in 2009 (3 points)

   I partnered Tom Shanklin at centre as Wales won the Grand Slam (2 points)

   I partnered Katya Virshilas on Strictly Come Dancing in 2010 (1 point)

2. At the age of 2 I moved to Hawaii and swam nearly everyday at Waikiki Beach (4 points)

   I set my 1st world record in 1967 in a time of 4 minutes and 10 seconds (3 points)

   In 1968 I won two Olympic gold medals in the pool in relay events (2 point)

   It was in 1972 that I astonished the world by winning seven swimming gold medals at a single Summer Olympic Games (1 point)

Round 4 – Home or Away

1. *Ray Clemence.* Which England goalkeeper played in a League

Cup final in the 70s, 80s and the 90s, for Nottingham Forest, Norwich City and Sheffield Wednesday respectively?

2. *Robin Cousins.* Between 1984 and 1988 which woman won two Olympic Figure Skating gold medals and four World Championships?

3. *Richard Krajicek.* Which Brazilian's three Grand Slam Singles victories all came on clay at Roland Garros between 1997 and 2001?

4. *Colin Montgomerie.* In 2003 Mike Weir became the first left handed golfer to win the US Masters and in doing so he became the first person from which country to win a Major?

Round 5 – Captain's Away

1. Of the horse racing courses in Britain which is the one with the least letters in its name?

2. In which competition did New Zealand beat England 13-10 in the final at the Stoop in 2010?

3. Between 1990 and 2010 name the two drivers who won the Formula One World Championship whose surnames begin with the letter V?

4. Which England batsman scored 177, 145 and 183 in the Ashes series in 2002/2003?
   a) Andrew Strauss
   b) Marcus Trescothick
   c) Michael Vaughan

Round 6 – What Happened Next

1. Pat Cash is playing John McEnroe in London in December 2000. Cash is about to serve, what happened next?
   a) As Cash serves, the ball explodes and leaves traces of tennis ball all over the court.
   b) Just before Cash serves, McEnroe whips a spare ball out of his pocket and sends it over the net leaving Cash and the crowd in hysterics.
   c) As Cash serves a pigeon flies onto the court and leaves bird droppings on the court right next to where Cash is standing.

2. Brazil have won a corner in the dying seconds of their World Cup group match with Sweden in 1978, the scores are level at 1-1, what happened next?
   c) Zico rises to head the ball in for Brazil to give them a 2-1 win that sets them on their way to winning the group and eventually the tournament.
   d) Zico heads the ball into the net but referee Clive Thomas blows the final whistle as the ball is in mid air and he doesn't allow the goal to stand.
   e) Zico heads the ball into the net and during the celebrations is sent off for celebrating in the face of Austria's goalkeeper Friedrich Koncilia.

Round 7 – On the Buzzer

This buzzer round is all about the year 1986.

1. Which English athlete won both the Commonwealth and European Decathlon?

2. Which club clinched their first League and Cup double, beating Everton in the FA Cup final?

3. Which British city staged the Commonwealth Games in this year, 16 years after hosting it for the first time?

4. Which opening batsman scored centuries for England in three successive Ashes Tests in Australia?

5. Which pair of brothers made their debuts for Scotland against France in the Five Nations?

6. Which Yorkshireman won the World Championship at the Crucible for the only time in his career?

7. Who in 1986 became the first American to win the Tour de France?

8. Which English jockey won the Grand National at Aintree for the first time in his career when he rode West Tip to victory?

9. Which American won the last of her 18 tennis Grand Slam Singles titles by beating Martina Navratilova in the final of the French Open?

10. Which Australian won at Turnberry by five shots to win his first Open Championship?

11. Which country beat West Germany 3-2 in the football World Cup final?

12. Which British boxer stunned American Donald Curry by beating him in a World Welterweight Title fight?

13. In August 1986 which Englishman passed Dennis Lillee's world record 355 Test wickets?

14. Who became the oldest winner of the US Masters when he won his final Major at the age of 46?

15. Which country defeated Sweden 3-2 to win the Davis Cup despite Paul McNamee losing both of his singles matches?

16. In which Commonwealth Games sport did England's Malcolm and Sarah Cooper win gold?

17. For which country did Kirsty Wade win the 1986 Commonwealth Champion in the 800m and 1500m?

18. Which Olympic champion won Commonwealth Games gold medals in the Single Sculls, the Coxless Pairs and the Coxed Fours in Edinburgh?

19. Which Brazilian driver won four races for Williams in the 1986 Formula One season on his way to finishing third in the Championship?

20. In which sport did England's Sarah Hardcastle win two individual Commonwealth gold medals?

Game 21

On this episode of A Question of Sport are...

Shane Warne (Cricket)
First appeared on the show as a guest in 2000

Matthew Pinsent (Rowing)
First appeared on the show as a guest in 1993

Keke Rosberg (Motor racing)
First appeared on the show as a guest in 1983

Richard Dunwoody (National Hunt racing)
First appeared on the show as a guest in 1987

Round 1 – Opening Rally

1. Name the ten Spanish football teams that have won the Copa Del Rey between 1990 and 2010.

Round 2 – One Minute Round

1. Who won the Wimbledon Junior Boys' Championship in 1978 but his best performance in the Men's Singles Championship saw him finish runner up in 1986 and 1987?

2. Which Wimbledon FA Cup winner went on to captain Wales?

3. Which Englishman scored a century on his 100th Test appearance for his country in August 2000?

4. Which Welsh golfer won the US Masters in 1991?

5. Which Cricket World Cup winning team is this an anagram of? A TRIAL USA

6. In which sport do teams play with a puck?

7. Which team did Jenson Button and Lewis Hamilton drive for in the 2010 Formula One Championship?

These sports stars all share their surnames with colours.

8. Robert _____ (Football)

9. Roger _____ (Athletics)

10. Alistair _____ (Cricket)

Round 3 – Mystery Guest

1. I was working in a sawmill when my career began in 1982 (4 points)

   I made my debut for Australia in that year and by the time I retired 14 years later I had won over 100 international caps (3 points)

   I won the Rugby Union World Cup in 1991 (2 points)

   I finished my career with 64 international tries and am considered to be one of the greatest wingers to have ever played the game (1 point)

2. I turned 45 in November 2010 having just become a national coach (4 points)

   At the age of 35 I moved to the Premier League and won a league title (3 points)

   I missed my country's World Cup final win in 1998 having been sent off in the semi-finals (2 points)

   I was well known for kissing my close friend Fabien Barthez on the head before games (1 point)

Round 4 – Home or Away

1. *Shane Warne.* Who, by dismissing Andrew Symonds in 2008 became the first Indian bowler to take 600 Test wickets?

2. *Matthew Pinsent.* Who were the British brothers who won gold

at the 1992 Olympic Games in the Coxed Pairs?

3. *Keke Rosberg.* When Michael Schumacher won the World Title in 2000 he became the first Ferrari driver to win it for 21 years. Which South African won the title for Ferrari in 1979?

4. *Richard Dunwoody.* In 2010 Tony McCoy finally won the Grand National at his 15th attempt. Which horse did he ride to victory at Aintree?

Round 5 – Captain's Away

1. Which American won the 1997 Open Championship at Troon and lost in a playoff in the competition two years later?

2. Which four letter indoor sport is an anagram of an outdoor sport, neither of which are part of the Olympic programme?

3. Name the two teams that played in an FA Cup final during the 2000s whose names end in a vowel?

4. Which country is Olympic silver medal winning sprinter Frankie Fredericks from?
   a) Namibia
   b) Trinidad and Tobago
   c) Jamaica

Round 6 – What Happened Next

1. Steffi Graf and Martina Hingis are in action in the French Open Singles final in 1999, Hingis is about to serve, what happened next?
   a) Hingis served the ball underarm to her opponent.

b) Hingis's mother and coach started shouting instructions to her and had to be removed by the match referee.

c) Hingis hit a powerful serve that hit the line judge at the back of the court and knocked him over.

2. Canadian gymnast Alexander Jeltkov is on the High Bar at the 2002 Commonwealth Games in Manchester, what happened next?

a) As Jeltkov is performing a double backwards spin his coach gets too close and is caught in the side of the face by the gymnast's trailing legs.

b) After a superb performance on the bar Jeltkov is just about to begin his big finale when the bar snaps ands he falls to the floor.

c) As Jeltkov goes to dismount he slips and lands face first on the mat ending his hopes of a medal.

Round 7 – On the Buzzer

All the answers to this buzzer round begin with the letter B. In the case of a person it's the surname that must start with that letter.

1. In 2010 which football team beat Cardiff City in the Championship playoff final to reach the Premier League for the first time?

2. Which American Football team lost in the Superbowl four times in the 1990s?

3. Which British cyclist won an Olympic gold medal in the 4000m Individual Pursuit in 1992?

4. Which Rugby League team which play their home games at Odsal won the Super League for the first time in 1997?

5. Which tennis player won the Wimbledon Men's Singles Title five years in a row from 1976 to 1980?

6. With which NBA team did Larry Bird win three NBA Championship Titles in the 80s?

7. Which country reached the semi-finals of the Football World Cup for the first time in their history in 1994?

8. Which Trinidad and Tobago athlete won Olympic medals in the 100m and 200m at both the 1996 and the 2000 Games?

9. Which country beat England, Ireland and the Netherlands at the 2011 Cricket World Cup?

10. Which city hosted the Summer Olympics in 1992?

11. In which country did Lewis Hamilton win the 2008 Formula One World Championship in the final race of the season?

12. In which sport did Gail Emms and Nathan Robertson win an Olympic silver medal in 2004?

13. Which English darts player won the World Championship in 1996 by beating Richie Burnett in the final?

14. Which European golfer won his first Open Championship title in 1979 at Royal Lytham and St Annes?

15. Which horse did Paul Carberry ride to victory in the Grand National in 1999?

16. Who are the only Rugby Union team beginning with B that played in the 2010/11 Guinness Premiership season?

17. Which Australian batsman retired from Test cricket in 1948

with an average of 99.94 and 29 international centuries?

18. Which baseball team won the World Series in 2004 for the first time in over 80 years?

19. Which American boxer was beaten to Heavyweight gold by Lennox Lewis in the Olympics in 1988 before going on to become the World Heavyweight Champion in 1992?

20. Which Englishman reached the final of the World Snooker Championship in 1995?

Game 22

On this episode of A Question of Sport are...

Ian Rush (Football)
First appeared on the show as a guest in 1987

Chris Hoy (Cycling)
First appeared on the show as a guest in 2003

Greg Chappell (Cricket)
First appeared on the show as a guest in 1972

Nick Faldo (Golf)
First appeared on the show as a guest in 1979

Phil Tufnell was selected as a permanent captain on the programme after a number of guest appearances as captain in 2007. He took over the job full time in January 2008, 18 years after his first appearance on the show.

Round 1 – Opening Rally

1. Name the ten snooker players that won the World Championship between 1990 and 2010?

Round 2 – One Minute Round

1. Which Englishman partnered Ian Poulter in both foursomes at the 2008 Ryder Cup?

2. In which month of the year is Royal Ascot held?

3. Which Rugby League team play their Super League home games at Odsal Stadium?

4. Which Romanian tennis player won four end of season ATP Masters Grand Prix between 1970 and 1975?

5. Which sporting event is this an anagram of? THE COMMAS GLEAM NOW

6. Which major sporting event began on June 11th in 2010 in Johannesburg?

7. What does the TT stand for in the Isle of Man TT?

These sports stars all share their surnames with places where you find lots of trees.

8. Grace _____ (Golf)

9. Craig _____ (Football)

10. Willie _____ (Bowls)

Round 3 – Mystery Guest

1. I was a large baby when I was born in 1982, my mother played A-grade netball and my father was a promising cricketer (4 points)

   In 1998 I won my 1st World Title aged just 15 (3 points)

   I won 4 gold medals for Australia at the 1998 Commonwealth Games whilst I was still at school (2 points)

   I won a total of 5 Olympic gold medals in 2000 and 2004 and am well known for my large feet (1 point)

2. I was born in September 1980 and represented Switzerland in the Fed Cup (4 points)

   I partnered Jana Novotna and Anna Kournikova amongst others to victories in Grand Slam Doubles finals (3 points)

   I became the youngest Grand Slam Singles winner of the 20th century by beating Mary Pierce at the Australian Open (2 points)

   I was voted out of *Strictly Come Dancing* in the first week of the show in 2009 (1 point)

Round 4 – Home or Away

1. *Ian Rush. Who* played in Manchester United's FA Cup final teams against Everton in both 1985 and 1995?

2. *Chris Hoy.* Which British cyclist finished fourth in the 2009 Tour de France a year after winning two Olympic gold medals?

3. *Greg Chappell.* Which Australian scored 380 against Zimbabwe in 2003 to break Brian Lara's record highest Test score?

4. *Nick Faldo.* Which American golfer beat two Australians in a playoff to win the 1989 Open Championship?

Round 5 – Captain's Away

1. What name links these three? An England Rugby Union captain, an Ashes bowler from 2010 and a British Olympic athletics bronze medallist?

2. Having not won the Challenge Cup for 35 years, which team beat the Huddersfield Giants and the Leeds Rhinos in the 2009 and 2010 finals?

3. Name the two Wimbledon Singles Champions from the 1990s whose surnames begin with a vowel?

4. What was unusual about Nigel Melville's England Rugby Union international debut?
   a) Scored 4 tries
   b) Was sent off in within 5 minutes
   c) Captained England

Round 6 – Great Sporting Moments

1. Having been level at half time, Brazil had taken a 3-1 lead mid way through the second half of the 1970 World Cup final. Brazil were playing some beautiful football which came to a climax when Clodoaldo danced his way up field with the ball. Rivelino, Jairzinho moved the ball along beautifully before Pele's perfectly weighted pass set up which player to score one of the greatest goals in World Cup history?

2. Tore Andre Flo was replaced for Chelsea in the 70th minute. The substitute had an immediate impact latching onto a wonderful Dennis Wise pass and with only his third touch of the game sent the ball high into the Stuttgart net to win the UEFA Cup Winners' Cup for Chelsea. Who struck the winner for the Blues?

Round 7 – On the Buzzer

This buzzer round is all about the year 2000.

1. Who retired from international football having won 63 caps and scoring 30 goals for England?

2. Who passed Roy Emerson's previous record of 12 Grand Slam Singles wins with victory at Wimbledon?

3. In 2000 which country staged its first Olympic Games in 44 years?

4. Ted 'the Count' Hankey won which World Title in January?

5. In which sport did Martin Pipe become an all time leading trainer overtaking Arthur Stephenson?

6. Dan Marino retired in 2000 after a 17 year career for which American Football team?

7. Which West Indian fast bowler became the all-time leading wicket taker in Test matches, overtaking Kapil Dev?

8. Tiger Woods won three of the four golf Majors in 2000, which Fijian won the US Masters?

9. Paul Grayson's 3 penalties helped which English team to win Rugby Union's Heineken Cup final?

10. After losing to Germany in the last game at the old Wembley which England manager resigned in 2000?

11. In June 2000 Scotland's Ken Buchanan was inducted into which sport's Hall of Fame?

12. Which Brazilian driver won his first Formula One race by winning the 2000 German Grand Prix?

13. Which French tennis player won the French Open Women's Singles Title by beating Conchita Martinez?

14. In which sport did Jason Queally win Britain's first Olympic gold medal of the 2000 Games?

15. Which British woman won Olympic bronze in the 800m?

16. In which sport did Britain's Shirley Robertson win an Olympic gold medal in 2000?

17. Which scrum half captained England in all five of his country's Six Nations Championship games?

18. Which country won the most medals at the 2000 Olympics, 97 in total of which 39 were gold?

19. Which golfer topped the European Money List, 10 years before becoming the world's number one?

20. Which country won the 2000 European Championships thanks to a golden goal?

Game 23

On this episode of A Question of Sport are...

Stuart Pearce (Football)
First appeared on the show as a guest in 1990

James Cracknell (Rowing)
First appeared on the show as a guest in 2001

Sue Barker (Tennis)
First appeared on the show as a guest in 1984

Mal Meninga (Rugby League)
First appeared on the show as a guest in 1990

Round 1 – Opening Rally

1. Other than the winners South Africa name the ten non-European countries that featured in the 2007 Rugby Union World Cup.

Round 2 – One Minute Round

1. What number does the starting hooker in Rugby Union wear?

2. Which former Barcelona player managed them to the treble in 2009?

3. Which Cricket World Cup winning team is this an anagram of? WIT IS DENSE

4. What nationality is the 2010 French Open winner Francesca Schiavone?

5. Which bird gives its name to a score on a hole of golf that is two under par?

6. Which County Championship team play their home games at Headingley?

7. Which jockey became the fastest man to ride 1000 career winners in National Hunt racing?

These sports stars all share parts of their names with things that are associated with fishing.

8. James _____ (Rugby Union)

9. _____ Laver (Tennis)

10. Jeff _____ (Golf)

Round 3 – Mystery Guest

1. I was born in Scotland in 1963 and raised in Yorkshire (4 points)

    I was leading European in my sport for seven successive years between 1993 and 1999 (3 points)

    I won the World Cup with Scotland in 2007 (2 points)

    I made my Ryder Cup debut in 1991 and captained the side to victory 19 years later (1 point)

2. After leaving school I made ceramic toilet roll holders in the Potteries (4 points)

    My first title was the Canadian Open in 1988 (3 points)

    I beat my mentor to win my first World Championship Title in 1990 (2 points)

    I won my 15th World Championship Title at the age of 49 (1 point)

Round 4 – Home or Away

1. *Stuart Pearce.* Between 1978 and 1993 which England full back played in League Cup finals with Nottingham Forest, Arsenal and Sheffield Wednesday?

2. *James Cracknell.* Which British woman won Olympic Rowing medals in 2000, 2004 and 2008?

3. **Sue Barker.** Who between 1961 and 1979 won a record 20 Wimbledon Titles including six Women's Singles?

4. **Mal Meninga.** Which player won the Man of Steel three times in the 1980s, once with Bradford and twice with Wigan?

Round 5 – Captain's Away

1. Which England player faced just one ball in the 2010/11 Ashes series with his dismissal giving Peter Siddle his hat trick?

2. In which sport have Japanese brothers Joe and Jumbo Ozaki competed?

3. Name the two teams that won the League Cup in the 2000s whose names begin with the letter L?

4. What was unusual about Allan Wells' winning of the Commonwealth Games 200m in 1982?
   a) Ran without spikes
   b) Won in a dead heat and shared the gold medal
   c) Left at the blocks but recovered to win

Round 6 – Great Sporting Moments

1. Alan Shearer gave England an early lead with a header before Stefan Kuntz levelled before half time. After a series of near misses for England the game went to penalties and, after both teams scored their first five penalties it went to sudden death. Which defender stepped up for England only to see his strike saved by Andreas Kopke before Andreas Moller sent Germany through?

2. With Marie-Jose Perec out of the picture she was now the clear favourite. In the final she came round the last bend level pegging with Lorraine Graham and Katharine Merry just behind with the crowd roaring her on. She powered to 400m Olympic glory over the last 80 metres to send her home crowd in the stands delirious. Who is she?

Round 7 – On the Buzzer

This buzzer round is all about sporting firsts.

1. In 2009 Juan Martin Del Potro became the first male player from which country to win the US Open since 1977?

2. Who in 2003 became the first left-hander to win the US Masters?

3. Which athlete became the first man to win three successive 100m World Championship gold medals?

4. After winning the 2008 FA Cup, which club played in Europe for the first time in their history the following season?

5. Tessa Sanderson became the first British woman to win an Olympic gold medal in which event?

6. Who became the first woman to train the winner of the Grand National at Aintree when Corbiere won in 1983?

7. Which country became the first to win the Rugby Union World Cup on two occasions?

8. Which England spinner's first Test wicket was Sachin Tendulkar in 2006?

9. Which basketball team won their first NBA Championship Title in 2006 by beating the Dallas Mavericks?

10. In which sport did Michaela Tabb become the first woman to referee a World final at the Crucible?

11. Who in 2008 became the first British woman to win a medal at the Olympic Games in two different sports, rowing and cycling?

12. In 1981 Neil Adams became the first British man to win a World Title in which sport?

13. Who in 1997 became the first Canadian to win the Formula One World Championship?

14. Who in 1995 became the first player to score 4 tries against England at a Rugby Union World Cup?

15. In which sport did Wales' Leighton Rees become the first World Champion in 1978?

16. Which county won their first Cricket County Championship Title in 2008 beating Nottinghamshire into second place?

17. In 1967 which American Football team won the first Superbowl ever played?

18. Which of the four golf Majors was held for the first time in 1934 and was won by American Horton Smith?

19. In 2008 in which sport did Tim Brabants become Britain's first Olympic gold medallist?

20. Which club became the first British team to win the European Cup by beating Inter Milan in 1967?

Game 24

On this episode of A Question of Sport are...

Rio Ferdinand (Football)
First appeared on the show as a guest in 1999

Cliff Morgan (Rugby Union)
First appeared on the show as a guest in 1970

Fatima Whitbread (Field athletics)
First appeared on the show as a guest in 1984

John Higgins (Snooker)
First appeared on the show as a guest in 1997

Jockey Willie Carson was a captain on *A Question of Sport* in 1982 and 1983.

Round 1 – Opening Rally

1. Name the ten teams that played in the top four tiers of English football in the 2010/2011 season whose names begin with the letter C?

Round 2 – One Minute Round

1. On which English racecourse are the 1000 and 2000 Guineas run annually?

2. With which sport would you associate William 'the Fridge' Perry?

3. In which event did Tim Benjamin win Britain's only track medal at the 2005 World Championships?

4. Which team did Jonathan Davies join in 1988 as his first Rugby League club?

5. Which former Olympic event is this an anagram of? TEN HOT PLAN

6. Which Portuguese midfielder played for both Barcelona and Real Madrid between 1995 and 2005?

7. Which team played their 2010/2011 Rugby Union Premiership home games at the Recreation Ground?

These sports stars all share their surnames with types of transport.

8. John _____ (Cricket)

9. Paul _____ (Golf)

10. Ray _____ (Football)

Round 3 – Mystery Guest

1. I was born in Milan in 1970 and despite my small stature I have reached the heights in my career (4 points)

   My father was successful in my sport winning the 2000 Guineas in 1975 and 1976 (3 points)

   In 2007 I finally won the Epsom Derby at the 15th time of asking (2 points)

   I famously won all seven races of the day at Ascot in 1996 to make some lucky punters very happy (1 point)

2. I was born in Plymouth and started my sport at the age of 7 (4 points)

   I was Britain's youngest competitor at my first Olympic Games (3 points)

   I won gold medals at the Commonwealth Games in 2010 with my partner Max Brick and individually (2 points)

   I was voted the BBC Young Sports Personality of the Year for the 3rd time in 2010 (1 point)

Round 4 – Home or Away

1. *Rio Ferdinand.* Having finished fourth in the Premier League

in 2005 which English team were beaten by Villarreal in the Champions League qualifying stages the following season?

2. *Cliff Morgan.* Who in 2011 against Ireland became only the 5th scrum half to win 50 international caps for Wales and celebrated the milestone with a try?

3. *Fatima Whitbread.* In which event did Heike Drechsler win World Championship gold in 1983 and then again ten years later?

4. *John Higgins.* Who became the first non-European player to win the World Championship in 30 years with his victory at the Crucible in 2010?

Round 5 – Captain's Away

1. In which sport did Nick Dempsey and his wife Sarah Ayton both win Olympic medals?

2. Which Russian tennis star who won the 2005 Australian Open has a sister who has also been a world number one tennis player?

3. Between 2000 and 2010 name the two golfers who won the Men's Open Championship whose surnames begin with a vowel?

4. How was Graham Gooch dismissed for England against Australia in 1993?
   a) Hit the ball twice
   b) Timed out
   c) Handled ball

Round 6 – Great Sporting Moments

1. Seven minutes from time, Kevin Keegan, playing in his last game for Liverpool before his move to Germany, won a penalty for his side following a challenge from Berti Vogts. Phil Neal stepped up to score, which gave Liverpool a 3-1 victory in the 1977 European Cup final. Which side did they beat to win the trophy?

2. With many fans still settling into their seats, it wasn't long before the Wembley crowd witnessed history. Within the first minute Chelsea stunned Middlesbrough to take an early lead in the FA Cup final, which midfield player gave Chelsea such a brilliant start?

Round 7 – On the Buzzer

This buzzer round is all about the southern hemisphere.

1. Which country won a Rugby Union World Cup final with a late drop goal from Joel Stransky?

2. Which Australian tennis player was known as the Scud during his playing days due to his powerful serve?

3. Which South African midfielder moved from Everton to Spurs in 2011?

4. Australians David Graham and Geoff Ogilvy have both won which golf Major?

5. Which country did 1500m runners John Walker and Jack Lovelock represent at the Summer Olympics?

6. What position did George Gregan play in over 100 Rugby

Union internationals for Australia?

7. What nationality is Formula One driver Rubens Barrichello?

8. In which city were the Summer Olympics held in the southern hemisphere for the first time?

9. Which Uruguayan striker scored five times in the 2010 Football World Cup to help his country to the semi-finals?

10. For which country did Billy Slater score 7 tries in the 2008 Rugby League World Cup to help them reach the final?

11. Who in 2011 hit 15 sixes in a score of 185 not out in only 96 balls against Bangladesh?

12. Which country is 2002 Wimbledon Singles finalist David Nalbandian from?

13. For which country did Andy and Grant Flower both play over 60 Tests?

14. In which sport was Chilean Marcelo Rios the world number one for six weeks in 1998?

15. Which golfer from Argentina won the 2007 US Open and the 2009 US Masters titles?

16. For which country did extravagant goalkeeper Jose Luis Chilavert score 8 times in his 74 national appearances?

17. Where in Australia do the Broncos play their Rugby League home games?

18. What nationality is four-time Olympic sprint silver medallist Frankie Fredericks?

19. In which sport did New Zealand's Eric Murray and Hamish Bond beat British pair Andrew Triggs Hodge and Peter Reed to World Championship gold in 2010?

20. Which country did 1979 Formula One World Champion Jody Scheckter come from?

Game 25

On this episode of A Question of Sport are...

Gianfranco Zola (Football)
First appeared on the show as a guest in 2003

Mark Foster (Swimming)
First appeared on the show as a guest in 1994

Andy Murray (Tennis)
First appeared on the show as a guest in 1984

Barry McGuigan (Boxing)
First appeared on the show as a guest in 1999

Round 1 – Opening Rally

1. Name the 12 drivers who won a Formula One Grand Prix between 2006 and 2010.

Round 2 – One Minute Round

1. Which Rugby League team play their Super League home games at the Twickenham Stoop?

2. Which country hosts the Formula One Grand Prix that is held at Monza?

3. Which NBA basketball team is this an anagram of? WONKY KNICKERS

4. With which sport would you associate with the Batley Bulldogs, Featherstone Rovers and the Dewsbury Rams?

5. Which city hosted the 2007 World Athletics Championships?

6. Which Football League team play their home games at Brunton Park?

7. On which golf course would you find the Swilcan Bridge and The Road Hole?

These sports stars all share parts of their names with American states.

8. Joe _____ (American Football)

9. _____ Bonora (Gymnastics)

10. MaliVai _____ (Tennis)

Round 3 – Mystery Guest

1. I was born in Oswestry and represented Wales at the World Cup on more than ten occasions, winning the tournament in 1987 (4 points)

    I once lived in a camper van to save money and won my first tournament in Switzerland in 1982 (3 points)

    I became the 1st Welshman to win the US Masters, receiving the Green Jacket from Nick Faldo (2 points)

    In 2001 I won the World Matchplay Golf Championship for the 3rd time, all in different decades (1 point)

2. I turned 50 in 2011 and am generally regarded as the greatest player in the history of my sport (4 points)

    I was born in Ontario and in 2010 I lit the Olympic Flame at the Winter Olympics in my home country (3 points)

    I played for the Edmonton Oilers and the Los Angeles Kings in the National Hockey League (2 points)

    I was known as 'the Great One' and my shirt number, 99, has been retired by all teams in the NHL (1 point)

Round 4 – Home or Away

1. *Gianfranco Zola.* Which Italian striker scored a hat trick on his Premier League debut in 1996?

2. *Mark Foster.* Which Scotsman became the first British male to

win an Olympic swimming title in 68 years when he won gold in Montreal?

3. *Andy Murray.* Who beat both Roger Federer and Rafael Nadal at the US Open in 2009 to win his first Grand Slam Singles Title?

4. *Barry McGuigan.* After unifying the three major Light-Welterweight Titles in 2001 which boxer was sensationally beaten by Ricky Hatton in 2005 for the WBA and IBF titles?

Round 5 – Captain's Away

1. Which British sprinter is the cousin of former West Bromwich Albion striker Cyrille Regis?

2. Whose first two wickets in Test cricket came on his England debut when he dismissed the Waugh brothers and in his next Test he scored 99 not out?

3. Between 1980 and 2000 name the two jockeys who won the Grand National at Aintree on more than one occasion?

4. Who at the age of 36 was the oldest ever British and Irish Lion during the 2005 tour to New Zealand?
   a) Richard Hill
   b) Lawrence Dallaglio
   c) Neil Back

Round 6 – Great Sporting Moments

1. With less than 30 seconds to go in extra time of the 1995 UEFA Cup Winners' Cup final the scores were still level. The ball was

just inside Arsenal's half and their goalkeeper, David Seaman, was starting to think about the penalty shoot-out ahead. Which former Tottenham Hotspur player won the match for his team Real Zaragoza by lobbing David Seaman whilst nearly 50 yards from goal?

2. The fight in Kinshasa was dubbed the Rumble in the Jungle. After six punishing rounds Muhammad Ali seemed to have absorbed all of the champions big punches using his rope-a-dope technique and the champion's energy levels seemed to be dropping. In the 7th round Ali began taunting him and in the 8th round Ali knocked him down onto the canvas and out of the fight. Who did Ali beat to claim the World Heavyweight Title?

Round 7 – On the Buzzer

This buzzer round is all about the year 1989.

1. Born in 1989 which Northern Ireland golfer was Europe's youngest Ryder Cup player in the 2010 team?

2. Ridden by Simon Sherwood which famous grey won the Cheltenham Gold Cup in this year?

3. Which British boxer was defeated in a World Heavyweight Title challenge to Mike Tyson in February in Las Vegas?

4. Who became only the third jockey to win 1000 National Hunt races when he raced to victory in February in this year?

5. Which 17 year old became the first American in 34 years to win the French Open Singles Title?

6. Which club did Gary Lineker help to beat Sampdoria in the final of the European Cup Winners' Cup?

7. Which Scottish fullback scored points in all three of the British and Irish Lions matches as they won the series against Australia?

8. Which field event's world record was broken by Cuban Javier Sotomayor in July?

9. Who captained Australia to a 4-0 win in the Ashes series in England?

10. Graeme Hick scored over 1500 runs as which county won the County Championship that year?

11. Which Scotsman beat Eric Bristow to win his second World Darts Championship, seven years after his first?

12. Which snooker player won his sixth World Championship of the decade by beating John Parrott 18-3 in the final?

13. With which stroke did Adrian Moorhouse and Nick Gillingham both win a European title in this year?

14. Which 17 year old Spaniard prevented Steffi Graf winning the Grand Slam by beating her in the French Open Singles final?

15. Which Spaniard partnered Seve Ballesteros in four matches at the Ryder Cup, winning 3 and a half points in the process?

16. Who scored a memorable winning goal to win the First Division for Arsenal at Anfield?

17. Which Rugby League side did Jonathan Davies and Martin Offiah score points for in the Premiership final?

18. In which sport did Virginia Leng win her third European Title?

19. Which race did American Greg LeMond win in a time of nearly 88 hours?

20. Which American Football team did Jerry Rice help to their third Superbowl victory of the 1980s?

Game 26

On this episode of A Question of Sport are...

Emlyn Hughes (Football)
First appeared on the show as a guest in 1974

Martin Johnson (Rugby Union)
First appeared on the show as a guest in 1997

Natalie Du Toit (Swimming)
First appeared on the show as a guest in 2004

Justin Rose (Golf)
First appeared on the show as a guest in 2004

In 1982 future host of the programme Sue Barker was incorrectly guessed in the mystery guest round as boxer Alan Minter by Willie Carson and as footballer Ray Clemence by Trevor Francis and Bill Beaumont.

Round 1 – Opening Rally

1. Name the 12 men to have captained the England cricket team in a Test match between 1990 and 2010.

Round 2 – One Minute Round

1. Which American city's NBA basketball team are called the Grizzlies?

2. Which British Olympic team won the BBC Sports Personality Team of the Year Award in 2008?

3. Which Rugby League team is this an angram of? DEFRAUDS IN DELIGHTS

4. Which Scotsman did Neil Robertson beat in the final to win the 2010 World Snooker Championship?

5. Which Football League team play their home games at the Valley?

6. In which sport did Jo Goode and Donna Kellogg win a European Title in 2000?

7. Which County Championship team play their home games at the Rose Bowl?

These sports stars all share parts of their names herbs and spices.

8. _____ D'Oliveira (Cricket)

9. Mel _____ (Football)

10. _____ McCain (Horse Racing)

Round 3 – Mystery Guest

1. I was born in Czechoslovakia in 1960 and my parents both played my chosen sport (4 points)

   I became an American citizen in 1992 and since retiring I have become a talented golfer (3 points)

   I reached 19 Grand Slam Singles finals in my career winning on 8 occasions (2 points)

   My main rivals throughout my career were Jimmy Connors, John McEnroe and Mats Wilander (1 point)

2. I was born in May 1955 and at the age of 14 competed in my first National Championship (4 points)

   I was the darling of my first Olympics where I won three gold medals (3 points)

   In 1972 and 1976 I won a total of 6 Olympic medals, four of them gold (2 points)

   In 1988 I was the first person to be inducted into the Gymnastic Hall of Fame (1 point)

Round 4 – Home or Away

1. *Emlyn Hughes.* Which English team won the UEFA Cup for the first time in their history by beating AZ 67 Alkmaar in 1981?

2. *Martin Johnson.* Who between 1991 and 2002 scored over 1000 points in his 87 internationals for Wales?

3. *Natalie Du Toit.* In which event did British swimmers Keri-Anne Payne and Cassie Patten win Olympic medals in Beijing?

4. *Justin Rose.* Which Scotsman captained Europe at the Ryder Cup three times during the 1990s having previously played in the competition eight times between 1969 and 1983?

Round 5 – Captain's Away

1. Which sport entered the Olympic Games timetable in 1992 with Britain's first silver medal coming in 2004 behind a Chinese pair?

2. A King, a Painter and a Shepherd were all British World finalists during the 2000s in which sport?

3. Name the two Formula One drivers who won the World Championship in the 1980s whose surnames begin with P?

4. Which international cricketer's cousin is British boxer Amir Khan?
   a) Sajid Mahmood
   b) Shoaib Aktar
   c) Shahid Afridi

Round 6 – What Happened Next

1. Australia were playing New Zealand in a One Day International in 1981, Brian McKenzie was on strike as Australia's Trevor Chappell stepped up to bowl the last delivery of the match, what happened next?
   a) McKenzie was bowled by Chappell to give the bowler a hat trick.

b) McKenzie smashed the ball for six to give New Zealand an unlikely win.

c) With New Zealand needing a six from the last ball to win, Chappell bowled the ball underarm at the batsman.

2. Inter Milan are playing Schalke 04 in the quarter-final of the Champions League, Schalke goalkeeper Manuel Neuer comes out of his area to head the ball away, what happens next?

    a) Neuer misjudges the flight of the ball and it bounces over his head into the empty goal behind him.

    b) Neuer collides with defender Per Metersaker and the ball trickles into the net.

    c) Neuer heads the ball clear towards the halfway line but Inter Milan midfielder Dejan Stankovic volleys the ball superbly over him and into the goal.

Round 7 – On the Buzzer

This buzzer round has a Scottish connection.

1. In which sport did Robbie Renwick win Scotland's first gold medal of the 2010 Commonwealth Games?

2. Which Scottish club won the European Cup Winners' Cup in 1983?

3. Which Scottish driver won the Formula One World Championship three times between 1969 and 1973?

4. Which golf course hosted the 2009 Open Championship for only the 4th time in the tournament's history?

5. In which sport did Scotsman Ricky Burns become a World Champion in 2010?

6. Which Scottish World Champion is nicknamed the Wizard of Wishaw?

7. Which Scottish athlete won the 100m gold medal at the 1980 Olympics?

8. Which Scottish stadium hosted Rugby League's Challenge Cup final in the year 2000?

9. On which racecourse did Beshabar win the 2011 Scottish Grand National?

10. In 2007 which Scotsman became the first British player in 20 years to win a Wimbledon title?

11. In which sport did Scotland's Rhona Martin skipper a British team to Winter Olympic gold?

12. Who played in the 1999 Cricket World Cup for Scotland before making his Test debut for England later that year?

13. Which cup is awarded annually to the winner of the Scotland and England Rugby Union Six Nations contest?

14. Which was the first Scottish city to host the Commonwealth Games?

15. Which Scotland striker scored for his country at the 1974, 1978 and 1982 World Cups?

16. In which sport has Richard Corsie won three Indoor World Titles?

17. Which Scotsman twice won the World Darts Championship in the 1980s?

18. Which Australian born Scotland player has scored over 1000 points in total in the Magners League for Glasgow Warriors and the Cardiff Blues?

19. Which Scotsman made his Formula One debut in 2011?

20. In 1988 which Scotsman became the first British golfer to win the US Masters?

Game 27

On this episode of A Question of Sport are...

Gary Speed (Football)
First appeared on the show as a guest in 1993

Rebecca Adlington (Swimming)
First appeared on the show as a guest in 2008

Tony McCoy (Horse racing)
First appeared on the show as a guest in 1997

Damon Hill (Motor racing)
First appeared on the show as a guest in 1994

Round 1 – Opening Rally

1. Name the ten golfers to win the US Masters between 1998 and 2011.

Round 2 – One Minute Round

1. Which event does the Olympic decathlon always finish with?

2. With which sport would you associate the Delhi Daredevils and the Kolkatta Knight Riders?

3. Who won the Wimbledon Junior Boys' Championship in 1998 five years before winning the Men's Singles Title at the Championships?

4. Which sporting event is this an anagram of? AN IGNORANT LAD

5. Which team did Adrian Sutil and Vitantonio Liuzzi drive for in the 2010 Formula One Championship?

6. Which Football League team play their home games at London Road?

7. Which country hosts the Formula One Grand Prix that is held on the Sepang International Circuit?

These sports stars all share parts of their names with the surnames of Presidents of the United States.

8. Ross _____ (Rugby Union)

9. Reggie _____ (American Football)

10. _____ Woods (Boxing)

Round 3 – Mystery Guest

1. Although I was born in Northern Ireland I turned professional and moved to Lancashire (4 points)

   Now in my 60s I can be heard commentating on the sport in which I became a World Champion (3 points)

   I am renowned for my glasses, which I need to spot the balls (2 points)

   In 1985 over 18 million viewers saw my epic World Championship final encounter conclude with Steve Davis (1 point)

2. I turned 50 in March 2011 and am widely considered as one of the greatest players of my generation (4 points)

   I represented my country on 150 occasions and played in 5 World Cups (3 points)

   I captained my country to World Cup victory in 1990 having beaten England in the semi-final (2 points)

   As well as starring for my country I played domestically in Germany, Italy and America (1 point)

Round 4 – Home or Away

1. *Gary Speed.* Which player won the Champions League with Porto and Barcelona before winning the English Premier League in 2010?

2. *Rebecca Adlington.* Which Dutchwoman won three individual swimming gold medals at the 2000 Sydney Olympics?

3. *Tony McCoy.* During the 2000s who was the only jockey to win the Aintree Grand National twice?

4. *Damon Hill.* When Michael Schumacher won his 52nd Grand Prix he overtook which driver as the most prolific in Formula One History?

Round 5 – Captain's Away

1. In which sport did England's men reach their first Champions Trophy final in August 2010 only to lose 4-0 to Australia?

2. Last included in 1904, which sport is due to make a return to the Olympic Games in Rio de Janiero?

3. Name the two American Football teams that played in the 2010 NFL season whose names begin with A?

4. By what nickname is Darts World Champion Martin Adams better known?
    a) Wolfie
    b) Grizzly Bear
    c) Hound Dog

Round 6 – What Happened Next

1. London Irish are playing Wasps in the Guinness Premiership and Juan Leguizamon is running clear to score a try, what happened next?
   a) Leguizamon attempts an elaborate dive over the line and drops the ball mid air.
   b) Leguizamon runs toward the try line and turns to wave to the crowd in celebration but runs straight into the post and falls over.
   c) Leguizamon runs towards the line but is tackled by a fan who has run onto the pitch.

2. Sao Paulo have a free kick just outside of the Corinthians' penalty box, Sao Paulo goalkeeper Rogerio Ceni is standing over the ball, what happened next?
   a) Ceni scores the free kick to give him his 100th career goal.
   b) Rivaldo flicks the ball high into the air for Ceni who attempts an audacious overhead kick but misses the ball completely.
   c) Ceni kicks the ball straight at the wall and Corinthians defender Fabio Santos kicks the ball up field and into the empty Sao Paulo net.

Round 7 – On the Buzzer

This buzzer round is all about the year 2002.

1. Which British city hosted the 2002 Commonwealth Games?

2. Whose two goals in the World Cup final helped him to become the competition's top scorer and guided his country to their fifth World Cup final victory?

3. Which South African won the 2002 Open Championship at Muirfield in a four way playoff?

4. Real Madrid beat Bayer Leverkusen in the Champions League final at which British ground?

5. Which British woman won the 5000m at the Commonwealth Games in 2002?

6. In which Commonwealth Games sport did New Zealand beat Fiji 55-15 in the gold medal match?

7. Which Australian won the Wimbledon Men's Singles final by beating David Nalbandian?

8. Who beat Switzerland 4-3 to win the Winter Olympic Women's Curling gold medal?

9. Which player scored a record 145 points for the LA Lakers as they beat the New Jersey Nets in the NBA final?

10. Which English gymnast won gold at the 2002 Commonwealth Games in the Women's Uneven Bars?

11. Who captained England in the Ashes series in Australia?

12. Which race did Frankie Dettori win on Marienbard at Longchamp on October 6th?

13. In the Six Nations game with France which English prop forward won his 100th cap?

14. Which reigning World Football Champions were knocked out in the first round in 2002?

15. When St Helens beat the Bradford Bulls to win the Super

League Grand Final which player scored a try, 3 goals and a late drop goal for them?

16. What nationality are 2002 Ryder Cup winners Pierre Fulke, Niclas Fasth and Jesper Parnevik?

17. Which English snooker player won the 2002 World Championship six years after reaching his first final?

18. Which country beat the USA to Ice Hockey gold at the 2002 Winter Olympics?

19. Which St Kitts and Nevis sprinter won Commonwealth gold in the men's 100m?

20. Ian Ward scored over 1700 runs for which side as they won the County Championship?

Game 28

On this episode of A Question of Sport are...

Peter Schmeichel (Football)
First appeared on the show as a guest in 2002

Zinzan Brooke (Rugby Union)
First appeared on the show as a guest in 2001

Darren Campbell (Track athletics)
First appeared on the show as a guest in 1998

Robbie Paul (Rugby League)
First appeared on the show as a guest in 1997

England footballer Emlyn Hughes took over as captain on the programme in 1979. He had two spells as captain, one between 1979 and 1982 and then between 1984 and 1989.

Round 1 – Opening Rally

1. Name the ten football clubs to have won the Scottish League Championship in the 20th century.

Round 2 – One Minute Round

1. For which team have cricketers Brian Lara, Allan Donald and Lance Gibbs all played in the County Championship?

2. In which sport have Lorena Ochoa, Cristie Kerr and Jiyai Shin all been World Number One?

3. Which English Football League team play their home games at Prenton Park?

4. Which country hosted the 2007 Rugby Union World Cup final?

5. Which sport is this an anagram of? OK SNORE

6. Which stadium hosted the weekend of matches that launched the start of the 2011 Super League season?

7. In which athletics event did Irving Saladino win Panama's only gold medal of the 2008 Summer Olympics?

Fill in the surnames of these famous sports stars.

8. James _____ – 2009 Ashes Winner

9. James _____ – British Formula One World Champion

10. James _____ – 2008 British Olympic gold medal winning boxer

Round 3 – Mystery Guest

1. I retired from internationals in 2003 before my 37th birthday (4 points)

   I was revered for my time in Lancashire as well as in my homeland (3 points)

   I helped my country beat England in the World Cup final in 1992 (2 points)

   I took over 400 Test wickets for Pakistan during my career (1 point)

2. I was born in London in 1965 and became a professional World Champion after winning Olympic gold (4 points)

   I learned how to compete in my sport after I moved away from England but returned to my homeland after my Commonwealth Games and Olympic glory (3 points)

   In 2004 I officially retired as the undisputed Heavyweight Champion of the World (2 points)

   I won my Olympic gold as a Canadian in 1988 by defeating Riddick Bowe (1 point)

Round 4 – Home or Away

1. *Peter Schmeichel.* Which striker became the first outfield player to represent England with five different Premier League clubs?

2. *Zinzan Brooke.* In 2007 which forward captained South Africa to their second World Cup final victory?

3. *Darren Campbell.* Who at the 2010 European Championships won both sprint gold medals and added a third in the sprint relay?

4. *Robbie Paul.* Which 17 year old appeared in Wigan's 1993 Challenge Cup winning side before winning the Man of Steel in both 1996 and 2004?

Round 5 – Captain's Away

1. Which American race is held at the Brickyard and run over 200 laps?

2. What is the maximum score you can achieve in a game of Ten Pin Bowling?

3. Name the two British horse racing courses that end in the letter W?

4. Which Major League Baseball team play their home games at Wrigley Field?
   a) Chicago Cubs
   b) Boston Red Sox
   c) Toronto Blue Jays

Round 6 – Great Sporting Moments

1. For 14 gruelling rounds he pounded his relentless challenger and for 14 rounds Muhammad Ali absorbed his opponents huge left and right punches. Both fighters struggled to summon up the energy for the 15th and final round as the crowd in Manila rose to acclaim the two great fighters. Referee Carlos Padilla stopped the fight signalling that Ali was the winner, who did he beat in the Thriller in Manila?

2. In the last minute of the game, Bobby Moore, as cool as ever under pressure deep inside his own half, looked up and saw his teammate Geoff Hurst making strides into the German half. Moore floated a long clearance into the path of Hurst who controlled the ball before sealing the win for England prompting commentator Kenneth Wolstenholme to utter which famous words?

Round 7 – On the Buzzer

All the answers to this buzzer round begin with the letter R. In the case of a person it's the surname that must start with that letter.

1. Who scored the winning goal for Everton in the 1995 FA Cup final?

2. Which Australian tennis player lost in two successive Men's Singles finals at Wimbledon in the 2000s?

3. Which team competition did Bernard Gallacher captain Europe in on three occasions in the 1990s?

4. Who scored England's try in the 2003 Rugby Union World Cup final?

5. Which batsman scored over 8000 Test runs for the West Indies between 1974 and 1991?

6. Which city hosted the Summer Olympics in 1960 and the World Athletics Championships in 1987?

7. At which venue did Seve Ballesteros win his first Open Championship title?

8. Which Italian team did Francesco Totti captain to the Serie A

Championship in 2001?

9. Which Finnish driver won the 1982 Formula One World Championship?

10. Which American boxer did Lennox Lewis fight twice in the 2000s for the World Heavyweight Title?

11. Which team, captained by Australian Shane Warne, won the first ever Indian Premier League Twenty20 tournament in 2008?

12. In which country will the 2014 Winter Olympics be held?

13. On which horse did Mick Fitzgerald win the 1996 Grand National?

14. Which British athlete won the Women's London Marathon three times between 2002 and 2005?

15. In which sport did Andrew Triggs Hodge, Peter Reed, Tom James and Steve Williams win Olympic gold in 2008?

16. What nationality is the five time Olympic gold medal winning gymnast Nadia Comaneci?

17. Which British cyclist won an Olympic gold medal in the Women's Individual Pursuit at the 2008 Summer Olympics?

18. Which rider won the first of his 500cc/Moto GP World Championships in 2001?

19. What common name is shared by a Major League Baseball team from Texas and a NHL Ice Hockey team from New York?

20. Which British sprinter won the 200m World Indoors Championship in 1989?

Game 29

On this episode of A Question of Sport are...

Dion Dublin (Football)
First appeared on the show as a guest in 1998

Jonah Lomu (Rugby Union)
First appeared on the show as a guest in 1996

Shirley Robertson (Sailing)
First appeared on the show as a guest in 2001

Phil Taylor (Darts)
First appeared on the show as a guest in 2001

Round 1 – Opening Rally

1. Between 1974 and 2010, name the ten host cities of the Commonwealth Games.

Round 2 – One Minute Round

1. What nationality are golfers Tim Clark and Rory Sabbatini?

2. With which sport would you associate Incheon United, Jeju United and the Pohang Steelers?

3. In which sport did Charlotte Edwards captain England's women to World Cup victory in 2009?

4. Which famous jockey's name is this an anagram of? GOT ST LEGER TIP

5. Which American won the Heavyweight Boxing gold medal at the 1964 Olympics?

6. Which country won the most gold medals at the 2008 Summer Olympic Games?

7. In which sport was Eddie Charlton beaten in two World Championship finals in the 1970s?

These sports stars all share parts of their names with the surnames of British Prime Ministers.

8. Mike _____ (Rugby Union)

9. Ben _____ (Football)

10. Ken _____ (Golf)

Round 3 – Mystery Guest

1. Because of my birthplace I was easily able to practise my chosen sport (4 points)

   I am revered in my country for winning gold in my home country in the 1976 Winter Olympics in Innsbruck (3 points)

   After I retired from my chosen sport I took up motor racing and won a round of the European Touring Car Championship (2 points)

   I won Olympic gold at the age of 22 by going downhill (1 point)

2. I was born in Welwyn Garden City. Whilst working as a carpet fitter I won the British Youth Championships (4 points)

   I reached my 50th birthday in 2007 20 years after I won my first Major (3 points)

   I famously overturned a six shot deficit on the final day of the US Masters in 1996 (2 points)

   I played in many Ryder Cup matches and captained Europe in 2008 (1 point)

Round 4 – Home or Away

1. *Dion Dublin.* Who in 2008 became the youngest player to score a hat trick for England, doing so in a World Cup qualifier against Croatia?

2. *Jonah Lomu.* Which is the only country to have been defeated in their first two World Cup finals?

3. *Shirley Robertson.* In 2008 Bryony Shaw became the first British woman to win an Olympic medal in which discipline?

4. *Phil Taylor.* Who in 1994 became the first overseas player to win a Darts World Championship?

Round 5 – Captain's Away

1. Between 1981 and 1986 which American woman partnered Martina Navratilova to five Wimbledon Doubles Titles?

2. In the 1980s which event did Welshman Steve Jones win in London, New York and Chicago?

3. Name the two cricketers who played for England in the 2009 Ashes series whose surnames begin with the letter P?

4. Which American Football team won the first ever Superbowl, in 1967?
   a) Chicago Bears
   b) Green Bay Packers
   c) Miami Dolphins

Round 6 – Great Sporting Moments

1. Having looked dead and buried only a few seconds before it appeared that Manchester United weren't finished yet. David Beckham whipped in a corner that Teddy Sheringham headed on for Ole Gunnar Solskjaer to turn into the net and pull off a superb comeback. Who did Manchester United beat to win the 1999 Champions League final in Barcelona?

2. Undefeated in three years the British crew had finished 4th in Lucerne just three months before the Olympic Games. Now a 38 year old the British athlete had been taking insulin for his diabetes but with the help of his teammates he managed to win a gold medal for an unbelievable 5th Olympics in succession. Who is he?

Round 7 – On the Buzzer

This buzzer round is all about 1987.

1. In which sport did the Durham Wasps beat the Murrayfield Racers to win a British title?

2. Who by beating France won the first Rugby Union World Cup final?

3. Who beat Ivan Lendl in the Wimbledon's Singles final to become the first Australian to win the title in the decade?

4. Which New Zealand Test bowler took a hat trick for Nottinghamshire against Kent in the County Championship?

5. Which American successfully defended his World Championship 400m Hurdles title?

6. Which Englishman beat Eric Bristow to win his second World Darts Championship, 8 years after claiming his first?

7. Three Spaniards featured for Europe in their 1987 Ryder Cup winning side, Jose Maria Olazabal, Seve Ballesteros and who else?

8. Which British driver finished runner up in the Formula One

World Championship for the second season in succession?

9. Who was the 'Hitman' who beat British boxer Dennis Andries to win the WBC Light Heavyweight Title?

10. Which club won the FA Cup for the first time in their history by beating Tottenham Hotspur 3-2 in the final?

11. Which team beat an England side captained by Mike Gatting in the Cricket World Cup final to win the tournament for the first time?

12. Who won the Hart Memorial Trophy for most valuable player in the NHL as his team the Edmonton Oilers won the Stanley Cup?

13. Which major horse race was won for a third successive year by See You Then and jockey Steve Smith Eccles?

14. Which sprinter retained his 100m World Championship title, beating Ray Stewart and Linford Christie into silver and bronze in the process?

15. Which British athlete won a World Championship gold medal with a throw of 76.64m?

16. In which sport did Canadian Brian Orser win a World Championship gold having won silver medals in the three previous championships?

17. Which British golfer won the US Women's Open in 1987 to give her a first win in the Majors?

18. Who in May 1987 scored his 33rd league goal of the season to finish as the top scorer in the League Championship?

19. The Twins won the World Series by beating the St Louis Cardinals, which state are the Twins from?

20. Which country won the Five Nations Grand Slam for the fourth time in their history?

Game 30

On this episode of A Question of Sport are...

Robbie Keane (Football)
First appeared on the show as a guest in 2001

Shaun Edwards (Rugby Union)
First appeared on the show as a guest in 1998

Iwan Thomas (Track athletics)
First appeared on the show as a guest in 1997

Stephen Hendry (Snooker)
First appeared on the show as a guest in 1988

Welsh Rugby Union international Gareth Edwards became captain of *A Question of Sport* for three series between 1979 and 1982, starring alongside fellow captain Emlyn Hughes.

Round 1 – Opening Rally

1. Name the ten countries which have provided a winner of the European Cup/Champions League.

Round 2 – One Minute Round

1. Which Frenchman won the European Player of the Year three times in the 1980s?

2. Which Rugby League team play their Super League home games at 'New' Craven Park?

3. In which American city is the sporting venue the Astrodome the home of a Major League Baseball team?

4. Which Winter Olympic host city is this an anagram of? ALL STATE ICKY

5. Over what distance is the Men's Steeplechase run at the Summer Olympics?

6. Which team did Michael Schumacher make a return to Formula One with in 2010?

7. In which sport did David Bryant and Tony Allcock win World Championship Titles in the 1980s?

These sports stars all share their surnames with special days of the year.

8. Alf _____ (Cricket)

9. Danielle _____ (Athletics)

10. Nick _____ (Rugby Union)

Round 3 – Mystery Guest

1. I turned professional in 1989 before I had turned 21 (4 points)

   I won the US Open in 1994 in a playoff (3 points)

   I emulated my compatriot Gary Player by winning the Open Championship, my victory coming in 2002 at Muirfield (2 points)

   I was born in Johannesburg in 1969 and am known as the 'Big Easy' (1 point)

2. I was born on Bonfire Night in 1935 and won my first race at the age of 12 with the help of The Chase (4 points)

   I followed in both my father and grandfather's footsteps by taking up my chosen sport (3 points)

   I won over 5000 races in my career and was Champion Jockey on 11 occasions (2 points)

   During my career I won 30 English Classics between 1954 and 1992 and I am considered to be the greatest flat jockey of all time (1 point)

Round 4 – Home or Away

1. *Robbie Keane.* Which country beat eventual winners Spain 1-0 in their first game of the 2010 World Cup?

2. *Shaun Edwards.* Who in 2009 played in his fourth Super League Grand Final for St Helens having already featured in five with Bradford Bulls?

3. *Iwan Thomas.* Who in 1996 became the first British athlete to win a Men's 400m Olympic medal since 1936?

4. *Stephen Hendry.* Which Englishman reached three successive Masters finals between 2008 and 2010, winning on two occasions?

Round 5 – Captain's Away

1. How many rounds did a boxing bout at the Beijing Olympics last if it went the distance?

2. Who were the only team in the 2010 Football World Cup not to lose a match?

3. Name the two French teams that won the Heineken Cup between 1996 and 2010?

4. Which of these is a fence at the Aintree Grand National?
    a) Lover's Leap
    b) Valentine's
    c) Fair Maiden

Round 6 – What Happened Next

1. During the 2000 Men's Doubles final at Wimbledon, Todd Woodbridge and Mark Woodforde were playing Paul Haarhuis and Sandon Stolle, what happened next?
    a) Stole and Haarhuis were becoming so frustrated with their play in the 3rd set that they suggested to the Woodies that they mix the teams up.

b) A point was interrupted when the umpires phone went off during play.

c) Woodbridge broke a string on his last racket and had to borrow one off Haarhuis.

2. Aston Villa defender Olaf Mellberg is about to take a throw in deep into his own half, what happened next?

a) Mellberg takes a long run up and performs a forward roll before launching the throw in up the field.

b) With limited options around him Mellberg throws the ball back to his goalkeeper Peter Encklman who misjudges the pass and it deflects of his foot into his own net.

c) Mellberg throws the ball straight to Birmingham City striker Clinton Morrison who runs into the box, rounds keeper Encklman and scores a simple tap in.

Round 7 – On the Buzzer

This buzzer round is all about hat tricks.

1. Who against the Netherlands in 2011 became the first West Indian to take a Cricket World Cup hat trick?

2. Which Rugby League club were beaten by Leeds Rhinos for the third time in a row in the Super League Grand Final in 2009?

3. Which major horse race was won by Best Mate for the third consecutive time in 2004?

4. Which basketball team won the NBA Championship three years in a row on two separate occasions in the 1990s?

5. Who in 1992 became the first snooker player to lose in three successive World Championship finals at the Crucible?

6. At which Irish venue in 2006 did Europe complete a hat trick of Ryder Cup wins?

7. Which country's women completed a hat trick of Winter Olympic Ice Hockey gold medals when they won on home soil in 2010?

8. Who in 1991 completed a hat trick of 100m World Championship titles with his victory in Tokyo?

9. Which England winger scored a hat trick of tries in the Six Nations against Italy in 2005?

10. Which Argentina striker was the only player to score a hat trick at the 2010 Football World Cup?

11. Who in 1994 scored a hat trick for Liverpool in 4 minutes and 33 seconds at Anfield against Arsenal?

12. In 2010 in which sport did Leisel Jones win her 3rd consecutive Commonwealth Games gold medal?

13. Which Ferrari driver completed a hat trick of fastest lap, pole position and race winner at the Italian Grand Prix in 2010?

14. For which country did cyclist Gregory Bauge win a hat trick of Men's Sprint Titles at the World Championships between 2009 and 2011?

15. Between 2003 and 2005 which American tennis player won a hat trick of Queen's Club Championships?

16. Which British sailor completed a hat trick of Olympic gold medals between 2000 and 2008?

17. In which sport did the Glasgow Hawks win the Scottish Club Championship on 3 successive occasions between 2004 and 2006?

18. For which Super League team did Chris Hicks score a hat trick in the 2010 Challenge Cup final?

19. Which Czech athlete completed a hat trick of Olympic gold medals in the Javelin when he claimed gold at the Sydney Olympics in 2000?

20. Which bowler took a hat trick for England in 2008 against New Zealand in Hamilton?

Game 31

On this episode of A Question of Sport are...

David Seaman (Football)
First appeared on the show as a guest in 1991

Jeremy Guscott (Rugby Union)
First appeared on the show as a guest in 1990

Kelly Sotherton (Athletics)
First appeared on the show as a guest in 2004

Ricky Hatton (Boxing)
First appeared on the show as a guest in 2002

Round 1 – Opening Rally

1. Other than Football name the 10 ball sports that featured in the 2008 Summer Olympics.

Round 2 – One Minute Round

1. In which sport do the winners of the amateur competition between USA and Great Britain and Ireland receive the Walker Cup?

2. Which team were bowled out for 54 at Lord's and 61 at Headingley by England in 2000?

3. Which tennis Grand Slam is played first in the calendar year?

4. Which Football League team play their home games at Deepdale?

5. Which 2010 Football World Cup country is this an anagram of? END ENTHRALS

6. Which famous horse won the Cheltenham Gold Cup three years in succession in the 1960s?

7. Which American state's MLB baseball team are called the Diamondbacks?

These sports stars all share parts of their names with food that can be fried.

8. _____ Beck (Golf)

9. Oscar _____ (Cycling)

10. Charles _____ (Athletics)

Round 3 – Mystery Guest

1. I turned 40 in 2009 and two years later was still competing in my chosen sport (4 points)

    My brother competed in the same sport as me but was never as successful as me (3 points)

    I voiced a character in the animated film *Cars* (2 points)

    I won my 7th World Championship Title in 2004 to make me the most successful man in the history of my sport (1 point)

2. I was born in Barcelona in 1971 and support my local football team (4 points)

    Both of my brothers also played professionally in my chosen sport (3 points)

    I was the first Spanish tennis player to be ranked number one in the world (2 points)

    At the age of 17 I beat Steffi Graf to win the French Open the first of my 4 Grand Slam Singles Titles (1 point)

Round 4 – Home or Away

1. *David Seaman.* Which South American won the European Cup Winners' Cup with Real Zaragoza and Chelsea in the 1990s?

2. *Jeremy Guscott.* Born in Venezuela which player scored a record 38 tries in his 93 Tests for France between 1980 and 1991?

3. *Kelly Sotherton.* Only two British women have won a medal in the Olympic 400m Hurdles. Sally Gunnell won gold in 1992 but who won bronze 16 years later in Beijing?

4. *Ricky Hatton.* Who did David Haye defeat in November 2009 to win the WBA World Heavyweight Title?

Round 5 – Captain's Away

1. Sarah Stevenson won a bronze medal for Britain at the Beijing Olympics in which martial arts event?

2. For which country did Andre Agassi's father compete in the Olympic boxing in 1948 and 1952?

3. Name the two American Football teams that played in the 2010 NFL season whose names begin with M?

4. Which of these cricketers didn't take a Test hat trick for England?
   a) Dominic Cork
   b) Darren Gough
   c) Andrew Caddick

Round 6 – Great Sporting Moments

1. On the 22nd of June 1986 the diminutive attacker received the ball on the halfway line, he skipped past Stevens, Butcher and Fenwick with ease and slotted the ball past Peter Shilton into England's goal. Who scored this famous goal for Argentina?

2. Grey Sombiero went into the lead after the first circuit of the course before Crisp took up the running. Spanish Steps, Rouge Autumn and Black Secret fell by the wayside so much so that by the Canal Turn only one horse was in a position to challenge Crisp. Which horse chased down Crisp to win the 1973 Grand National?

Round 7 – On the Buzzer

This buzzer round is all about the year 1993.

1. What was unusual about the running of the Grand National in 1993?

2. Which English circuit staged the European Formula One Grand Prix?

3. In which event did Jan Zelezny twice break a world record in 1993?

4. Which 25 year old during the middle of the Ashes series replaced Graham Gooch as England captain?

5. Which European won the second US Masters Title of his career in April 1993?

6. Which of his compatriots did Pete Sampras beat in the Wimbledon Singles final?

7. Which German city hosted the 1993 World Athletics Championship?

8. After losing his World Heavyweight Title to Riddick Bowe who regained the title in November?

9. Which pair of brothers both scored tries for England against Scotland in the Calcutta Cup match in March?

10. Who in April 1993 retired as manager of Nottingham Forest after 18 years in charge?

11. In which sport did Scotland's Graeme Obree win a World Track Title?

12. Which British athlete won a World Championship gold medal in 1993 in a world record time of 12.91 seconds?

13. Which side won the 1993 County Championship captained by Mike Gatting?

14. Which famous Formula One Grand Prix did Ayrton Senna win for a record sixth time in 1993?

15. Which woman was leading 4-1 in the third and final set of the Wimbledon Singles final but lost to Steffi Graf and famously cried on the shoulder of the Duchess of Kent?

16. In which sport did Alexander Popov win gold medals at the European Championships?

17. Which team did Arsenal beat in both the FA Cup and League Cup finals?

18. Which five times Open Championship winner captained the USA to their Ryder Cup win at the Belfry?

19. Which Wigan winger won his first Challenge Cup winners medal before playing in two Rugby Union World Cup finals later in his career?

20. Which Canadian Major League Baseball team retained the World Series Title?

Game 32

On this episode of A Question of Sport are...

Peter Reid (Football)
First appeared on the show as a guest in 1985

Lawrence Dallaglio (Rugby Union)
First appeared on the show as a guest in 1996

Steve Harmison (Cricket)
First appeared on the show as a guest in 2004

Neil Hodgson (Motorcycle racing)
First appeared on the show as a guest in 2003

England international Rugby Union player Bill Beaumont became captain in 1982, and over the course of the next 15 years he appeared in a then record 319 shows. Bill became the first team captain to host the show when he stood in for David Coleman in 1996.

Round 1 – Opening Rally

1. Name the 10 countries or territories in Europe that competed in the Commonwealth Games.

Round 2 – One Minute Round

1. For which country did Sean Lamont score a try in the 2011 Six Nations Championships?

2. Which Spanish football team play their home games at the Camp Nou?

3. With which sport would you associate the Brisbane Broncos and the Parramatta Eels?

4. Which cricket term is this an anagram of? SEWER SERVING

5. Which major event was held in Lake Placid, America in 1932 and 1980?

6. Which golf course features holes called Firethorn, Golden Bell and Pampas?

7. In which sport has Cuban Felix Savon won three Olympic gold medals?

Fill in the surnames of these famous sports stars.

8. Michael _____ – 1991 Wimbledon Champion

9. Michael _____ – 2005 Ashes Winner

10. Michael _____ – 2001 European Footballer of the Year

Round 3 – Mystery Guest

1. I first came to prominence in 1982 at the University of North Carolina (4 points)

    I won an Olympic gold medal in 1984 and 1992 (3 points)

    I am a six time NBA Champion (2 points)

    I starred in the 1996 film *Space Jam* as myself and famously wore the number 23 in my career (1 point)

2. I was born in 1957 and am revered on both sides of the Atlantic (4 points)

    At the age of 19 I led the Open Championship after three rounds (3 points)

    I won the European Order of Merit six times, the first in 1976 (2 points)

    I became the first Spaniard to win a golf Major when I won the Open Championship in 1979, a tournament I won on three occasions (1 point)

Round 4 – Home or Away

1. *Peter Reid.* Who against Manchester United in 2004 became only the third player manager to play in the FA Cup final?

2. *Lawrence Dallaglio.* Who in 2008 captained Wales to their second Six Nations Grand Slam victory of the decade?

3. *Steve Harmison.* For which country did Peter Petherick in 1976 and James Franklin in 2004 take their country's first two Test hat tricks?

4. *Neil Hodgson.* Which British rider won the World Superbike Championship four times during the 1990s?

Round 5 – Captain's Away

1. In Sydney in 2000 Joanne Wright-Goode and Simon Archer won Britain's first Olympic medal in which indoor sport?

2. Who in 1997 became the first Danish golfer to represent Europe in the Ryder Cup?

3. Name the two Australian Formula One drivers who won a World Championship between 1960 and 2010?

4. Which of these people has won a Bowls World Championship?
   a) David Bryant
   b) Ed Coode
   c) Nathan Robertson

Round 6 – What Happened Next

1. Eric Moussambani Malonga from Equatorial Guinea is about to swim his heat of the Olympic 100m freestyle in 2000, what happened next?
   a) Malonga swam the heat in a time of 1 minute 53 seconds, over a minute outside of the world record.
   b) Malonga stunned the crowd by setting the fastest time of the heats so far and breaking the world record in the process.

c) Malonga didn't hear the starters signal as he was still putting his goggles on and by the time he'd jumped into the pool the others were on their second lap.

2. Carlisle United are playing Plymouth Argyle in the last game of the season, Carlisle need to win to stay in the Football League and in the last minute of the game they win a corner, what happens next?
    a) Carlisle keeper Jimmy Glass comes up for the corner and volleys the ball into the net to give them a remarkable win.
    b) Glass is fouled in the penalty box and wins a penalty for Carlisle that he takes himself but sends high over the bar.
    c) Glass comes up for the corner but the Plymouth Argyle keeper catches the cross and boots the ball down field into the empty Carlisle goal.

Round 7 – On the Buzzer

All the answers to this buzzer round begin with the letter T, in the case of a person it's the surname that must start with that letter.

1. Who in 2007 became the first Rugby Union player to win 100 caps for Wales?

2. Which European city hosted the 2006 Winter Olympic Games?

3. In which sport did China win Olympic gold, silver and bronze in both the Men's Singles and the Women's Singles in 2008?

4. Which British athlete won gold at the Commonwealth Games in the Decathlon in 1978, 1982 and 1986?

5. Who are the only NBA basketball team that are based outside of the United States of America?

6. For which team did Sebastian Vettel win the Italian Grand Prix in 2008 to give him and his team their first Formula One victory?

7. On which course did Stewart Cink win the Open Championship in 2009?

8. In which event did Sweden's Christian Olsson win Olympic gold in 2004, a year after winning the World Championship in the same event?

9. Which team won the UEFA Cup in 1972 by beating Wolverhampton Wanderers and again in 1984 by beating Anderlecht?

10. Which centre captained England in their opening game of the 2011 Six Nations Championship?

11. Who scored his 98th and 99th international centuries during the 2011 Cricket World Cup?

12. In which city did Lynn Davies win an Olympic gold in the Long Jump?

13. Who scored in the Champions League final penalty shoot-out in 2008 to help his side win the tournament and a year later joined Manchester City?

14. Which American tennis player won the 1977 Australian Open and lost to Bjorn Borg in the final of Wimbledon two years later?

15. In which sport have British athletes Simon Lessing, Timothy Don and Alistair Brownlee all been World Champions?

16. Which American golfer won the USPGA Championship in 2001 and was on the losing side in the Ryder Cup on three occasions in the 2000s?

17. In which sport do Europe and the USA compete against one another for the Weber Cup?

18. Which American Football team won the first Superbowl in their history when they beat the Oakland Raiders to the title in 2003?

19. Which American boxer defeated Bernard Hopkins in July 2005 to become the Middleweight Champion of the World?

20. Which country did Ato Boldon represent as he won the 100m at the 1998 Commonwealth Games?

Game 33

On this episode of A Question of Sport are...

Graeme Le Saux (Football)
First appeared on the show as a guest in 2002

Jayne Torvill (Ice dancing)
First appeared on the show as a guest in 1981

Graham Gooch (Cricket)
First appeared on the show as a guest in 1980

Lee Westwood (Golf)
First appeared on the show as a guest in 1997

Round 1 – Opening Rally

1. Name the ten Football League teams beginning with the letter B that played in the FA Cup final during the 20th century.

Round 2 – One Minute Round

1. Which Rugby Union player of the 1990s was appointed England captain at the age of 22?

2. Which English football team is this an anagram of? THE NUTS NAMED ERIC

3. In which sport have Mardy Fish, Sam Querrey and James Blake all represented the USA?

4. Which international major sporting event took place in India in October 2010?

5. Which Scottish football team play their home games at Easter Road?

6. Which men's golf Grand Slam is played first in the calendar year?

7. What colour is the bullseye in Olympic archery?

These sports stars all share their surnames with types of metal or alloy.

8. Peter _____ (Squash)

9. David _____ (Cricket)

10. David _____ (Football)

Round 3 – Mystery Guest

1. I was born in San Diego in 1977 and in 2010 I played for my country for the 100th time (4 points)

   I won a European Cup with my club in 2006 and 2008 (3 points)

   I played for the British and Irish Lions in 2009, the same year that I became the record points scorer in the Six Nations for my country (2 points)

   I have scored over 1000 international points (1 point)

2. I was born in June 1985 and began taking my sport more seriously at the age of just 7 (4 points)

   I qualified for the USA Olympic team in 2000 at the age of just 15 (3 points)

   Six months later I broke a world record to become the youngest man to set a swimming world record (2 points)

   Since then I went onto to win an unprecedented eight gold medals at the Beijing Olympics (1 point)

Round 4 – Home or Away

1. *Graeme Le Saux.* Who in 2010 won a Champions League winners' medal, a Serie A title and was a losing finalist in the World Cup?

2. *Jayne Torvill.* Which American was a Figure Skating World

Champion five times between 1996 and 2003 but her best Olympics saw her win silver in Nagano?

3. *Graham Gooch.* Who scored 340 against India in August 1997 to become the first Sri Lankan batsman to score a Test triple century?

4. *Lee Westwood.* Who finished 3rd in the US Masters for three years in a row between 2001 and 2003 before winning the tournament for the first time the following year?

Round 5 – Captain's Away

1. Which sport is played at Wrigley Field, Fenway Park and at the Dodgers Stadium?

2. Portsmouth played in the 2008 and 2010 FA Cup finals but who was the only player to start both games for the club?

3. Name the two Welsh snooker players to have reached a World Championship final between 1990 and 2010?

4. Which of these British boxers did not win a World Heavyweight Title in their career?
   a) Herbie Hide
   b) Henry Akinwande
   c) Danny Williams

Round 6 – What Happened Next

1. The men's 100m at the Super League meeting in Gateshead is just about to take place, the competitors are in the starting blocks, what happened next?

a) The starters gun wouldn't work so he had to use a mega phone to shout go.

b) Just as the starter's gun sounded and the race began an official walks on to the track oblivious of the race entirely.

c) Despite a false start being called three of the sprinters complete the entire race before realising it didn't count.

2. Celtic are playing a Champions League qualifier in Hungary against MTK Hungaria, what happened next?

a) The game was held up for four minutes as a sprinkler went off in the middle of the pitch and began soaking the players.

b) The match had to be abandoned as MTK Hungaria had five men sent off for dissent by a particularly pedantic referee following a contentious penalty decision.

c) The game was plunged into darkness by a brief floodlight failure and when they turned back on seconds later Celtic had scored a goal.

Round 7 – On the Buzzer

This buzzer round is all about the year 1996.

1. Ridden by Mick Fitzgerald which horse won the Grand National as the 7-1 favourite?

2. Which famous English umpire retired from Test cricket in June after 66 matches?

3. In which sport did Finnish driver Tommi Makinen become a World Champion for the first time?

4. Despite leading the Premier League by 12 points in January which team did Manchester United overtake to win the title?

5. Which British athlete won Olympic silver behind Michael Johnson in the Olympic 400m?

6. Who lost a six shot lead on the final day of the US Masters to lose to Nick Faldo?

7. On which racecourse did Frankie Dettori win all seven races on the card in September?

8. In February 1996 which club's 9 year, 43 match unbeaten run in the Challenge Cup came to an end against Salford?

9. Who missed the sudden death penalty for England in the European Champions semi-final penalty shoot-out against Germany?

10. Which singer led an impromptu sing along on July 3rd at Wimbledon as rain held up play?

11. Steve Beaton beat the defending champion Richie Burnett in which sport's World final?

12. Which club won a third successive Rugby Union Pilkington Cup final, beating Leicester in the final in all three years?

13. Which 19 year old Briton won a sailing Olympic silver medal prior to winning successive gold medals in the next three Olympics?

14. In which sport did the Birmingham Bullets beat the London Towers 78-72 in a Premier League playoff final?

15. Captain Mike Watkinson and opener Michael Atherton helped which county to cup final wins in the Benson and Hedges and the NatWest Trophy?

16. Which Wigan Rugby League player captained England at the age of 21?

17. In what sport did the Scottish Claymores beat the Frankfurt Galaxy in the World Bowl '96?

18. Which country beat Australia in the final to lift the cricket World Cup for the first time?

19. Which Ethiopian won the first of his two Olympic gold medals in the 10,000m at the Atlanta Games?

20. Which American won the Open Championship in 1996 and held the top spot in the World Rankings for a week?

Game 34

On this episode of A Question of Sport are...

David Ginola (Football)
First appeared on the show as a guest in 1995

Brian O'Driscoll (Rugby Union)
First appeared on the show as a guest in 2001

Allan Lamb (Cricket)
First appeared on the show as a guest in 1985

Rhona Martin (Curling)
First appeared on the show as a guest in 2002

England star Ian Botham became the first cricketer to become a full time captain on *A Question of Sport* in 1989. He battled it out with Bill Beaumont for the next eight years.

Round 1 – Opening Rally

1. Name the 12 teams that started the 2011 Formula One season.

Round 2 – One Minute Round

1. Which Australian became the first man to take 700 Test wickets?

2. Which Football League team play their home games at Fratton Park?

3. Which country does three time French Open Men's Singles title champion Gustavo Kuerten come from?

4. Which famous jockey's name is this an anagram of?
    PROCEEDS MATURE

5. In which sport did American Bode Miller win a Winter Olympic gold medal in Vancouver?

6. What nationality is 10 time Major winning golfer Annika Sorenstam?

7. Which Canadian won the Super Heavyweight Boxing gold medal at the 1988 Olympics?

Fill in the surnames of these famous sports stars.

8. Ian _____ – Scored over 100 English Premier League goals

9. Ian _____ – 2010 Ryder Cup Winner

10. Ian _____ – 2005 Ashes Winner

Round 3 – Mystery Guest

1. Although I was born in South America I moved to Britain to further my career (4 points)

   My nephew has followed my footsteps into the sport that I was considered a great in (3 points)

   I won three World Championships between 1988 and 1991 (2 points)

   I tragically died at the age of 34 in a high speed crash in San Marino (1 point)

2. I was born in Derbyshire in 1976 and I developed a love of sailing at a very young age (4 points)

   In 1994 I won the Young Sailor of the Year Award (3 points)

   In June 2000 I sailed Kingfisher from Plymouth to Newport, Rhode Island in less than 15 days (2 points)

   I beat Francis Joyon's world record for a single-handed non-stop circumnavigation of the globe in June 2005, following this achievement I was named a Dame (1 point)

Round 4 – Home or Away

1. *David Ginola.* Who played in five World Cups between 1982 and 1998 captaining the winners in 1990?

2. *Brian O'Driscoll.* Which team in 2002 became the first English side to win successive Heineken Cup finals?

3. *Allan Lamb.* Which Test captain scored 277 against England in 2003 and followed it up with another double century one week later in the next Test?

4. *Rhona Martin.* At the 2010 Winter Olympics which European country retained their Women's Curling title by beating the host nation in the final?

Round 5 – Captain's Away

1. In which sport did Britain's Daniel Keatings win a World Championship silver medal in 2009?

2. Which British field athlete won Olympic silver in 2008 and World Championship gold the following year?

3. Name the two teams that played in the top four tiers of English football in 2010/2011 whose names begin with the letter E?

4. Which of these is not a Commonwealth Games sport?
   a) Squash
   b) Handball
   c) Netball

Round 6 – Great Sporting Moments

1. With 90 minutes gone and the 40,000 plus crowd shouting for the final whistle, Lee Dixon cleared the ball from deep in the Arsenal half to Alan Smith who lobbed it into the path of the on rushing midfielder. He controlled the ball and struck it past the goalkeeper to win the League Championship for his team at Anfield on goal difference. Who scored the goal for Arsenal?

2. Despite an error in the triple jump the British Olympian mesmerised the American crowd with a stunning sequence of manoeuvres, and was especially outstanding in the spins. His programme included three great triple jumps, two cherries and a salchow, pleasing both the audience and the judges in Lake Placid. Which British skater won Olympic gold with this routine?

Round 7 – On the Buzzer

This buzzer round is all about sporting locations.

1. In which country did Liverpool overturn a 3-0 half time deficit to win the Champions League in 2005?

2. On which ground did Graham Gooch record his highest Test score of 333 for England?

3. On which English racecourse are the Derby and the Oaks contested?

4. In which city did Kelly Holmes win her two Olympic gold medals for Britain?

5. In which city did England win the Rugby Union World Cup in 2003 thanks to Jonny Wilkinson's drop goal in extra time?

6. Which famous golf course's first three holes are called Tea Olive, Pink Dogwood and Flowering Peach?

7. Barry McGuigan won his World Title at Loftus Road in 1985. Which football team play their home games there?

8. What annual event is held at Hickstead in Sussex?

9. In which state did the Green Bay Packers win the Superbowl in 2011?

10. Which Rugby League team played their home games at Knowsley Road before relocating at the end of the 2010 season?

11. Which Major League Baseball team play their home games at Fenway Park?

12. Which British couple won Winter Olympic gold medals in Sarejevo?

13. In which city would you find the Albert Park motor racing circuit?

14. In which city does the Tour de France traditionally end with a sprint finish?

15. In which city did Jesse Owens famously win 4 Summer Olympic gold medals for the USA?

16. Which famous horse race did Sea the Stars win in October 2009 at Longchamp?

17. In which venue do both the New York Knicks and the New York Rangers play their home games?

18. At which London venue did Andy Roddick and Lleyton Hewitt win 4 titles each during the 2000s?

19. Which Canadian city hosted the Commonwealth Games in 1994?

20. In which city did the tearful Paul Gascoigne pick up his booking in the 1990 World Cup semi-final?

Game 35

On this episode of A Question of Sport are...

Niall Quinn (Football)
First appeared on the show as a guest in 1991

Matt Dawson (Rugby Union)
First appeared on the show as a guest in 1999

Fred Trueman (Cricket)
First appeared on the show as a guest in 1976

Zara Phillips (Equestrianism)
First appeared on the show as a guest in 2006

Round 1 – Opening Rally

1. Name the ten countries that have won tennis' Davis Cup between 1980 and 2010.

Round 2 – One Minute Round

1. Which Football League team play their home games at Portman Road?

2. Which famous horse race did ESB win in 1956, Red Alligator in 1968 and Rag Trade in 1976?

3. Which American tennis player is the main court at Flushing Meadows named after?

4. Which Champions League winning team is this an anagram of? ABLE ACORN

5. Which County Championship team play their home games at Lord's?

6. What nationality is the 1991 Open Championship winner Ian Baker-Finch and the runner up Mike Harwood?

7. What is the maximum number of frames that can be played in the snooker World Championship final?

These sports stars all share parts of their names with months of the year.

8. _____ Croft (Swimming)

9. Fiona _____ (Athletics)

10. Ricky _____ (Rugby Union)

Round 3 – Mystery Guest

1. Like many in my sport I was born in Northern Ireland, in my case in 1974 (4 points)

   I started my career in England in 1994 and have gone on to win over 3000 races in my career (3 points)

   My first names are Anthony Peter and in 2010 I achieved something I had been striving to achieve for 15 years (2 points)

   In 2010 I became the first jockey to win BBC Sports Personality of the Year (1 point)

2. I turned 30 in 2009 and was born in Kingston (4 points)

   I am known for my big hitting and in 2007 I hit the first century in Twenty20 internationals (3 points)

   I have scored a triple Test century on more than one occasion (2 points)

   I made my West Indies debut in 2000 and I regularly open the batting (1 point)

Round 4 – Home or Away

1. *Niall Quinn.* Which Scottish international won the Champions League with Borussia Dortmund in 1997?

2. *Matt Dawson.* Which country won the last Five Nations Championship in 1999, captained by Gary Armstrong?

3. *Fred Trueman.* Who became the first player to take all 10 wickets in a Test match, doing so against Australia in 1956?

4. *Zara Phillips.* Which British rider won an Olympic bronze medal in Individual Three Day Eventing in both 1984 and 1988?

Round 5 – Captain's Away

1. Who set a Long Jump world record at the 1968 Summer Olympics, a record that was not beaten for 23 years?

2. Who won the Football World Cup as a captain in 1974 and as a manager in 1990?

3. Name the Northern Irish golfers who played for Europe in the 2010 Ryder Cup?

4. In which sport do the Leicester Riders compete in the British League?
   a) Basketball
   b) Netball
   c) Field Hockey

Round 6 – What Happened Next

1. Brazil have just been awarded a free kick against Zaire in the 1974 World Cup, the Zaire wall has just been moved back ten yards, what happened next?
   a) As the Brazil attackers prepared to take the free kick a fan runs onto the pitch and steals the ball.

b) As the referee blew the whistle a Zaire player broke out of the wall and kicked the ball away.

c) Three Brazilian attackers all attempt to take the free kick at the same time and collide with each other.

2. It's the 1981 London Marathon and runners Dick Beardsley and Inge Simonsen are neck and neck approaching the finish line, what happened next?

a) The two runners decide to cross the line together so hold hands and tie the race.

b) Beardsley trips just before the line but Simonsen helps him up and carries him over the line.

c) Beardsley runs the wrong way mistaking a break in the crowd for the course so Simonsen canters through for victory.

Round 7 – On the Buzzer

This buzzer round is all about the year 1990.

1. With victory over American Zina Garrison in the final who won a ninth Wimbledon Singles Title?

2. In July which British athlete set a new world record in the javelin with a throw of over 90 metres?

3. Which side beat Liverpool 4-3 in the FA Cup semi-final but lost to Manchester United in the final in a replay?

4. Which opening batsman captained England to their first Test defeat of the West Indies in 16 years?

5. Captained by David Sole which country recorded their third Five Nations Grand Slam?

6. After the 1990 World Cup who replaced Bobby Robson as manager of the England football team?

7. Which Swede beat Boris Becker to win his second Wimbledon Singles Title?

8. Which female sprinter from Jamaica won both the 100m and 200m at the Commonwealth Games?

9. Which British golfer won two of the four Majors in 1990, the US Masters and the Open Championship?

10. Which race did Mr Frisk win in a record time of 8 minutes and 48 seconds in April?

11. In which sport did Australian Hayley Lewis win five Commonwealth gold medals?

12. Which trophy did the Edmonton Oilers win in 1990 for the fifth time in seven years?

13. Which young snooker player won the Masters, the UK Championship and the World Championship in 1990?

14. Which Rugby League team did Ellery Hanley lead to a record third consecutive Challenge Cup final victory?

15. Which driver won six Grand Prix races on the way to winning the Formula One World Championship?

16. Who did James 'Buster' Douglas sensationally defeat in February to become the World Heavyweight Champion?

17. In which sport did England's Sara Sankey partner Fiona Smith to win Commonwealth gold?

18. Which legendary darts player won his first World Championship winning the final 6 sets to 1 at the Lakeside Country Club?

19. In which sport did the Detroit Pistons defeat the Portland Trail Blazers to a National Championship?

20. Which famous quarterback was named as Superbowl MVP as his side the San Francisco 49ers won the game?

Game 36

On this episode of A Question of Sport are...

Joe Cole (Football)
First appeared on the show as a guest in 2001

Bill Beaumont (Rugby Union)
First appeared on the show as a guest in 1980

Audley Harrison (Boxing)
First appeared on the show as a guest in 2000

John Surtees (Motor racing)
First appeared on the show as a guest in 1970

After retiring as captain Ian Botham came back onto the show as a guest and famously failed to identify his son Liam as a mystery guest.

Round 1 – Opening Rally

1. Name the 12 Italian football teams that have won the Serie A Championship between 1960 and 2010.

Round 2 – One Minute Round

1. For which country did Luke McLean score a try in the 2011 Six Nations Championships?

2. Which Open Championship golf course features holes called The Monk, Rabbit and Postage Stamp?

3. Which England cricketer's name is this an anagram of? NEW MANAGERS

4. Which country hosted the last race of the 2008 Formula One Championship season?

5. With which sport would you associate the Tasmanian Tigers and the Victorian Bushrangers?

6. In which sport did Britain's Louis Smith win an Olympic bronze medal at the 2008 Games?

7. Which football team won the FA Cup final in 1991 beating Nottingham Forest in the final?

Fill in the surnames of these famous sports stars.

8. David _____ – Scored five goals at the 2010 World Cup

9. David _____ – Over 8000 Test runs for England

10. David _____ – 2001 Open Champion

Round 3 – Mystery Guest

1. I was born in Stockport in 1909 and after a spectacular career as a sportsman my name is still very well known today (4 points)

    I helped Britain to victories in a major team event in the 1930s (3 points)

    I was a World Table Tennis Champion before winning Wimbledon (2 points)

    I gave my name to a design of tennis clothing that is still worn today (1 point)

2. I was born in Cheshire in 1973 and gained a first-class honours degree in Modern European Studies from Loughborough University (4 points)

    In 1992 I won the Junior Race at the World Cross Country Championships and 9 years later won gold at the Championships in the Senior Race (3 points)

    I endured a hard time of things at the 2004 Olympics missing out on the chance to win gold by being forced to withdraw through injury halfway through the race (2 points)

    I won the London Marathon on three occasions in the 2000s and in 2002 I set the world record in the marathon (1 point)

Round 4 – Home or Away

1. *Joe Cole.* In 2010 two penalties were missed in normal play of

an FA Cup final for the first time. Frank Lampard missed for Chelsea but who missed a spot kick for Portsmouth?

2. *Bill Beaumont.* Besides Gareth Edwards which other back was an ever present in Wales' three Grand Slam winning sides in the 1970s?

3. *Audley Harrison.* Which future World Heavyweight Champion beat Riddick Bowe to win the Olympic Super Heavyweight Title in 1988?

4. *John Surtees.* In 1984, Alain Prost lost the World Championship by half a point to his McLaren team mate. Who was he?

Round 5 – Captain's Away

1. In December 2001 Michael Vaughan became only the 7th player to be given out in a Test match by which method of dismissal?

2. Who led the 2001 Open Championship but was given a two stroke penalty after he was found to accidentally have 15 golf clubs in his bag?

3. Name the two German teams to have won the Champions League between 1990 and 2010?

4. In which sport did Cannock and East Grinstead compete in the 2010/2011 Premier League?
   a) Field Hockey
   b) Netball
   c) Ice Hockey

Round 6 – What Happened Next

1. Gabriela Szabo is in pole position on the final straight of the Women's 3000m in Paris 2002, what happened next?
    a) Szabo slows down as she thinks she is well clear of the rest of the field and begins to celebrate but Berhane Adere catches her and pips her to the line.
    b) Szabo trips just before the line and loses out on first place but manages to crawl across the line to take second.
    c) Szabo wins the race and goes over to the crowd to celebrate with her boyfriend who proposes to her at the side of the track.

2. Wales are playing Ireland in the 2011 Six Nations Championship at the Millennium Stadium and Jonathan Sexton is just about to kick the ball into touch, what happened next?
    a) Sexton's kick hits Wale's coach Warren Gatland on the head on the sidelines and he is forced to receive medical treatment.
    b) The ball goes out of play and Matthew Rees collects a different ball off the official and takes a quick lineout to Mike Phillips who scores a try which is given despite being against the rules.
    c) Sexton's kick is about to go out of play but an over eager touch official catches the ball before it goes out of play.

Round 7 – On the Buzzer

This buzzer round is all about defending champions.

1. Which Spanish driver successfully defended his Formula One World Championship in 2006 whilst driving for Renault?

2. Who in 1968 became the first American Football team to

defend their Superbowl title?

3. In 1990 which European golfer beat Raymond Floyd in a playoff to defend his US Masters Title?

4. Between 1998 and 2007 which British boxer successfully defended his Super Middleweight World Title on more than 20 occasions?

5. In which sport did Russians Oksana Grishuk and Evgeny Platov defend their Winter Olympic gold medals in the 90s?

6. Which Italian rider won the Moto GP World Championship in 2001 and defended the title for the next four seasons?

7. Which defending champions were knocked out of the 2011 FA Cup on penalties by Everton, the team they beat in the final the previous year?

8. In which sport did Stuart Bingham knock out the then reigning World Champion in the first round of the 2000 tournament?

9. Which horse won the 2007 Cheltenham Gold Cup but was beaten into second place the following year by Denman?

10. Which team missed out on winning their third successive Cricket World Cup final when they lost to India in 1983?

11. Which defending World Cup Champions were famously beaten by Senegal in the opening match of the 2002 World Cup in Seoul?

12. Which American successfully retained her Wimbledon Singles title by defeating Vera Zvonareva in 2010?

13. Which baseball team beat defending champions Philadelphia Phillies in the 2009 World Series to win their 27th Championship?

14. Which Rugby League team defended the Challenge Cup successfully for seven years after their victory over Halifax in 1988?

15. Who in 2011 became the first England captain in over 20 years to win an Ashes series in Australia?

16. In which sport did Martin Adams beat Dean Winstanley in 2011 to retain his World Championship title?

17. Which English Rugby Union team beat defending champions Toulouse in the 2004 Heineken Cup final at Twickenham?

18. Which team defended their NBA Championship in 2010 by defeating the Boston Celtics?

19. Which Chinese athlete failed to defend his 110m hurdles Olympic title in Beijing due to injury in the heats?

20. Which British rower defended his Olympic title in the Coxless Pairs with Steve Redgrave in 1996?

Game 37

On this episode of A Question of Sport are...

Jamie Redknapp (Football)
First appeared on the show as a guest in 1996

Bradley Wiggins (Cycling)
First appeared on the show as a guest in 2004

Willie Carson (Horse racing)
First appeared on the show as a guest in 1981

Ian Woosnam (Golf)
First appeared on the show as a guest in 1985

Round 1 – Opening Rally

1. Name the ten American Football teams that have won the Superbowl between 1998 and 2011.

Round 2 – One Minute Round

1. In which sport did Paul Lim make World Championship history in 1990?

2. Which US Masters Champion did Davis Love III partner to four successive Golf World Cup titles between 1992 and 1995?

3. Which sport is this an anagram of? LEGGY BUREAU

4. Which country in 1924 hosted the first ever Winter Olympic Games?

5. In which sport did Britain's Zac Purchase win an Olympic gold medal at the 2008 Games?

6. Which country hosted football's European Championships in 2004?

7. In which sport do Australian teams compete for the Sheffield Shield Trophy?

In which sports have these Frenchmen been World Champions?

8. Raymond Roche – _____

9. Jean Claude Killy – _____

10. Arnaud Tournant – _____

Round 3 – Mystery Guest

1. I was born in 1964 and played 72 times for my country (4 points)

    In that time I scored 33 tries in 11 years of international rugby (3 points)

    I played for Llanelli for the most of my career but I had a season at Bath and we won the Heineken Cup during my time there (2 points)

    I played on the wing on three British and Irish Lions Tours and in 1995 I captained Wales at the Rugby Union World Cup (1 point)

2. I was born in 1976 and made my international debut before I turned 21 (4 points)

    I made over 500 dismissals in Test cricket passing the total in 2010 (3 points)

    My 75 consecutive Tests between 1997 and 2005 was a South African record (2 points)

    My dismissals all came from behind the stumps (1 point)

Round 4 – Home or Away

1. *Jamie Redknapp.* Who between 2002 and 2006 became the first player to score more than 20 Premier League goals in five consecutive seasons?

2. *Bradley Wiggins.* Who beat Chris Hoy in the Sprint semi-final at the 2011 World Championships before winning silver in the final?

3. *Willie Carson.* In 1970 which horse won the Triple Crown of Epsom Derby, 2000 Guineas and the St Leger?

4. *Ian Woosnam.* Who spent 331 weeks as the World's Number One golfer and won the Open Championship in both 1986 and 1993?

Round 5 – Captain's Away

1. Who became the first 21 year old since Stephen Hendry to contest a Snooker World Championship final?

2. In British greyhound racing the dog wearing the orange jacket runs from which trap?

3. Name the two Rugby Union teams that played in the 2010/2011 Premiership whose names begin with N?

4. In which sport did Coventry Blaze win the 2010 Elite League?
   a) Field Hockey
   b) Basketball
   c) Ice Hockey

Round 6 – Great Sporting Moments

1. After scoring the winning goal in the League Cup final Steve Morrow was met by a delighted captain Tony Adams and his teammates. As part of the celebrations Morrow was hoisted into the air, what happened next?

2. Needing only a six from the par 4 18th hole at Carnoustie to win the Open Championship, he hit one shot into the water, one shot into a bunker and proceeded to make a triple bogey. Although he recovered to compete in the playoff, Scotsman Paul Lawrie triumphed and his chance to lift the Claret Jug had passed. Whose downfall at the Open is this?

Round 7 – On the Buzzer

This buzzer round is all about the year 2006.

1. Which race was won by Niall Madden on Numbersixvalverde in April?

2. Which Bolton Wanderers player became the first person to play in 500 Premier League games?

3. Which golfer won the 2006 US Open to become the first Australian since 1981 to win the tournament?

4. Which British boxer won the World Light Welterweight Title by beating DeMarcus Corley?

5. In August 2006 which British driver won his first Formula One Grand Prix?

6. Which club won their first Heineken Cup beating Biarritz in the final at the Millennium Stadium in Cardiff?

7. Russia won the Davis Cup thanks to wins in the Singles by Marat Safin and which other player?

8. In which event did Shelley Rudman win a Winter Olympic silver medal for Britain?

9. In January which Australian scored centuries in both innings of his 100th Test match?

10. Which English athlete won 1500m Commonwealth gold beating Sarah Jamieson and Hayley Tullett into second and third?

11. Which city staged the 2006 Commonwealth Games 50 years after staging the Summer Olympics?

12. Who scored a penalty and was sent off in the 2006 Football World Cup final?

13. James Graham won the Young Rugby League Player of the Year award in 2006 whilst playing for which club?

14. Which Scottish snooker player beat Peter Ebdon 18-14 in the final of the World Championships?

15. When Scotland beat England to win the Calcutta Cup at Murrayfield which player scored 15 points to secure victory for his side?

16. Which Surrey and former England batsman finished the County Championship season with an average of over 100?

17. Which country won netball gold at the 2006 Commonwealth Games?

18. Who in January scored 81 points in a single NBA game for the Los Angeles Lakers?

19. Which Germany player was the leading goalscorer at the 2006 World Cup helping his country to a third place finish?

20. Which cyclist won the Men's 20km Scratch Race at the 2006 Commonwealth Games to give the Isle of Man their only gold medal of the Games?

Game 38

On this episode of A Question of Sport are...

Michael Johnson (Athletics)
First appeared on the show as a guest in 2003

Will Greenwood (Rugby Union)
First appeared on the show as a guest in 2003

Christopher Dean (Ice dancing)
First appeared on the show as a guest in 1984

Martina Hingis (Tennis)
First appeared on the show as a guest in 2004

John Parrott became the first snooker player to become a captain on the programme when he teamed up with Ally McCoist in 1996. The pair were on opposing sides for seven series up until 2002.

Round 1 – Opening Rally

1. Name the 12 footballers whose surnames begin with the letter B who have won a cap for England between 2000 and 2009.

Round 2 – One Minute Round

1. Which Football League team play their home games at Sincil Bank?

2. Which country has won the Men's Ice Hockey gold medal at the Winter Olympics on 8 occasions?

3. In which sport do the Hertfordshire Mavericks and the Loughborough Lightning compete in the Super League?

4. In 1967 Robert DeVicenzo became the first golfer from which country to win a Major?

5. Which fielding position in cricket is this an anagram of? TO PROVINCE

6. Who partnered Todd Woodbridge to 15 Grand Slam Men's Doubles finals between 1990 and 2000?

7. In which country's league would you find the cricket teams Central Stags, Otago Volts and the Northern Knights?

Fill in the surnames of these famous sports stars.

8. Steven _____ – England 2010 World Cup scorer

9. Steve _____ – 2005 Ashes Winner

10. Steve _____ – 1996 Super Middleweight World Champion

Round 3 – Mystery Guest

1. I was born in 1952 in the Caribbean though my career saw me move around the world a lot (4 points)

   I was a good footballer but played my main sport internationally for 17 years before retiring in 1991 (3 points)

   As the West Indies captain I never lost a Test series (2 points)

   I'm fondly remembered in Somerset where I struck up a close friendship with Ian Botham (1 point)

2. I became a professional a year after winning Olympic gold (4 points)

   In 1973 I became Heavyweight World Champion by defeating Joe Frazier before losing the title a year later in Zaire (3 points)

   At the age of 45 I became a World Champion once again by beating Michael Moorer (2 points)

   Since retiring I have become known to another generation for my range of cooking grills (1 point)

Round 4 – Home or Away

1. *Michael Johnson.* Who in the year 2000 became the first British sprinter to win an Olympic medal in the 200m since Allan Wells won silver in 1980?

2. *Will Greenwood.* Who in 2011 broke Ian Smith's record to become the top try scorer in the Six Nations Championships?

3. *Christopher Dean.* In which year did Robin Cousins win the Men's Figure Skating Olympic gold medal in Lake Placid?

4. *Martina Hingis.* Which European woman won her third US Open Singles Title in 2010 by beating Vera Zvonareva?

Round 5 – Captain's Away

1. What colour jersey did Mark Cavendish wear as the point classification winner in the 2010 Vuelta a Espana?

2. Which British golfer won a 76th career title at Flamingos Gold Club on the Costa del Sol in 2010?

3. Name the two teams that played in the top four tiers of English football in 2010/2011 whose names begin with the letter O?

4. Which of these teams did Ayrton Senna not drive for in Formula One?
   a) Williams
   b) McLaren
   c) Ferrari

Round 6 – Great Sporting Moments

1. Having tasted joy in Rome only seven years earlier, Liverpool were on the verge of winning their fourth European Cup final following Francesco Graziani's miss in the penalty shoot-out for Roma. Liverpool needed to score their next penalty to win the shoot-out and the trophy, which full back slotted home the winning penalty?

2. In the 51st minute Diego Maradona pushed forward and moved the ball to Jorge Valdano on the right hand side. Steve Hodge managed to intercept the ball but his attempted clearance was miscued in the direction of goalkeeper Peter Shilton and Diego Maradona who had continued his run. What happened next?

Round 7 – On the Buzzer

This buzzer round is all about the north of England.

1. Which North West club played in the Premier League for the first time in 2010?

2. Which Superbike World Champion was born in Blackburn in 1965?

3. The Salford City Reds are a professional team in which sport?

4. Who are the Tykes who won rugby's Powergen Cup final for the first time in 2005?

5. Born in Fleetwood in which sport did Jane Crouch become Britain's first officially licensed sportswoman?

6. Which snooker ranking event was held in York between 2001 and 2006 before being moved to Telford?

7. Which Liverpudlian athlete won a bronze medal in the high jump at the 1996 Olympics?

8. Known more for horse racing which North West venue hosted the British Grand Prix on five occasions between 1955 and 1962?

9. Which English county cricket team play their home games at the Riverside?

10. Which Bolton Wanderers played made his England debut at the age of 33 in October 2010?

11. Which Yorkshire born cricket umpire was born Harold Dennis but is more commonly known as 'Dickie'?

12. In which stadium in the North East did Asafa Powell equal his own 100m world record in June 2006?

13. Which of the English Classics is held at the Doncaster Racecourse?

14. England fly half Rob Andrew played for which team between 1995 and 1999 before becoming their Director of Rugby?

15. Who are the Wolves who play their Rugby League at the Halliwell Jones Stadium?

16. Which Wirral golf course staged its first Open Championship in 29 years in 2006?

17. In which sport did Yorkshire born Anita Lonsbrough win an Olympic gold medal in 1960?

18. Which footballer won his first England cap with Newcastle United in 2010 and his second cap with Liverpool in 2011?

19. Which city has hosted Snooker's World Championship since 1977?

20. In which sport did Stoke's Adrian Lewis become a World Champion in 2011?

Game 39

On this episode of A Question of Sport are...

Ray Wilkins (Football)
First appeared on the show as a guest in 1980

Thomas Castaignede (Rugby Union)
First appeared on the show as a guest in 2001

Greg Rusedski (Tennis)
First appeared on the show as a guest in 1996

Jonathan Edwards (Athletics)
First appeared on the show as a guest in 1995

Round 1 – Opening Rally

1. Name the ten European golfers to win a men's Major between 1985 and 2010.

Round 2 – One Minute Round

1. With which sport would you associate the Urawa Red Diamonds, Nagoya Grampus and Gambo Osaka?

2. For which team have cricketers Jacques Kallis, Waqar Younis and Sourav Ganguly all played for in the County Championship?

3. Which Scottish football ground is this an anagram of? TRICK PLACE

4. What nationality is 2002 Australian Open Men's Singles Title Champion Thomas Johansson?

5. Which famous horse did Brian Fletcher and Tommy Stack both ride to victory in the Grand National at Aintree?

6. In which sport might you be penalised for a double dribble?

7. Which American won the Heavyweight Boxing gold medal at the 1968 Olympics?

These sports stars all share parts of their names with types of weather.

8. Dominic _____ (Football)

9. _____ Irwin (Golf)

10. John _____ (Cricket)

Round 3 – Mystery Guest

1. I was born in Nottingham and it was here I met someone that would shape my career (4 points)

   I won an Olympic gold medal at the age of 26 and ten years later I won bronze (3 points)

   I have a piece of music by Maurice Ravel to thank for my worldwide fame (2 points)

   You can now see me on television as part of the programme Dancing on Ice (1 point)

2. I was born in 1982 in Sydney and my father was a Rugby League player (4 points)

   At the age of 20 I made my debut for Australia against England before I had played in the Super 12s (3 points)

   I came on as a substitute in the 2003 Rugby Union World Cup final but couldn't prevent my team from losing (2 points)

   In 2010 I scored my 600th point for Australia to become only the third player from my country to reach that milestone (1 point)

Round 4 – Home or Away

1. *Ray Wilkins.* Which Liverpool player was the only person to score in FA Cup finals in two different years in the 1970s?

2. *Thomas Castaignede.* Which forward is the only person to have played in England's World Cup final sides in both 1991 and 2003?

3. *Greg Rusedski.* Between 2000 and 2010 which player has been beaten by Roger Federer in three Wimbledon Singles finals?

4. *Jonathan Edwards.* Who in 2009 broke her own world record by reaching a height of 5.06m in the pole vault at the Golden League meeting in Zurich?

Round 5 – Captain's Away

1. Traditionally how many fences are jumped only once during the Grand National at Aintree?

2. Which Nigerian international in 1993 became the first player to score four goals in an English Premier League match?

3. Name the two first class cricket counties that begin with the letter W?

4. Which of these courses has not hosted the Open Championship?
    a) Gleneagles
    b) Birkdale
    c) Portrush

Round 6 – Great Sporting Moments

1. Having already hit the post earlier in the game, the Spanish striker was not to be denied in the 33rd minute. Xavi's clever pass created uncertainty for the German defender Philipp Lahm and his goalkeeper Jens Lehmann and the striker latched onto it to find the net. Who was the forward that won the European Championship for Spain with his goal?

2. Despite a fine third leg from Coby Miller, Marlon Devonish

was able to hand over the baton some two metres ahead of the Americans who had Maurice Greene to run the anchor leg. Which sprinter was able to hold off Greene to win the 100m relay for Great Britain at the 2004 Olympics?

Round 7 – On the Buzzer

This buzzer round is all about 2003.

1. Which Dutchman won the World Darts Championship at Frimley Green for the third time?

2. On which racecourse did Richard Johnson partner Rooster Booster to win the Champion Hurdle?

3. Which European team did England beat in the Rugby Union World Cup semi-final?

4. Which British female rider won a second successive Badminton Horse Trials on Supreme Rock?

5. Who scored 140 for Australia in their World Cup final victory over India?

6. Which British athlete set a world record when winning the London Marathon in 2 hours and 15 minutes?

7. In which sport did Britain's Katherine Grainger and Cath Bishop win a World Pairs Title?

8. Which American golfer won his first Major by winning the US Open at Olympia Fields?

9. Who scored a hat trick for Real Madrid as they lost 4-3 to Manchester United at Old Trafford?

10. Which Colombian Formula One driver won the 2003 Monaco Grand Prix?

11. Two women from which European country contested the French Open Singles final?

12. In which event did Carl Myerscough add 23cms to Geoff Capes 23 year old British Record?

13. Who equalled Billie Jean King's record of 20 Wimbledon titles when she partnered Leander Paes to the Mixed Doubles Title?

14. Which jockey won the Grand National for the first time on Monty's Pass?

15. In which sport did Britain's James Gibson and Katy Sexton win a World Championship gold medal?

16. Which American won his 8th and last Grand Slam Singles Title by winning the Australian Open in 2003?

17. At the age of 22 years and 26 days which Spaniard became the youngest ever Formula One Grand Prix winner?

18. Who won BBC Sports Personality of the Year having helped his team win the 2003 World Cup?

19. Porto beat which British team to win the UEFA Cup winning 3-2 after extra time?

20. Which Irishman did Mark Williams beat in the snooker World Championship final?

Game 40

On this episode of A Question of Sport are...

Ian Wright (Football)
First appeared on the show as a guest in 1991

David Campese (Rugby Union)
First appeared on the show as a guest in 2000

Chris Boardman (Cycling)
First appeared on the show as a guest in 1995

Pippa Funnell (Equestrianism)
First appeared on the show as a guest in 2001

Princess Anne became the first member of the Royal Family to appear on the show, doing so in 1987. Her appearance coincided with *A Question of Sport* receiving its highest ever audience figures of approximately 19 million viewers.

Round 1 – Opening Rally

1. Other than England, name the 12 countries which have played in 4 or more ODI Cricket World Cups.

Round 2 – One Minute Round

1. For which country did Daniel Nestor and Sebastien Lareau win a gold medal at the 2000 Summer Olympics?

2. Which English tennis player won the BBC Sports Personality of the Year Award in 1977?

3. Which country finished third at the 1987 Rugby Union World Cup?

4. Which sport is this an anagram of? KEY CHOICE

5. Which Football League team play their home games at Home Park?

6. Which of the four golf Majors did Mark Brooks, Steve Elkington and Wayne Grady all win in the 1990s?

7. Which Sri Lankan finished the 2011 Cricket World Cup as the top run scorer of the tournament?

Fill in the surnames of these famous sports stars.

8. Peter _____ – 1980s Champion Jockey

9. Peter _____ – 2002 Snooker World Champion

10. Peter _____ – 1999 Champions League Winner

Round 3 – Mystery Guest

1. I was born in 1967 and captained Wales at the age of 20 (4 points)

   I could have played professional football and was also an English Schools Athletics Champion (3 points)

   I scored a very famous try for the Barbarians against the All Blacks in 1973 (2 points)

   I was a captain on *A Question of Sport* and during my career developed a superb understanding with half back partner Barry John (1 point)

2. I followed my father into the national side and was joined by my brothers internationally (4 points)

   I am looked upon as being my country's greatest ever cricketer (3 points)

   I helped Clive Rice to win the County Championship (2 points)

   I was knighted for my services to cricket and was later named as chairman of selectors for New Zealand (1 point)

Round 4 – Home or Away

1. *Ian Wright.* Which international defender won the Premier League with Blackburn Rovers and Manchester United in the 90s?

2. *David Campese.* Who between 1984 and 1996 scored 49 tries in his 85 England games to become his country's record try scorer?

3. **Chris Boardman.** Which British cyclist won at least four stages of the Tour de France in 2008, 2009 and 2010?

4. **Pippa Funnell.** What country are the Olympic Three Day Eventing Champions Mark Todd and Blyth Tait from?

Round 5 – Captain's Away

1. Which Australian scored a century on his Test debut in 2009 and has played for Derbyshire, Durham, Gloucestershire, Hampshire and Lancashire?

2. Chicago were eliminated first, then Tokyo, then Madrid, leaving Rio de Janeiro as the winners in the bidding process to host which event?

3. Name the two Swedish golfers who played for Europe in the 2006 Ryder Cup?

4. Which of these sports is not included in the Olympic Heptathlon?
    a) 200m
    b) 400m
    c) 800m

Round 6 – What Happened Next

1. Manchester City travelled to Sheffield United in the 2008 FA Cup 4th Round. Lee Martin is about to cross the ball into the box, what happened next?
    a) Martin crossed into the penalty box that was littered with balloons and City defender Michael Ball lost sight of the football amongst the balloons leaving striker Luke Shelton to score the opening goal.

b) Martin's cross hit a divot and bounced over City keeper Joe Hart's head and into the goal.

c) Martin missed the ball and kicked the assistant referee on the touchline by mistake as he had gotten too close to the action.

2. It's the final of the Men's 1000m Speed Skating at the Winter Olympics in 2002, and with only the final corner to go Australian Stephen Bradbury is in last place, what happened next?

a) An unaware official walks out onto the ice and collides with Bradbury, ruining his race.

b) Bradbury's four opponents all collided in front of him allowing the Australian to skate through and take the gold medal.

c) As Bradbury bends over to enter the final corner his skin-tight lycra suit rips revealing his backside to the crowd.

Round 7 – On the Buzzer

All the answers to this buzzer round begin with the letter M. In the case of a person it's the surname that must start with that letter.

1. Which Formula One Grand Prix did Ayrton Senna win five years in a row between 1989 and 1993?

2. Which country hosted the 1998 Commonwealth Games?

3. Which American golfer won his third US Masters title in 2010?

4. Which American Football team did Dan Marino reach the Superbowl with in 1985?

5. Which English snooker player won the 2005 World Championship final at the Crucible?

6. Who was beaten in his first Grand Slam final by Roger Federer at the 2008 US Open?

7. For which team did Irishman Denis Leamy score a try to help them win the 2008 Heineken Cup final?

8. In 1997 which team reached the final of the FA Cup and the League Cup as well as being relegated?

9. Known as Pretty Boy which American boxer won a World Title at five different weights between 1998 and 2007?

10. On which horse did Richard Dunwoody win his second Grand National victory, doing so in 1994?

11. In which event did Kenyan Samuel Wanjiru win gold at the 2008 Summer Olympics?

12. In 2005 which British yachtswoman broke the world record for the fastest solo circumnavigation of the globe?

13. Which team won the County Championship three times during the 1980s and play their home games at Lord's?

14. Who managed Porto to Champions League victory in 2004 and six years later was in charge as Inter Milan lifted the trophy?

15. Which European golfer held a four shot lead at the start of the final day's play of the 2011 US Masters before eventually finishing tied for 15th place?

16. In which city were the 1976 Summer Olympic Games held?

17. In 2010 which New Zealand Rugby Union player was named the IRB Player of the Year for the third time?

18. Which French woman won her only Wimbledon Singles Title in 2006 by beating Justine Henin in the final?

19. In 2007 which Australian bowler took his 563rd and final Test wicket by dismissing James Anderson in Sydney?

20. Which British swimmer won four gold medals at the European Championships between 1983 and 1989?

Game 41

On this episode of A Question of Sport are...

François Pienaar (Rugby Union)
First appeared on the show as a guest in 2000

Victoria Pendleton (Cycling)
First appeared on the show as a guest in 2007

Michael Vaughan (Cricket)
First appeared on the show as a guest in 2003

John McEnroe (Tennis)
First appeared on the show as a guest in 1999

Emlyn Hughes famously failed to identify Princess Anne on the Pictureboard, believing she was jockey John Reid instead.

Round 1 – Opening Rally

1. Other than Dave Beasant name the 10 goalkeepers that have featured in an England World Cup squad since 1990?

Round 2 – One Minute Round

1. Which country hosted football's European Championships in 1996?

2. For which team have cricketers Ricky Ponting, Graeme Smith and Justin Langer all played in the County Championship?

3. Which country hosted the 2011 Formula One Grand Prix on the Albert Park circuit?

4. Which European golfer's name is this an anagram of?
   ROMANCES RAT

5. Which Nottingham fighter won the WBC Super Middleweight World Title by beating Jean Pascal in 2008?

6. For which country did Morgan Stoddart score a try in the 2011 Six Nations Championships?

7. Who was the only Spaniard to play for Europe in the 2010 Ryder Cup?

In which sports have these Americans been World Champions.

8. Shawn Johnson – _____

9. Tara Lipinski – _____

10. Kenny Roberts – _____

Round 3 – Mystery Guest

1. I am a qualified pilot and emerged on the international stage as a 20 year old (4 points)

   I captained my country for the first time in 2004 at only 23 and I led them three years later at the World Cup (3 points)

   I surpassed Sean Fitzpatrick's record of 39 Test wins as All Blacks captain (2 points)

   The IRB named me as the International Rugby Player of the Year in 2006, an award I have won more than once (1 point)

2. I was born in Cheshire but was raised by the coast in Cornwall for much of my childhood and it was here I got my sea legs (4 points)

   By the age of 17 I was a World Youth Champion and aged 19 I won my first Olympic medal in 1996 (3 points)

   At the Sydney Olympics in 2000 I became an Olympic Champion for the first time (2 points)

   In 2008 I won my third successive Olympic gold medal to become Britain's most successful sailor (1 point)

Round 4 – Home or Away

1. *François Pienaar.* Who between 1995 and 2004 scored a then All Blacks record of 967 points in his 70 Tests?

2. *Victoria Pendleton.* Which cyclist won the Olympic Women's Road Race in Beijing to become the Britain's first gold medal winner of the games?

3. *Michael Vaughan.* Which England Test batsman scored 405 not out for Worcestershire in 1988, one of 136 centuries he scored in a First Class career that ended in 2008?

4. *John McEnroe.* Andre Gomez became the first player from which South American country to win a Grand Slam Singles Title?

Round 5 – Captain's Away

1. Which is the only English city to have hosted top-flight games in every season of league football?

2. With which sport would you associate the scoring term bed and breakfast?

3. Name the two Welsh golfers who played for Europe in the Ryder Cup between 1997 and 2002?

4. Which of these horse racing venues doesn't hold National Hunt races?
   a) Chester
   b) Ludlow
   c) Exeter

Round 6 – Great Sporting Moments

1. In the first period of extra time the tireless Alan Ball chased a long pass forward down the right hand channel. Having caught

it towards the corner flag he pulled it back across the German penalty box for the forward to hit the ball onto the crossbar and down toward the goal line, which, despite protests from the Germany players was given as a goal by the referee. Who scored this controversial goal for England in the 1966 World Cup final?

2. With Liverpool a goal down they were presented with the perfect opportunity to get back on level terms when referee Brian Hill adjudged Clive Goodyear to have fouled John Aldridge. The striker picked himself up to take the penalty only to see it saved by the Wimbledon goalkeeper. By making that save the goalie became the first man to save a penalty in a Wembley FA Cup final, who was he?

Round 7 – On the Buzzer

This buzzer round is all about the year 2007.

1. Which former World Champion became the first snooker player in history to record 700 competitive centuries?

2. Who became the first British tennis player in 20 years to win a title at Wimbledon by winning the Mixed Doubles final with Jelena Jankovic?

3. Which European darts player won his first PDC World Championship title by beating Phil Taylor 7-6 in the final?

4. In which sport's World Championships did Aaron Peirsol and Natalie Coughlin break world records?

5. Who after 15 years of trying finally won the Epsom Derby on Authorised to give him his first win in the race?

6. Which 13 year old from Plymouth won two Senior National Diving Titles in Sheffield?

7. Who won Britain's first gold of the 2007 World Athletics Championships beating Nicola Sanders into second place?

8. In which sport did Britain's Louis Smith win a World Championship bronze medal?

9. Who scored for Chelsea in both the League Cup final and the FA Cup final?

10. Which European won her third consecutive French Open Singles Title by beating Ana Ivanovic 6-1 6-2 in the final?

11. Which wicketkeeper scored a century on his England Test debut at Lord's against the West Indies?

12. In which form of motor sport did Sebastien Loeb win his fourth consecutive World Championship Title?

13. Which South African was the top points scorer at the 2007 Rugby Union World Cup?

14. Which American male won gold at the 2007 World Athletics Championship in the 100m and the 200m?

15. Which basketball team won their 4th NBA Championship in nine years by beating the Cleveland Cavaliers?

16. Which fellow European did Padraig Harrington beat in a playoff at Carnoustie to win the Open Championship?

17. Who in his first season in Formula One won the Canadian Grand Prix to give him victory in only his sixth race?

18. Which 19 year old became the youngest player to score a televised maximum 147 break, doing so at the Masters?

19. Which English team beat Besiktas 8-0 in a Champions League group game in November?

20. Against the West Indies in June which English spinner completed his first 10 wicket haul in Tests?

Game 42

On this episode of A Question of Sport are...

Gary Lineker (Football)
First appeared on the show as a guest in 1986

Justin Langer (Cricket)
First appeared on the show as a guest in 2007

Ed Moses (Athlete)
First appeared on the show as a guest in 2005

Jimmy White (Snooker)
First appeared on the show as a guest in 1987

Round 1 – Opening Rally

1. Name the ten tennis players that have won the Wimbledon Women's Singles Title between 1990 and 2010.

Round 2 – One Minute Round

1. Which Football League team play their home games at Turf Moor?

2. Which city was named as the host of the 2014 Winter Olympics?

3. With which sport would you associate icing, face offs and hooking?

4. Heath Streak was the first bowler to take 100 Test wickets for which country?

5. Which basketball term is this an anagram of? DAMN SULK

6. Which Chinese tennis player did Kim Clijsters beat in the 2011 Australian Open Singles final?

7. Which famous horse race has been held at the Flemington Racecourse on the first Tuesday in November since 1861?

These sports stars all share their surnames with points on the compass.

8. Sam _____ (Cricket)

9. Andy _____ (Golf)

10. Melanie _____ (Tennis)

Round 3 – Mystery Guest

1. I turned 40 in 2010 and was still heavily involved in the sport in which I made my name (4 points)

    I played for New Zealand at Under 21 level but I returned to England in 1990 (3 points)

    I had my greatest moment as a player in 2003 as an inspirational winning captain (2 points)

    Since retiring from playing Rugby Union I have become England's national coach (1 point)

2. I was born in January 1940 and am the most successful player in the history of my sport (4 points)

    I was twice a US Amateur Champion and like me, my son has played professionally (3 points)

    In 1986 I proved I still had what it takes by winning the US Masters at the age of 46 (2 points)

    In all I won a record 18 Majors and am affectionately known as the 'Golden Bear' (1 point)

Round 4 – Home or Away

1. *Gary Lineker.* Who won the Champions League as a player with AC Milan and Ajax before coaching Barcelona to victory in the competition in 2006?

2. *Justin Langer.* In 2010 which Australian took the first Ashes hat trick since Darren Gough achieved the feat 11 years earlier?

3. *Edwin Moses.* For which country did 100m sprinter Kim Collins win gold medals at both the World Championships and the Commonwealth Games?

4. *Jimmy White.* Having won the World Championship at his first attempt in 1979 which player was beaten in his second final 9 years later?

Round 5 – Captain's Away

1. Who partnered John McEnroe to four Wimbledon Men's Doubles finals?

2. Gareth Rees of London Wasps and Harlequins played in four Rugby Union World Cups for which country?

3. Name the two Spanish golfers who played for Europe in the 2008 Ryder Cup?

4. Which of these horse races isn't one of the five English Classics?
   a) The Oaks
   b) 1000 Guineas
   c) Champion Stakes

Round 6 – What Happened Next

1. American decathlete Paul Terek is about to begin the 110m hurdles at the World Championships, what happened next?
   a) An announcement is read out over the PA system about a

car that is being towed and it turns out to be his so he runs off to sort it out.

b) Terek has a very disappointing race and ends up knocking over all 10 hurdles he is faced with.

c) Terek forgets his running trainers so has to borrow a pair from the crowd but as he wins the race he buys them off the spectator.

2. Robert Wagner has just beaten Gary Robson 3-1 at the Darts World Championships, what happened next?

a) Wagner celebrates his victory by ripping the dartboard down and holding it above his head like a trophy.

b) Wagner gets booed by the crowd who wanted local favourite Robson to win so he bares his bottom to the crowd.

c) Wagner surprises the crowd with his flexibility as he celebrates with a somersault on stage.

Round 7 – On the Buzzer

The questions in this buzzer round all have an Irish connection.

1. Who played in goal in FA Cup winning sides for Arsenal and Tottenham Hotspur?

2. For which county did Eoin Morgan and Ed Joyce play in 2008?

3. Who in 2011 against England became the record try scorer in the Six Nations?

4. In which sport did Michael Carruth win his country's first Olympic gold medal in 1992?

5. Which racecourse stages five Irish Classics each year?

6. Which Irishwoman won World Championship gold in the 5000m in 1995?

7. Who in 1997 became the first snooker player from the Republic of Ireland to win the World Championship?

8. Which Irish golfer retained the Open Championship in 2008?

9. Who captained Northern Ireland at the 1982 World Cup two years after winning the European Cup with Nottingham Forest?

10. The Sam Maguire is which sport's principal championship?

11. In which event did Northern Ireland's Mary Peters win an Olympic gold medal?

12. Stephen Roche won which famous race in July 1987?

13. Which Irish boxer won a World Title by defeating Eusebio Pedroza in 1985?

14. Which British and Irish Lions hooker scored four tries for Ireland against the USA in the 1999 World Cup?

15. In 1985 which Ireland player became the first player to be sent off in an FA Cup final?

16. Which famous race is run at Fairyhouse in Ireland on Easter Monday every year?

17. Who scored a century for Ireland as they beat England in the 2011 Cricket World Cup?

18. Which Irish golfer holed the winning putt for Europe at the 2002 Ryder Cup?

19. Who became the first player to reach 100 caps for the Republic of Ireland?

20. Who in 1999 became the first Irish team to win Rugby Union's Heineken Cup?

Game 43

On this episode of A Question of Sport are...

Steve Redgrave (Rowing)
First appeared on the show as a guest in 1987

Nasser Hussain (Cricket)
First appeared on the show as a guest in 1994

Donovan Bailey (Track athletics)
First appeared on the show as a guest in 1998

Seve Ballesteros (Golf)
First appeared on the show as a guest in 2000

Steve Davis became the first person to appear as a studio guest on the programme 20 times and holds the record for the most appearances on the panel without being a captain.

Round 1 – Opening Rally

1. Name the 12 countries to have played in the men's Football World Cup final.

Round 2 – One Minute Round

1. Which American state's NHL Ice Hockey team are called the Avalanche?

2. In which team sport did Sean Kerly win an Olympic gold medal at the 1988 Games?

3. Who replaced Ian Healy as Australian wicketkeeper and scored 149 not out in only his second Test match?

4. Which World Athletics Championship host city is this an anagram of? LIKE SHIN

5. Which bird gives its name to a score on a hole of golf that is three under par?

6. Which team won the Super Rugby tournament on 7 occasions between 1998 and 2008?

7. Which Football League team play their home games at the Riverside Stadium?

These sports stars all share parts of their names with cities that have hosted the Commonwealth Games.

8. Lewis _____ (Motor Racing)

9. Justin _____ (Football)

10. _____ Pendleton (Cycling)

Round 3 – Mystery Guest

1. If I hadn't chosen sport as my career I could possibly have become a professional musician (4 points)

   In 2004 I became the youngest World Champion in my class (3 points)

   Although I was born in Doncaster in 1980, I often reside in the Isle of Man (2 points)

   In 2007 I famously played piano on the BBC's Sports Personality of the Year programme (1 point)

2. I won an Olympic gold medal in 2008 at the age of 27 (4 points)

   I was number one in the world in my chosen sport for a record 237 consecutive weeks (3 points)

   I won my 16th Grand Slam in 2010 in Australia (2 points)

   I am one of the most successful Swiss sport stars of all time (1 point)

Round 4 – Home or Away

1. *Steve Redgrave.* For which country did the Abbagnale brothers win Olympic rowing gold medals in 1984 and 1988 in the Coxed Pairs?

2. *Nasser Hussain.* For which country did Ryan ten Doeschate score two World Cup centuries in 2011, one against England and one against Ireland?

3. *Donovan Bailey.* Who in 2009 became the first woman to win three successive World Championship gold medals in the 200m?

4. *Seve Ballesteros.* Who in 2001 became the third South African to win the US Open following in Gary Player's and Ernie Els' footsteps?

Round 5 – Captain's Away

1. Which player lost in FA Cup finals in the 2000s with Millwall and Everton?

2. In which event did Teddy Tamgho break a World Indoor Record with a distance of 17.92m in 2011?

3. Name the two Rugby Union teams that played in the 2010/2011 Premiership whose names begin with S?

4. Which one of these horse races isn't held at Cheltenham?
   a) Champion Hurdle
   b) Whitbread Gold Cup
   c) Queen Mother Champion Chase

Round 6 – What Happened Next

1. Tanzanian runner Francis Naali is about to win the Commonwealth Games Marathon in Manchester, what happened next?
   a) As Naali completed the final lap he didn't realise the race

was over and kept on running.

b) Naali began to slow down on the final straight to celebrate and didn't see Kenya's Joshua Chelanga sprint past him to win gold.

c) Naali's father comes out of the crowd and runs the down the final straight with his son.

2. England are playing Colombia in a friendly in 1995, Jamie Redknapp is just about to shoot, what happened next?

a) Redknapp's shot hits the woodwork so hard that the net came apart and the game had to be halted whilst it was fixed.

b) Colombian goalkeeper Rene Higuita performed a scorpion kick and saved the shot with his heels above his head.

c) Colombia defender Luis Herrera saw that his keeper was well out of position so decided to save the shot himself with a stunning one handed tip over the bar, which he was understandably sent off for.

Round 7 – On the Buzzer

All the answers to this buzzer round begin with the letter C. In the case of a person it's the surname that must start with that letter.

1. Which American city is home to a Major League Baseball team called the Cubs and a NBA team called the Bulls?

2. Which famous horse race did Sam Waley Cohen win on Long Run in 2011?

3. Which team famously beat Tottenham Hotspur in the 1987 FA Cup final?

4. Which American tennis player won the French Open in

1991 and 1992?

5. Which city hosted the Commonwealth Games in 1974?

6. Which Welsh forward scored a hat trick of tries in 2001 against Romania?

7. Which England batsman scored a double century in 2010 in the opening Test of the Ashes series?

8. Which country won the Men's 100m relay gold medal at the 1996 Olympics anchored by Donovan Bailey?

9. Which English snooker player reached his first World Championship final in 2008?

10. In which country did Jorge Lorenzo win the 2010 Moto GP in Brno?

11. Which golfer from South America won the 2009 US Masters in a playoff?

12. On which racecourse is the Welsh Grand National run, traditionally in late December?

13. Which country won all but one of the gold medals available in the diving at the 2008 Summer Olympics?

14. Which Winter Olympic sport requires players to throw their stones in to the house?

15. Which Rugby League team reached the Challenge Cup final for the first time in their history in 2007?

16. Which city hosted the 1988 Winter Olympic Games?

17. Which British boxer won the BBC Sports Personality of the Year award in 1967 and 1970?

18. Which British rower won Olympic gold in the Coxless Fours in both 2000 and 2004?

19. Marcos Baghdatis became the first tennis player from which country to reach a Grand Slam Singles final?

20. Which country hosted the 1962 Football World Cup?

Game 44

On this episode of A Question of Sport are…

Jonny Wilkinson (Rugby Union)
First appeared on the show as a guest in 1999

Jane Sixsmith (Field hockey)
First appeared on the show as a guest in 1991

Kim Collins (Track athletics)
First appeared on the show as a guest in 2004

Dennis Taylor (Snooker)
First appeared on the show as a guest in 1985

Round 1 – Opening Rally

1. Between 1975 and 2010 name the ten Track and Field athletes who have won BBC Sports Personality of the Year.

Round 2 – One Minute Round

1. Which Football League team play their home games at the Valley Parade?

2. Which Rugby League team won the BBC Sports Personality Team of the Year Award in 1994?

3. Which European country made their Cricket World Cup debut in 2007?

4. Which Champions League winning football team is this an anagram of? RED ADMIRAL

5. With which sport would you associate with Dutchmen Co Stompe, Roland Scholten and Michael van Gerwen?

6. Which country hosts the Formula One Grand Prix which is held at Interlagos?

7. What nickname is English snooker player Jimmy White commonly known by?

These sports stars all share their surnames with types of music.

8. Fred _____ (Golf)

9. David _____ (Rugby Union)

10. Pat _____ (Baseball)

Round 3 – Mystery Guest

1. I celebrated my 60th birthday in 2007 and made my senior debut at the age of 17 (4 points)

   I helped my club to three European Titles in the 1970s (3 points)

   During those glory years I was voted the best player in Europe three times (2 points)

   I captained the Netherlands at the 1974 Football World Cup before coaching Barcelona to European glory (1 point)

2. I followed my father and two uncles by turning professional (4 points)

   My father fought Sugar Ray Leonard and my uncle Jeff fought Oscar de la Hoya (3 points)

   In 2007 I fought Oscar de la Hoya myself and by beating him I won a World Title at a fifth different weight (2 points)

   Known as a 'Pretty Boy' I stopped Ricky Hatton in the 10th round in Las Vegas (1 point)

Round 4 – Home or Away

1. *Jonny Wilkinson.* In 2010 Tom Prydie became the youngest player to represent which country at full international level?

2. *Jane Sixsmith.* At the 2010 Commonwealth Games which country defended both their Men's and Women's Field Hockey titles?

3. *Kim Collins.* Which Jamaican's record did Usain Bolt break when he set his first 100m world record in 2008?

4. *Dennis Taylor.* In 1978 Perrie Mans became the first player from which country to reach the World Championship final?

Round 5 – Captain's Away

1. Which sport is governed by the Marquess of Queensbury rules?

2. What have Australian Test players Andrew Symonds, Rex Sellers, Brendon Julien, Dav Whatmore and Kepler Wessels all have in common in a non-cricketing capacity?

3. Name the two Dutch teams to have won the European Cup between 1980 and 2000?

4. Which of these golfers have captained Europe at the Ryder Cup?
   a) Barry Lane
   b) Mark James
   c) Peter Baker

Round 6 – Great Sporting Moments

1. Just over halfway through the 1984 Olympic Women's 3000m final South African born Zola Budd was just in front of the chasing pack. She collided with an American opponent a couple of times, the second tussle leading to the American favourite falling in front of her home crowd. The crowd voiced their

displeasure at Budd who tailed off and finished well down the field but who was the American athlete whose race was cut short?

2. On 30 June 1998, England and Argentina faced each other in the World Cup knockout stages in St Etienne. David Beckham released a young teenage striker who, with lightning speed and quick feet left Jose Chamot and Roberto Ayala trailing in his wake to fire the ball into the net and give England the lead. Who was the 18 year old announcing himself on the world stage with this goal?

Round 7 – On the Buzzer

This buzzer round is all about the year 1994.

1. In which sport did Herbie Hide become a World Champion by beating Michael Bentt?

2. Which major event was held in Lillehammer in February 1994?

3. Which cricketer scored a world record 375 in a Test match against England?

4. Which 28 year old Spaniard won his first US Masters?

5. Which famous race did Britain's Sean Yates lead in July 1994?

6. Nicknamed the 'Divine Ponytail' which Italian missed a penalty in the 1994 World Cup final?

7. Which major sports final was cancelled for the first time in its 90 year history due to a players strike?

8. In which track event did Duaine Ladejo lead a British 1, 2 at the European Athletics Championships?

9. For which club did All Black Frano Botica kick 5 goals in the Challenge Cup final?

10. Which county did Dermot Reeve and Tim Munton lead to their first County Championship since 1972?

11. Which Scotswoman won the 10,000m at the Commonwealth Games?

12. 27 year old John Part became the first player from outside of Britain to reach a World Championship final in which sport?

13. Which player moved from Norwich City to Blackburn Rovers to form a potent partnership with Alan Shearer?

14. Which pole vaulter broke his 17th world record?

15. Which 24 year old became only the second South African to win the US Open, doing so in a playoff?

16. Which 51 year old won the Epsom Derby for the 4th time in his career, doing so on Erhaab in his 26th race in the English Classic?

17. Which British rider won the first of his four Superbike World Championships in 1994?

18. Which country provided three of the four Women's Grand Slam Singles Champions?

19. Which British swimmer won the Men's 50m freestyle at the 1994 Commonwealth Games?

20. Which NHL Ice Hockey team based at Madison Square Garden won their first Stanley Cup for over 50 years?

Game 45

On this episode of A Question of Sport are...

John Parrott (Snooker)
First appeared on the show as a guest in 1987

Tanni Grey Thompson (Track athletics)
First appeared on the show as a guest in 1993

Wasim Akram (Cricket)
First appeared on the show as a guest in 1998

Walter Payton (American football)
First appeared on the show as a guest in 1987

A Question of Sport celebrated its 40th anniversary in 2010 and featured Michael Johnson, Laura Davies, Pat Cash and David Coulthard on the celebratory show.

Round 1 – Opening Rally

1. Russia is due to host the 2014 Winter Olympics; name the ten countries that have already hosted the Games.

Round 2 – One Minute Round

1. Who became the 6th South African golfer to win a men's golf Major with victory at the 2011 US Masters?

2. Which country hosted football's European Championships in 1984?

3. Later known as 'Sugar' which American won the Light Welterweight Boxing gold medal at the 1976 Olympics?

4. Which sporting competition is this an anagram of?
    PLAGUESOME CHINA

5. For which team have cricketers Shane Warne, Malcolm Marshall and Chaminda Vaas all played in the County Championship?

6. In which sport have Carlos Sainz, Petter Solberg and Marcus Gronholm all been World Champions?

7. What nationality is 2002 Australian Open Women's Singles Champion Jennifer Capriati?

In which sports have these Germans been World Champions.

8. Steffan Nimke – _____

9. Britta Steffen – _____

10. Max Schmeling – _____

Round 3 – Mystery Guest

1. I was born in Sheffield in 1986 and have a degree in psychology (4 points)

   In 2006 I competed at the Commonwealth Games where an English woman won gold in my event (3 points)

   I finished 3rd in the BBC Sports Personality of the Year Award in 2009, receiving the award in my home city (2 points)

   I was the only British woman to win gold at World Athletics Championships in 2009 (1 point)

2. I was born in Scotland in 1987 and my grandfather played professional football (4 points)

   I won the BBC Young Sports Personality of the Year in 2004 (3 points)

   My brother plays the same sport as me and we've represented Great Britain together (2 points)

   In Australia in 2011 I lost in my third Grand Slam Singles final (1 point)

Round 4 – Home or Away

1. *John Parrott.* In 1983 who became the first player to record a maximum 147 break at the Snooker World Championship at the Crucible?

2. *Tanni Grey Thompson.* Which Canadian won 5 Paralympic gold medals in both 2004 and 2008 taking her overall total to 14 in the T54 Class?

3. *Wasim Akram.* Which New Zealander's best Test score was 299 whilst his brother's highest was 128 against England in 1984?

4. *Walter Payton.* Which team played in four consecutive Superbowl games in the 1990s, losing on all four occasions?

Round 5 – Captain's Away

1. In which sport are the balls four different colours – blue, red, black and yellow?

2. Which football manager's unbeaten run of 150 Home League matches came to an end when his side were beaten by Sporting Gijon in April 2011?

3. Name the two cities that have hosted the Summer Olympic Games that begin with the letter L?

4. Which of these isn't a horse racing course in Ireland?
   a) Fairyhouse
   b) Leopardstown
   c) Kelso

Round 6 – What Happened Next

1. It's the 1956 Grand National at Aintree and Devon Loch is leading the Grand National with less than 50 yards still to race, what happened next?
   a) Devon Loch turned around and began to run the other way.

b) Devon Loch suddenly jumped into the air and landed on its stomach allowing ESB to run past him and take victory.

c) Devon Loch ran through to win the race but unseated its jockey, Dick Francis, as soon as he crossed the line and went running around the Aintree course once more.

2. German pole vaulter Tim Lobinger has just won the World Athletics final in Monaco in 2003, what happened next?

   a) Lobinger starts dancing in celebration and manages to get a large section of the crowd to copy his dance moves.

   b) Lobinger grabs a German flag from the crowd, attaches it to his pole and runs onto the field, plants it firmly into the ground and proceeds to clamber up the pole.

   c) In protest at an incident earlier in the day Lobinger strips off his shorts and bares his buttocks to the crowd.

Round 7 – On the Buzzer

This buzzer round is all about debuts.

1. Who on his Champions League debut in 2004 scored a hat trick for Manchester United?

2. Former Rugby League star Lesley Vainikolo scored 5 tries on his debut for which English club in 2007?

3. On which horse did Niall 'Slippers' Madden win the Grand National at his first attempt?

4. Which driver finished 3rd in his first Formula One race at the Melbourne Grand Prix in 2007?

5. Which Italian brothers made their Ryder Cup debuts for Europe in 2010?

6. Which future England cricket captain scored a Test century on his debut against New Zealand in 2004?

7. Which team made their Super League debut in 2009?

8. Which 17 year old lost to Shaun Murphy in the first round of the World Championship in his first match at the Crucible?

9. After his athletics career Welshman Nigel Walker made an international debut in which sport in 1993?

10. Teddy Sheringham's debut in league football saw him play for which London club?

11. Whose first marathon saw her win in London in 2002 with a time of 2 hours 18 minutes and 55 seconds?

12. Which Major did American golfer Ben Curtis win on his debut in 2003?

13. Which country won the women's Olympic football gold medal in 1996, the first time the competition had been held?

14. For which team did Scottish driver Paul Di Resta make his Formula One debut in 2011?

15. With which country did Michael Beer and Usman Khawaja make their Test debuts in 2011?

16. Which Englishman came through the qualifiers to win the World Darts Championship at the first attempt in 1983?

17. Which sport made its Olympic debut in 1996 with its competitors playing in the sand?

18. Which England great scored on his debuts for Chelsea, Spurs,

West Ham United, AC Milan and England?

19. Which youngster shocked Kevin Curren in the Wimbledon Men's Singles final in 1985 to win on his first appearance at the tournament?

20. Who having scored a century on his Test debut in 2004 became the Australia captain in 2011?

Game 46

On this episode of A Question of Sport are...

Ryan Giggs (Football)
First appeared on the show as a guest in 1994

Philippe Sella (Rugby Union)
First appeared on the show as a guest in 2003

Ronnie O'Sullivan (Snooker)
First appeared on the show as a guest in 1996

Linford Christie (Track athletics)
First appeared on the show as a guest in 1986

Round 1 – Opening Rally

1. Name the 12 countries that won the most medals at the 2010 Commonwealth Games.

Round 2 – One Minute Round

1. In which sport does America compete against the Rest of the World in the President's Cup?

2. For which team have cricketers Stephen Fleming, Gary Sobers and Richard Hadlee all played in the County Championship?

3. Who competed in her fourth Olympics by featuring for Great Britain's Field Hockey team at the 2000 Games?

4. With which sport would you associate the Chicago Fire, Houston Dynamo and the Los Angeles Galaxy?

5. Which country does 2004 French Open Men's Singles Title Champion Gaston Gaudio come from?

6. Which team played their 2010/2011 Rugby Union Premiership home games at Sandy Park?

7. Which Scottish football team is this an anagram of? BEEN DEAR

These sports stars all share their surnames with things you might find in a court room.

8. Alan _____ (Football)

9. Jo _____ (Tennis)

10. Simon _____ (Speedway)

Round 3 – Mystery Guest

1. I was born in Kent in 1970 and first competed in my chosen sport at the age of 12 but I joined the Army as an 18 year old (4 points)

   In the Army I became a Judo Champion but returned to my chosen sport and at the age of 34 I achieved my ultimate goal (3 points)

   In 2005 I retired from athletics having won medals in the 800m and 1500m at the Olympics, the World Championships and the European Championships (2 points)

   As a result of my double Olympic gold medal winning exploits in 2004 I was made a Dame in the New Years Honours List the following year (1 point)

2. I was born in the Loire region of central France in 1955 (4 points)

   If you think of my nickname you'd think I'd be a university lecturer but I preferred much faster pursuits (3 points)

   I won the first of my four World Championship Titles in 1985 and the last in 1993 (2 points)

   I am 'the Professor' and won my World Titles in a McLaren and a Williams (1 point)

Round 4 – Home or Away

1. *Ryan Giggs.* In 2011 which club became the first team in Premier League history to come from 4-0 behind to rescue a point?

2. *Philippe Sella.* Which English team did Philippe Saint André coach to their first Guinness Premiership Title in 2006?

3. *Ronnie O'Sullivan.* Which Englishman lost in his first Crucible final to Stephen Hendry in 1996 but returned six years later to beat him in the final 18-17?

4. *Linford Christie.* Who in 1999 became the first man to win the World Championship sprint double of 100m and 200m at the same championship?

Round 5 – Captain's Away

1. Which all rounder played for England whilst with Somerset, Worcestershire and Durham?

2. In which sport did Desmond Douglas dominate the British game in the 1970s and 1980s?

3. Name the two NBA basketball teams that are based in Florida?

4. Which of these isn't a term used in Figure Skating?
    a) Lutz
    b) Triple Salchow
    c) Souple

Round 6 – Great Sporting Moments

1. In May 1982, only 105 days since Tony Barton took over as manager, the game was level before Gary Shaw, Gary Williams and Tony Morley combined to leave the Bayern Munich defence at sixes and sevens. Morley's pass found it's way to Peter Withe who slotted home to win the European Cup for which team?

2. It was the 1981 FA Cup final; Tony Galvin's pass was short and orthodox. What happened next was far from orthodox; the midfielder set off on a mazy run past Caton twice and Ranson once before slotting the ball into the Wembley net. Who scored this famous Cup final goal for Spurs?

Round 7 – On the Buzzer

This buzzer round has a Welsh connection.

1. Which Welshman scored for Liverpool in the 1986, 1989 and 1992 FA Cup finals?

2. Which teenager scored two tries on his Welsh Rugby Union debut against South Africa in 2010?

3. At which weight did Welsh boxer Nathan Cleverly win a European boxing title in 2010?

4. In which sport did Jazmin Carlin win two Commonwealth Games medals for Wales in 2010?

5. Which Welsh snooker player won his first World Championship in 2000?

6. Defending champion Michaela Breeze won a silver medal at

the 2010 Commonwealth Games in which sport?

7. Which 2011 Rugby League team played their home Super League games at Wrexham's Racecourse Ground?

8. Which team beat Cardiff City in the 2008 FA Cup final?

9. With which sport do you associate the Cardiff Devils?

10. Which Welsh athlete won long jump gold in the 1964 Olympics?

11. In March 2008 which Welshman lost in a World Cruiserweight fight to David Haye?

12. Who captained Wales to the Grand Slam in the 2008 Six Nations Championship?

13. In which sport would you associate the 1970 World Champion David Broome and Beethoven?

14. In which year were the Commonwealth Games held in Cardiff?

15. Which Welsh forward played for both Manchester United and Chelsea in FA Cup finals during the 1990s?

16. Which Welsh snooker player won the World Championship on 6 occasions in the 1970s?

17. In which track and field event did Matt Elias win a silver medal for Wales behind England's Chris Rawlinson at the 2002 Commonwealth Game?

18. Who became the first player to reach 100 international caps for the Welsh Rugby Union team?

19. Which Glamorgan spinner made his debut for England against Pakistan in 1996?

20. In which sport did Welshman Leighton Rees become the first World Champion in 1978?

Game 47

On this episode of A Question of Sport are...

Shane Williams (Rugby Union)
First appeared on the show as a guest in 2008

Duncan Goodhew (Swimming)
First appeared on the show as a guest in 1981

Christine Ohuruogu (Track athletics)
First appeared on the show as a guest in 2006

Alec Stewart (Cricket)
First appeared on the show as a guest in 1991

Matt Dawson said that his mum was more impressed the day he became a *Question of Sport* team captain than when he first played for England.

Round 1 – Opening Rally

1. Name the twelve tennis players who between 1973 and 1995 were ranked Number One in the world on the ATP Tour.

Round 2 – One Minute Round

1. Which football team won the last FA Cup final to be played at the Millennium Stadium?

2. Which Ukrainian won the Super Heavyweight Boxing gold medal at the 1996 Olympics?

3. What nationality are golfers Raphael Jacquelin and Gregory Havret?

4. Which Test playing cricket nation is this an anagram of?
   DANGLE BASH

5. With which sport do you associate the Adelaide Thunderbirds, the Northern Mystics and the Canterbury Tactix?

6. In which competition did Leinster beat Leicester Tigers in a 2009 final?

7. Which American city's NBA basketball team are called the Celtics?

These sports stars all share their surnames with musical instruments.

8. Frank _____ (Baseball)

9. Barry _____ (Football)

10. Simon _____ (Field Hockey)

Round 3 – Mystery Guest

1. I turned 50 in August of 2007 and since retiring I have become a sports pundit (4 points)

    I come from a sporting family, my father played in goal for Millwall and I had my greatest moment in America in 1980 (3 points)

    I won an Olympic gold at Lake Placid in 1980 emulating my compatriot John Curry's achievement (2 points)

    I was inducted into the World Figure Skating Hall of Fame and became a judge on the television programme Dancing on Ice (1 point)

2. At the age of 27 I reached the very pinnacle of my sport and became an icon in my homeland (4 points)

    Between 1990 and 2002 I won four Commonwealth gold medals (3 points)

    In 2000 I became the first competing athlete to light the Olympic Flame (2 points)

    On home soil at the Sydney Olympics I won the 400m gold to become only the second Australian Aboriginal Olympic Champion (1 point)

Round 4 – Home or Away

1. *Shane Williams.* Thomas Castaignede scored the only try as which team beat Cardiff in the first Heineken Cup final?

2. *Duncan Goodhew.* Which swimmer won his eighth gold medal of the 2008 Summer Olympics with victory in the Medley Relay?

3. *Christine Ohuruogu.* Behind which British athlete did Tony Jarrett win World, European and Commonwealth silver medals?

4. *Alec Stewart.* Who was the only England player to score over 400 runs in the 2011 Cricket World Cup with a highest score of 92 coming against Ireland?

Round 5 – Captain's Away

1. In which sport might you find yourself in a cradle and then be subjected to a flying mare?

2. Between 1999 and 2010 Jiri Novak, Yevgeny Kafelnikov, Tim Henman, Mario Ancic, Rafael Nadal and Tomas Berdych were the only players to beat which man in a Wimbledon Singles match?

3. Name the two Italian teams to have won the European Cup between 2000 and 2010?

4. Which of these isn't an Olympic Fencing discipline?
    a) Rapier
    b) Foil
    c) Epee

Round 6 – What Happened Next

1. At the 2001 Open Championship at St Andrews Ian Woosnam is well placed after sharing a tie of the lead overnight heading into the final day's play. What happened next?
   a) Woosnam broke his driver on the first tee so had to make do for the remainder of the round without it.
   b) Woosnam's caddie Miles Byrne fell ill overnight so Woosnam carried his own clubs for the round.
   c) Woosnam's caddie miscounted the number of clubs in his bag and the Welshman went onto the course with 15 clubs instead of the regulation 14, resulting in a two stroke penalty that ended his chances of winning.

2. Turks and Caicos athlete Elvis Smith is just about to throw the javelin at the 2002 Commonwealth Games, what happened next?
   a) Smith trips and falls on his face stabbing the javelin into the ground only a few inches in front of where he lay.
   b) Smith attempted to release the javelin but as he brought his arm back to throw he dropped the javelin out of the back of his hand.
   c) Smith released the javelin at a strange angle and it landed on the running track 50 yards to his left.

Round 7 – On the Buzzer

This buzzer round is all about the year 2010.

1. Who won his 2nd World BDO Darts Title beating fellow Englishman Dave Chisnall in the final 7-5?

2. Which country staged the Winter Olympics in 2010 – the second time this country had hosted the Games?

3. In which sport were Eve Muirhead and David Murdoch Britain's leading players at the Winter Olympics?

4. Which city hosted the 2010 Commonwealth Games?

5. Which former Manchester United striker scored for Atletico Madrid in the Europa League semi-final and the final, both against English clubs?

6. Who scored the winning goal for Spain in the 2010 Football World Cup final?

7. Who did England beat in the Twenty20 World Cup final in Barbados?

8. Against India in July 2010 which bowler became the first player to take 800 wickets in Test cricket?

9. Who against Wales in February became the first player to reach 100 caps for Scotland in Rugby Union internationals?

10. Which Welshman won a European and Commonwealth Games 200m medal?

11. Who shot a record equalling 63 on the opening day of the Open Championship at St Andrews and eventually finished third?

12. Which team beat the Indianapolis Colts to win their first Superbowl?

13. Who beat Rafael Nadal at the Australian Open in January, the only man to beat him in a tennis Grand Slam all year?

14. Zoe Smith became the first English woman to win a Commonwealth Games medal in which sport?

15. Which Rugby League team retained the Challenge Cup by beating Leeds 30-6 at Wembley?

16. At which Grand Prix was Sebastian Vettel crowned the Formula One World Champion?

17. Which jockey rode Don't Push It to Grand National victory at Aintree in April?

18. Which Major League Baseball team were crowned World Series Champions in November?

19. Which country completed the Grand Slam in Rugby Union's Six Nations Championship for the first time in six years?

20. Who became golf's world number one for the first time in his career but by the end of 2010 was still searching for his first Major win?

Game 48

On this episode of A Question of Sport are...

Colin Jackson (Track athletics)
First appeared on the show as a guest in 1989

Peter Scudamore (National Hunt racing)
First appeared on the show as a guest in 1982

Ray Reardon (Snooker)
First appeared on the show as a guest in 1983

Eric Bristow (Darts)
First appeared on the show as a guest in 1981

Round 1 – Opening Rally

1. At the end of the 2009/2010 Premier League season who were the top 10 scorers in English football Premier League history.

Round 2 – One Minute Round

1. Which Spanish football team play their home games at the Mestalla?

2. Which Australian won the 2010 Snooker World Championship?

3. Which basketball player was voted the NBA's Most Valuable Player in both 2008/9 and 2009/10?

4. Which Olympic sport is this an anagram of? MYSTIC NAGS

5. Between 1987 and 2007 which is the only European country to win the Rugby Union World Cup?

6. The Thomas Cup and Uber Cup are the World Team Championships in which racquet sport?

7. What title is given to the cyclist who wins the white and red polka dot jersey at the Tour de France?

These sports stars all share their surnames with things you might find in a larder.

8. Phil _____ (Cricket)

9. Gary _____ (Athletics)

10. Donald _____ (Baseball)

Round 3 – Mystery Guest

1. I was born in 1961 and demonstrated my ability in Helsinki in 1983 (4 points)

   My parents were great enthusiasts of my sport and my sister represented America at the World Championships (3 points)

   In my homeland in 1984 I emulated Jesse Owens' feat of winning four Olympic gold medals in the same games (2 points)

   Whilst being renowned as a sprinter I also won four successive Olympic Titles in the Long Jump (1 point)

2. I grew up in South Africa where my father was an Archdeacon and learned to play my chosen sport here (4 points)

   I was born in Bournemouth and returned to England at the age of 15. I studied mathematics and physics at the University of Sussex, graduating in 1966 (3 points)

   My most famous moment came in 1977 when I won on home soil in front of the Queen (2 points)

   I won the Wimbledon Singles Title in 1977 having won the Australian and the French Open earlier in my career (1 point)

Round 4 – Home or Away

1. *Colin Jackson.* Who having won successive Olympic 110m hurdles gold medals broke Renaldo Nehemiah's 8 year old world record in 1989?

2. *Peter Scudamore.* Which horse won the 2009 Grand National at odds of 100-1?

3. *Ray Reardon.* Who as a 150-1 rank outsider won his first ever match at the Crucible in 1986 and went on to lift the trophy?

4. *Eric Bristow.* Which Australian lost in the BDO World Championship final two years before being beaten in the PDC World Championship final?

Round 5 – Captain's Away

1. Manchester in 2002, Melbourne in 2006 and Delhi in 2010 all hosted the Commonwealth Games. Which city was awarded the 2014 Commonwealth Games?

2. How did the second Test between the West Indies and England in 2009 create Test cricketing history?

3. Name the two Rugby Union teams that have won the Heineken Cup between 1996 and 2010 whose names begin with the letter L?

4. Which of these is not an award given to Rugby League players?
    a) Lance Todd Trophy
    b) Harry Vardon Trophy
    c) Man of Steel

Round 6 – Great Sporting Moments

1. Coming back from a goal down the Scots scored twice either side of the half time interval to take a 2-1 lead. The talented Scottish midfielder picked up a loose ball on the right side of

the penalty area, cut inside two men before scoring one of the most memorable World Cup goals of all time. Who scored this famous third goal for Scotland against the Netherlands?

2. Nottingham Forest had dominated the first half of the 1979 European Cup final. As the half time whistle approached John Robertson beat two Malmo defenders on the left and curled over a cross into the box for which player to head home the winner?

Round 7 – On the Buzzer

This buzzer round is all about the Summer Olympics.

1. Which is the only country to have won over 2000 medals at the Summer Olympics?

2. In which sport did Gary Herbert help a pair of brothers to Olympic gold in 1992?

3. For which country did Donovan Bailey win Olympic sprint gold medals?

4. Richard Dodds captained which British team to an Olympic gold medal in 1988?

5. In which city did American Mark Spitz win 7 Olympic gold medals?

6. In which sport are two of the gold medals won in the Trap and Skeet competitions?

7. Who left Liverpool for Barcelona in 2010 having played in Argentina's Olympic gold medal winning team in 2004 and 2008?

8. What nationality is five time Olympic gold medal winning gymnast Nadia Comaneci?

9. Which French woman won both the 200m and the 400m gold medals at the 1996 Olympics in Atlanta?

10. In which sport has Chilean Fernando Gonzalez won an Olympic gold, silver and bronze medal?

11. Which country won both the men's and the women's basketball competitions at the 2008 Olympics?

12. Which track and field athlete broke world records in three different events at the 2008 Summer Olympics?

13. Which Oscar winning film depicted the exploits of 1924 British Olympics Champions Harold Abrahams and Eric Liddell?

14. Which city hosted the Summer Olympics in 1968 and hosted the World Cup final two years later?

15. In which sport did Cuban Felix Savon win 3 successive Olympic gold medals?

16. Over which distance is the longest track and field event at the Summer Olympics?

17. Which British Olympian won gold medals in the Keirin, the sprint and the team sprint in 2008?

18. In which sport could you win Olympic gold in the Canadian Singles and the Canadian Pairs?

19. Which American athlete won gold medals in the long jump and the heptathlon at the 1988 Summer Olympics?

20. Which city became the first to host the modern Olympic Games on more than one occasion?

Game 49

On this episode of A Question of Sport are...

George Best (Football)
First appeared on the show as a guest in 1986

Ieuan Evans (Rugby Union)
First appeared on the show as a guest in 1993

Jo Durie (Tennis)
First appeared on the show as a guest in 1985

Ian Poulter (Golf)
First appeared on the show as a guest in 2004

A Question of Sport has had a whole host of world class sports stars appear on the show over the years, none more so than in the Mystery Guest segment. Sporting greats such as Pele, Maradona and Greg Norman have all featured on the show in this round.

Round 1 – Opening Rally

1. Name the first ten batsmen to reach 9,000 runs in Test cricket.

Round 2 – One Minute Round

1. Which team beat Wigan Athletic 4-0 on their Premier League debut in 2010?

2. Which famous jockey's name is this an anagram of? TAKEN IT FOR RIDE

3. In which sport did Javier Gomez and Emma Moffatt win the World Championships in 2010?

4. Who captained the USA at the 2010 Ryder Cup?

5. Who in 2011 became only the second female jockey to win the Irish Grand National?

6. Which sport would you associate with the Vendee Globe, the Admirals Cup and the Route du Rhum?

7. Which country hosted the first race of the 2010 Formula One Championship season?

These sports stars all share their surnames with things you might find on a bush.

8. Murray _____ (Swimming)

9. George _____ (Football)

10. Willie _____ (Snooker)

Round 3 – Mystery Guest

1. I was born in 1986 and always thought I'd like to be a fast bowler, a very popular sport in my home country (4 points)

   I switched sports in my youth and was well over 6 foot by the time I reached 16 years of age (3 points)

   In 2002 I won the 200m at the World Junior Championships in my home country (2 points)

   In 2009 I broke two of my own world records in the space of a week at the World Athletics Championships in Berlin (1 point)

2. I was born in the same county as Ian Poulter and Ashley Young (4 points)

   My father got me in to my chosen sport at a very young age (3 points)

   I won a World Championship Title in 2008 (2 points)

   I was named after American sprinter Carl Lewis (1 point)

Round 4 – Home or Away

1. *George Best.* Which of England's 1970s World Cup squad won the League Championship with Manchester City and Derby County?

2. *Ieuan Evans.* Which Englishman scored six tries in the first two games of the 2011 Six Nations Championship?

3. *Jo Durie.* Which British player partnered Jelena Jankovic to the Wimbledon Mixed Doubles Title in 2007?

4. *Ian Poulter.* Which Danish golfer finished runner up to Tiger Woods in the 2000 Open Championship three years after becoming the first person from his country to play in a Ryder Cup?

Round 5 – Captain's Away

1. West Indian opening Test batsman Alvin, Geoff and Gordon all shared which surname without being related?

2. In which sport would you find the hog line, sweepers and stones?

3. Name the two Major League Baseball teams that begin with the letter P?

4. Which of these sports is not included in the Olympic Modern Pentathlon?
   a) Fencing
   b) Shooting
   c) Archery

Round 6 – What Happened Next

1. It's the 2003 World Athletics Championships and the second men's 100m quarter-final is about to start, Jon Drummond is in the blocks, what happened next?
   a) Drummond is disqualified for a false start but believes he is innocent so he lies on the track and refuses to move.
   b) Drummond trips as the starting gun goes off and falls flat on his face.

c) Drummond's boot gets stuck in the blocks and isn't able to free himself until after the other competitors have completed the race.

2. England are playing Australia in a One Day International, England bowler Ronnie Irani is loosening up on the boundary rope, what happened next?
   a) Nasser Hussain sneaks up behind him and pulls Irani's trousers down.
   b) Irani is so engrossed in his warm up routine that he misses an easy catch which lands right next to him.
   c) The Australian crowd start copying Irani's warm up stretching their arms above their heads in time with his movements.

Round 7 – On the Buzzer

This buzzer round is all about the year 1998.

1. Which British skier was selected for his 5th Winter Olympic Games?

2. Which American golfer won both the US Masters and the Open Championship in 1998?

3. In February which Liverpool footballer became England's youngest player of the 20th century?

4. Ashian Hansen broke the world indoor record whilst winning gold in which event at the European Championships in February?

5. Which club completed one of the biggest shocks in Rugby League history by beating Wigan in the Challenge Cup final?

6. Which Surrey player against South Africa replaced Michael Atherton as England's Test captain?

7. Who were the Falcons who clinched Rugby Union's Premiership Title for their first time?

8. Which famous Australian race did Jezabeel win at the Flemington racecourse in November?

9. Which British Olympic gold medal winning cyclist briefly led the Tour de France after the prologue stage?

10. Which 17 year old British amateur finished 4th in the Open Championship at Birkdale?

11. Which Welshman won both the Commonwealth and European Men's 400m gold medals?

12. Which Finnish driver won the Formula One World Championship with McLaren?

13. In which city were the 1998 Commonwealth Games held?

14. Which Austrian skier won both the Super G and Giant Slalom Winter Olympic gold medals?

15. England's Rugby Union side suffered their biggest defeat in 127 years when losing 76-0 against which country?

16. Which Scottish snooker player won his first World Championship by beating Ken Doherty at the Crucible?

17. Which Englishman won the Commonwealth Games 50m freestyle?

18. Tim Henman reached his first Wimbledon semi-final only to lose to which American who went on to win the tournament?

19. Which country ended England's World Cup hopes by beating them 4-3 on penalties in St Etienne?

20. Which Worcestershire batsman became only the 24th player in history to score 100 hundreds in First Class cricket?

Game 50

On this episode of A Question of Sport are...

Ian Botham (Cricket)
First appeared on the show as a guest in 1979

Steve Cram (Track athletics)
First appeared on the show as a guest in 1982

Boris Becker (Tennis)
First appeared on the show as a guest in 2006

Mick Fitzgerald (National Hunt racing)
First appeared on the show as a guest in 1996

Round 1 – Opening Rally

1. Name the 10 venues that have hosted golf's Open Championship since 1950.

Round 2 – One Minute Round

1. Which stadium hosted the FA Cup final between 2001 and 2006?

2. Which American city's NFL American Football team are called the Cowboys?

3. Which country won the 2010 Twenty20 Cricket World Cup in the West Indies?

4. Which American Olympic gold medal winning athlete is this an anagram of? WISE DEMONS

5. Which Scottish Football League team play their home games at Tannadice Park?

6. Which English snooker player won the BBC Sports Personality of the Year Award in 1988?

7. Which country hosted a Moto GP race in 2010 at Laguna Seca?

These sports stars all share their surnames with things that you can drink from.

8. Jimmy _____ (Football)

9. Allan _____ (Athletics)

10. Jake _____ (Swimming)

Round 3 – Mystery Guest

1. I made my international debut in 1993 and just two years later I experienced the greatest moment in my career (4 points)

    The image of me receiving the World Cup winners' trophy is one of the most memorable moments in my sport (3 points)

    In 2005 I was inducted into the International Rugby Hall of Fame (2 points)

    Matt Damon portrayed me in the 2009 film Invictus about our successful World Cup campaign in 1995 (1 point)

2. In January 2009 I celebrated my 50th birthday (4 points)

    After my retirement I coached my country as a bowling consultant, although I was one of the world's great all-rounders (3 points)

    I was voted my country's cricketer of the century although I think that honour would now fall to Sachin Tendulkar (2 points)

    I captained India to victory in the World Cup final in 1983 (14 point)

Round 4 – Home or Away

1. *Ian Botham.* Which West Indian bowler claimed more Test wickets than any other bowler in the 1980s, 323 at an average of just 19.91?

2. *Steve Cram.* In 2010 at the European Championships in Barcelona which British athlete won gold in both the 5000m and the 10,000m?

3. *Boris Becker.* Which American won all four Grand Slam Singles Titles during the 1990s?

4. *Mick Fitzgerald.* In 2011 which jockey became the first amateur to win the Cheltenham Gold Cup since 1981?

Round 5 – Captain's Away

1. Seve Ballesteros, Bernhard Langer, Ian Woosnam, Nick Faldo and Lee Westwood are all European golfers that have been ranked number one in the world. Who in 2011 became the next player in the sequence?

2. Which award was won by Paul Hanagan following his 191 race wins in the 2010 season?

3. Name the two teams that played in the top four tiers of English football in 2010/2011 that played their home games at a ground called St James Park?

4. Which of these circuits has not hosted a Formula One British Grand Prix?
   a) Donington Park
   b) Brands Hatch
   c) Silverstone

Round 6 – Great Sporting Moments

1. Having lost the first set 4-6 she recovered to win the second 6-3 and so the Wimbledon crowd began to sense a rare victory.

Leading 4-0 the Dutch player was given a lifeline and won the 5th game to reduce the arrears to 4-1 but by this stage the end was in sight. Which British star won the next two games to complete a win on home soil?

2. The FA Cup final was finely balanced with the scores at 0-0. Liverpool's goalkeeper David James punched the ball away following David Beckham's corner only to see it deflect off Ian Rush. Which player half volleyed the ball into the back of Liverpool's net to send the Manchester United fans in the stadium wild?

Round 7 – On the Buzzer

This buzzer round is all about 100 or more.

1. Who was the first player to score 100 goals in the English Premier League?

2. How many laps do drivers have to do to complete the Indianapolis 500 motor race?

3. Which German scored twice against Argentina in the 2010 Football World Cup on his 100th appearance for them?

4. Which opening batsman in the first Test against India in 2006 scored a century on his England Test debut?

5. Who was the first Englishman to play in 100 international games for his country in Rugby Union?

6. Alain Prost, Mika Hakkinen and David Coulthard all drove in over 100 Formula One Grand Prix races for which team?

7. Between 1977 and 1987 athlete Ed Moses went unbeaten in an unprecedented 122 races in which event?

8. Which country won 177 medals at the 2010 Commonwealth Games in Delhi?

9. Who in 2003 became the first snooker player to record 100 century breaks at the Crucible?

10. In Super League's first season for which team did Bobby Goulding finish as leading goalkicker with 120 goals?

11. Who in the 1980s became the first National Hunt jockey to win over 200 races in a season?

12. What is the highest score you can check out with three darts?

13. For which country did Rugby Union's Percy Montgomery play over 100 times between 1997 and 2008?

14. Which rider won for the 100th time in his professional motor racing career by taking victory at Assen in 2009?

15. Who became the first man to top golf's world rankings for over 100 weeks?

16. How many pots are required to achieve a maximum break of 147 in snooker?

17. Who in 1996 became only the third tennis player to win over 100 WTA singles titles in her career?

18. Who scored 149 for Australia in the 2007 Cricket World Cup final?

19. Who in 2010 against Wolverhampton Wanderers scored his 100th Premier League goal for Manchester United?

20. Which country won 110 medals at the 2008 Summer Olympics?

Game 51

On this episode of A Question of Sport are...

Andrew Strauss (Cricket)
First appeared on the show as a guest in 2004

Sandy Lyle (Golf)
First appeared on the show as a guest in 1980

John Francome (National Hunt racing)
First appeared on the show as a guest in 1983

David Haye (Boxing)
First appeared on the show as a guest in 2003

By the end of the 2010 series there had been 920 episodes recorded of *A Question of Sport* and the show had featured over 2,750 different sports stars.

Round 1 – Opening Rally

1. Name the 14 tennis players that have won the Wimbledon Men's Singles Title between 1980 and 2010.

Round 2 – One Minute Round

1. Which country has reached the Cricket World Cup semi-finals on six occasions without ever reaching the final?

2. Which Scottish Football League team play their home games at Rugby Park?

3. Which sport is this an anagram of? TRAGIC MORON

4. Which British woman won her ninth BDO World Darts Championship in January 2011?

5. In which sport have Tommy, Nina and Paul Carberry all competed?

6. Who did Marc Warren partner to win the 2007 Golf World Cup for Scotland?

7. In which sport did Britain's Wendy Houvenaghel win an Olympic silver medal at the 2008 Games?

In which sports have these Australians been World Champions.

8. Drew Ginn – _____

9. Stephanie Rice – _____

10. Troy Bayliss – _____

Round 3 – Mystery Guest

1. I was born in 1975 and made my 140th Test appearance in 2010 (4 points)

   I scored hundreds in five successive Tests between 2003 and 2004 (3 points)

   In 2005 I was named the ICC's Test Player of the Year thanks to my all-round displays (2 points)

   Shaun Pollock and I became the first South Africans to play in a hundred Test matches (1 point)

2. I was born in Scotland and at school I was a sporting all-rounder that excelled at rugby and rowing (4 points)

   I became the first British person to win three gold medals at a single Olympic Games since 1908 (3 points)

   In 2008 I won the BBC Sports Personality of the Year Award following my Olympic success in the summer (2 points)

   I was knighted due to my sporting success and well known for having large thighs (1 point)

Round 4 – Home or Away

1. *Andrew Strauss.* Who having played in the winning World Cup final side in 1996 finished on the losing side in the World Cup final 15 years later?

2. *Sandy Lyle.* Between 1985 and 2010 which English course

hosted the Ryder Cup on four occasions which included the tie in 1989?

3. *John Francome.* Brian Fletcher rode Red Rum to Grand National victory in 1973 and 1974 but which jockey was on board when the horse won the race in 1977?

4. *David Haye.* Which Middleweight boxer became the only British fighter to win an Olympic gold medal in Beijing?

Round 5 – Captain's Away

1. Jamie Baker and James Ward helped Britain to beat Tunisia in which major sporting contest in 2011?

2. Complete this Olympic Games gold medal winning British quartet, Marlon Devonish, Darren Campbell, Mark Lewis-Francis and which other sprinter?

3. Name the two Canadian cities that have hosted the Winter Olympic Games?

4. Which of these sports is not included in the Olympic Decathlon?
   a) Hammer
   b) Discus
   c) Shot Put

Round 6 – What Happened Next

1. It's the half-time show in the NBA game between the Phoenix Suns and the Charlotte Bobcats, what happened next?
   a) During a slam dunk contest one competitor misjudged his leap and ended up falling through the net himself.

b) The Phoenix Sun's cheerleaders form a spectacular human pyramid which collapses when hit by a stray basketball.

c) The Bobcats get locked in their dressing room and are delayed coming back out onto the court.

2. Goalkeeper Hans Jorg Butt is just about to take a penalty for Bayer Leverkusen in the German Bundesliga against Schalke, what happened next?

a) Butt scores the penalty but whilst he is celebrating Schalke restart the game and score from the halfway line.

b) Butt sends the penalty into the bottom corner of the goal but it goes right through the netting and the referee disallows it thinking the ball went wide.

c) Butt dummies the penalty and his teammate Ze Roberto runs in and scores the penalty.

Round 7 – On the Buzzer

This buzzer round is all about the year 2008.

1. Which British club lost in the UEFA Cup final to Zenit St Petersburg in Manchester?

2. Who recorded a 147 maximum at the Crucible on his way to reaching his first World Championship final?

3. Which British boxer beat Bernard Hopkins in a Light Heavyweight contest?

4. Which 14 year old became the first British winner of the Wimbledon Junior Girl's Singles Title since 1984?

5. Which Englishman finished runner up behind Padraig Harrington in the Open Championship at Birkdale?

6. Who during the 2008 Six Nations Championship against Scotland became the top points scorer in Rugby Union internationals?

7. For which county did Steve Harmison take 60 wickets to help them win their first County Championship?

8. In which event did Britain win its only athletics gold medal at the Beijing Summer Olympics?

9. At the end of the season which driver retired from Formula One racing having won 13 of his 246 races?

10. Who rode Comply or Die to victory in the Grand National at Aintree?

11. In which sport did Britain's Paul Manning win an Olympic medal for the third successive games?

12. Which country did Nathan Cayless captain to victory in the 2008 Rugby League World Cup final?

13. Who scored Spain's winning goal in the 2008 European Championship final defeat of Germany?

14. Which former England captain made his 339th and final London Wasps appearance by captaining the team to the Guinness Premiership Title?

15. By winning the Canadian Grand Prix Robert Kubica became the first driver from which country to win a Formula One race?

16. In a game between the Manchester Phoenix and the Nottingham Panthers Tony Hand played his 1000th game in which sport?

17. Who did Blake Aldridge partner for Britain at the 2008 Summer Olympics?

18. In 2008 which 23 year old American made his Ryder Cup debut and beat Sergio Garcia 5&4 in the first singles match?

19. Which country won their second Six Nations Championship Grand Slam in four years?

20. Which race did Spaniard Carlos Sastre win in July 2008?

Game 52

On this episode of A Question of Sport are...

Jenson Button (Motor racing)
First appeared on the show as a guest in 2002

Dennis Lillee (Cricket)
First appeared on the show as a guest in 1975

Joe Calzaghe (Boxing)
First appeared on the show as a guest in 1998

Edwin Van Der Sar (Football)
First appeared on the show as a guest in 2002

Round 1 – Opening Rally

1. Other than cycling name the 10 sports in which Britain won at least one medal at the 2008 Summer Olympics in Beijing.

Round 2 – One Minute Round

1. Which American city's NBA basketball team are called the 76ers?

2. In which year did Europe and USA play each other in the Ryder Cup at Kiawah Island in what was described as 'The War on the Shore'?

3. Which England cricketer's name is this an anagram of? SPIKE INTERVENE

4. In which sport do teams compete against each other at the World Cup to win the Webb Ellis Cup?

5. On which surface is the French Open Championship tennis tournament played?

6. In which field event have Nelson Evora, Christian Olsson and Charles Friedek all been World Champions?

7. Which football ground do Italian teams AC Milan and Inter Milan share?

These sports stars all share their surnames with things you might find in a church.

8. Martin _____ (Rowing)

9. Danny _____ (Football)

10. Graham _____ (Skiing)

Round 3 – Mystery Guest

1. I was born in London in 1966 and growing up it became clear that speed was a great asset for me (4 points)

   A north west club spent a world record fee of £440,000 to sign me but I'd like to think I repaid them during my time there (3 points)

   I won the Lance Todd Trophy on two occasions for my performances in the Challenge Cup final (2 points)

   I was nicknamed Chariots and I scored over 500 Rugby League tries (1 point)

2. I celebrated my 30th birthday in 2010 (4 points)

   My two middle names are Ebony Starr and I was born in California (3 points)

   Although I am considered one of the greatest players of my generation you could argue I'm not even the best player in my family (2 points)

   Between 2001 and 2003 I lost to my sister in 5 Grand Slam Singles Titles (1 point)

Round 4 – Home or Away

1. *Jenson Button.* Which Finnish driver won back to back Formula One World Championships in 1998 and 1999?

2. *Dennis Lillee.* Who in the Ashes series of 1981 and 1989 captured over 40 wickets for Australia to become the first player in history to achieve the feat twice?

3. *Joe Calzaghe.* In the 1990s which boxer became the first Irishman to win versions of the World Title at two different weights?

4. *Edwin Van der Sar.* Who scored a golden goal winner as France beat Italy in the final of Euro 2000 but missed a penalty against them in a World Cup final penalty shoot-out six years later?

Round 5 – Captain's Away

1. What was unusual about Shane Watson and Marcus North's inclusion on the Lord's honours board as bowlers in 2010?

2. In which sport did Great Britain play Lithuania at the Vitas Gerulaitis Centre in 2010?

3. Name the two cities that have hosted the Commonwealth Games that begin with the letter E?

4. Which of these horse races takes place over the shortest distance?
    a) Epsom Derby
    b) Cheltenham Gold Cup
    c) Grand National

Round 6 – What Happened Next

1. England are playing South Africa in a Test match at Lord's, South African batsman Morne Morkel has just been dismissed, what happened next?
    a) Morne Morkel is dismissed and walks off the ground the wrong way ending up in the groundsman's shed.
    b) Morkel is dismissed but he refuses to leave the field believing the umpire got the decision wrong and he eventually gets escorted off by captain Graeme Smith.
    c) Morkel is dismissed and the next man in, Andre Nel, walks to the crease but has forgotten his bat.

2. The 5:50pm race is about to start at Yarmouth, the horses are in the stalls, what happened next?
    a) The wrong side of the starting gates are opened and the horses reverse out and start running in the opposite direction.
    b) As the gates are opened, jockey Jamie Spencer is left standing on the stalls as his horse 'New Christmas' leaves without him.
    c) One of the stable hands walks across the gates to do a final check but they are opened and he has to quickly dodge the horses.

Round 7 – On the Buzzer

The questions in this buzzer round all have a European connection.

1. Who did Virginia Wade defeat in the 1977 Wimbledon Singles final?

2. In which country are horse racing classics held at Chantilly?

3. What nationality is multiple World Champion motorcyclist Max Biaggi?

4. Which goalkeeper captained Spain to their World Cup final victory in 2010?

5. Which Dutchman won the BDO World Darts Championship 4 times between 1998 and 2005?

6. The San Marino Grand Prix is held at which circuit?

7. Pieter van den Hoogenband successfully defended his Olympic title in 2004 but in which sport?

8. In which country would you find the famous toboggan course the Cresta Run?

9. Which Frenchman sensationally imploded on the 18th hole at Carnoustie in the Open Championship in 1999?

10. What nationality are World Champion cyclists Kevin Sireau and Gregory Bauge?

11. Which pair of Italian brothers had both won over 80 Rugby Union caps by the end of the 2011 Six Nations?

12. Who in 1994 became the first Spanish woman to win the Wimbledon Singles Title?

13. With which sport do you associate with the Giro d'Italia?

14. Which country won the 1996 European Championships by beating the Czech Republic via a golden goal?

15. Which Swedish athlete succeeded Denise Lewis as the Olympic Heptathlon gold medal winner in 2004?

16. For which country did Ryan ten Doeschate score a century against England in the 2011 Cricket World Cup?

17. Who was the first Italian to play Ryder Cup golf for Europe?

18. Who by winning in Canada in 2008 became the first Polish driver to win a Formula One Grand Prix?

19. Which French Rugby Union team won the Heineken Cup for a record 4th time in 2010?

20. Which Spanish football team won the first 5 European Cup finals?

Game 53

On this episode of A Question of Sport are...

Phil Tufnell (Cricket)
First appeared on the show as a guest in 1991

Alan Wells (Track athletics)
First appeared on the show as a guest in 1979

Chris Eubank (Boxing)
First appeared on the show as a guest in 1991

James Hunt (Motor racing)
First appeared on the show as a guest in 1975

The lowest score ever recorded on *A Question of Sport* was on 18 February 2011 by Matt Dawson, Brian Blessed and Chris Coleman – the team scored a paltry four points in the entire show.

Round 1 – Opening Rally

1. Since the men's world rankings began in 1986 name the first 12 golfers to have been number one in the world.

Round 2 – One Minute Round

1. Which country's best performance at the Cricket World Cup is reaching the final, a feat they achieved in 1979, 1987 and 1992?

2. In which year did Tiger Woods win his first golf Major?

3. With which sport would you associate the Bulls, the Brumbies and the Waratahs?

4. Which city hosted the 2010 ATP World Tour final between Roger Federer and Rafael Nadal?

5. Which stadium hosted the 2011 Champions League Cup final?

6. In which sport did Britain's Paul Goodison win an Olympic gold medal at the 2008 Games?

7. Which country that has won the Football World Cup is this an anagram of? AN INGRATE

In which sports have these Italians been World Champions.

8. Giacomo Agostini – _____

9. Alberto Tomba – _____

10. Federica Pellegrini – _____

Round 3 – Mystery Guest

1. I was born in West Bromwich in 1972 and 28 years later I became an Olympic Champion (4 points)

    I finished second in the BBC Sports Personality of the Year Award on two occasions (3 points)

    I have been an athletics pundit for the BBC and I finished as runner up on Strictly Come Dancing with my dance partner Ian Waite (2 points)

    At the 2000 Summer Olympics I was the only British Track and Field athlete to win a gold medal, doing so in the Heptathlon (1 point)

2. In my career I had spells in Ireland, England and Scotland (4 points)

    I made my debut as a youngster at Anfield (3 points)

    Since retiring I have managed Ipswich Town and Sunderland (2 points)

    I won the FA Cup and Premier League with Manchester United in 1999 but missed out on playing in the Champions League final that year due to suspension (1 point)

Round 4 – Home or Away

1. *Phil Tufnell.* Which former England bowler has played County Cricket in each of the last four decades and has taken over 1100 First Class wickets?

2. *Allan Wells.* Which British sprinter won four European Indoor 60m titles as well as the World Indoor 60m title in 2004?

3. *Chris Eubank.* Which boxer lost in a World Title fight to Joe Calzaghe in 2007 but then gave Carl Froch his first professional defeat three years later?

4. *James Hunt.* Having won the Indy 500 in 1969 which Italian born American won his only Formula One World Championship nine years later?

Round 5 – Captain's Away

1. What was unusual about John White's Grand National victory on Esha Ness in 1993?

2. Red, green and black are three colours of the Olympic rings, what colours are the other two?

3. Name the two golfers who represented Europe at the 2010 Ryder Cup whose surnames begin with the letter H?

4. Which of these races takes place over the longest distance?
   a) The University Boat Race
   b) 3000m Steeplechase
   c) Cheltenham Gold Cup

Round 6 – Great Sporting Moments

1. In Bobby Robson's second season in charge England had failed to qualify for the European Championship. Their summer tour to South America in 1984 however helped to salvage some pride, especially the famous 2-0 win over Brazil in the Maracana. Whose mazy run from the left wing into the box

past countless Brazilian defenders gave England a 1-0 lead just before half time?

2. The batsman now faced Nash's final ball of the over hoping to become the first ever batsman to score six successive sixes off an over. Which legendary batsman completed the feat in Swansea in 1968?

Round 7 – On the Buzzer

All the answers to this buzzer round begin with the letter P, in the case of a person it's the surname that must start with that letter.

1. Which team won the 2008 FA Cup final and lost in the final two years later to Chelsea?

2. In 2009 which American Football team won their sixth Superbowl by beating Arizona Cardinals with a last minute touchdown?

3. Which South African golfer became the first non-American to win the US Masters when he won the tournament in 1961?

4. Which boxer beat Ricky Hatton for the Light Welterweight World Title in Las Vegas in 2009 by knockout in only the 2nd round?

5. In which event did Yelena Isinbayeva win an Olympic gold in both 2004 and 2008?

6. Who retired as captain of Australia in 2011 having led the team in 77 Tests in his seven year career as captain?

7. Which swimmer known as the Baltimore Bullet won a record eight gold medals at the 2008 Summer Olympics?

8. Which country famously held England to a 1-1 draw at Wembley in October 1973 to prevent them from qualifying for the 1974 Football World Cup?

9. Which horse did Ruby Walsh ride to victory in the 2000 Grand National to give the jockey his first Grand National win?

10. Which Rugby Union international successfully kicked 36 consecutive goals for Scotland between August 2007 and June 2008?

11. Which city hosted the Summer Olympics in both 1900 and 1924?

12. Which English snooker player was crowned the Junior Pot Black Champion in 1982 and 1983?

13. Which French team did Toulouse beat in the 2003 Heineken Cup final?

14. Which British rower partnered Steve Redgrave to Olympic gold in the Coxless Pairs in 1992 and 1996?

15. Which country won the 2009 Twenty20 Cricket World Cup by beating Sri Lanka in the final at Lord's?

16. Which Major League Baseball team won the World Series for the first time in over 28 years by beating the Tampa Bay Rays in 2008?

17. Which American won Olympic silver medals behind Carl Lewis in the Long Jump in 1988 and 1992?

18. For which country did Nelson Evora win an Olympic gold medal in the Triple Jump in 2008?

19. Which Canadian won the BDO Darts World Championship in 1994 before winning the PDC version of the World Title in 2003 and 2008?

20. With which basketball team did Charles Barkley reach the NBA Championship finals in 1993 losing to the Chicago Bulls?

Game 54

On this episode of A Question of Sport are...

Courtney Walsh (Cricket)
First appeared on the show as a guest in 2007

Peter Alliss (Golf)
First appeared on the show as a guest in 2000

Sammy Sosa (Baseball)
First appeared on the show as a guest in 2002

Carl Fogarty (Superbike racing)
First appeared on the show as a guest in 1995

Round 1 – Opening Rally

1. Name the 12 African countries to have played at the Football World Cup finals between 1990 and 2010.

Round 2 – One Minute Round

1. Which Irish boxer won the BBC Sports Personality of the Year Award in 1985?

2. Which Football League team play their home games at the Priestfield Stadium?

3. Which American won the 2009 Open Championship at Turnberry?

4. Which fielding position in cricket is this an anagram of?
WEEK CREEP KIT

5. Which Italian city hosted the 2006 Winter Olympic Games?

6. In which sport is the Hopman Cup an annual international tournament?

7. Which African country's best performance at the Cricket World Cup was reaching the semi-finals in 2003?

In which sports have these South Africans been World Champions.

8. Trevor Immelman – _____

9. Roland Schoeman – _____

10. Kork Ballington – _____

Round 3 – Mystery Guest

1. I celebrated my 40th birthday in October 2010 and was able to reflect on my successes at the Olympics and the World Championships (4 points)

   I learned my sport at Eton and thanks to my record at the Olympics was asked to be Britain's flag-bearer at the Sydney Olympics in 2000 (3 points)

   I won several World Championship gold medals with my Olympic teammate James Cracknell (2 points)

   I was famously very emotional on the podium in 2000 having won my 4th rowing Olympic gold medal (1 point)

2. I was born in 1972 in Kandy (4 points)

   I have played my sport all around the world but it is in the sub-continent that I have really made my name (3 points)

   I received an amazing reception during my final game for my country on home soil in 2011 (2 points)

   I finished my career with 800 Test wickets for Sri Lanka and played my last game for them in the 2011 Cricket World Cup (1 point)

Round 4 – Home or Away

1. *Courtney Walsh.* Who with a score of 333 in November 2010 became only the second West Indian batsman to score two triple centuries in Test cricket?

2. *Peter Alliss.* Who won the 1997 USPGA Championship and 14 years later was named as Corey Pavin's successor as the USA's Ryder Cup captain?

3. *Sammy Sosa.* Which team in 1992 became the first side from outside of the United States of America to win baseball's World Series?

4. *Carl Fogarty.* In 1990, Raymond Roche became the first rider from which country to win the World Superbike Championship?

Round 5 – Captain's Away

1. Complete this Olympic Games gold medal winning British quartet, James Cracknell, Matthew Pinsent, Ed Coode and which other rower?

2. Which country featured in the Twenty20 Cricket World Cup for the first time when they played against India in 2010?

3. Name the two members of England's 2010 Football World Cup squad whose surnames begin with the letter G?

4. Which of these is not an Olympic diving event?
   a) 3m Springboard
   b) 5m Pairs
   c) 10m Platform

Round 6 – What Happened Next

1. England are playing the West Indies at Old Trafford, Dwayne Bravo is about to bowl to Kevin Pietersen, what happened next?

a) Pietersen's helmet is knocked off by Bravo's delivery and it falls on to the stumps resulting in a wicket.
b) Bravo completely messes up his delivery and bowls a beamer that flies over wicketkeeper Dinesh Ramdin's head and over the boundary rope.
c) Pietersen hits the ball for a huge six which smashes the TV commentary box window.

2. Boxers Tyson Fury and Lee Swaby are in the middle of a Heavyweight contest in Birmingham, what happened next?
   a) The referee steps in to try and separate the boxers but ends up taking a punch on the chin.
   b) As Fury throws a punch, Swaby ducks to avoid it and Fury falls through the ropes into the crowd.
   c) As Fury throws an uppercut, he misses Swaby and punches himself in the face.

Round 7 – On the Buzzer

This buzzer round is all about the year 2001.

1. Who in January 2001 announced his decision to leave Lazio and take over as England manager?

2. Trina Gulliver became the first Women's World Champion in which sport?

3. Who in 2001 became the fastest woman to solo circumnavigate the globe?

4. Against which country did England win a Six Nations Rugby Union international 80-23?

5. Which European won the Wimbledon Men's Singles Title at the fourth time of asking by beating Patrick Rafter in the final?

6. The Sheffield Steelers completed a Grand Slam of four titles in which sport?

7. Which Englishman won his first World Snooker Championship by beating John Higgins in the final?

8. Which club won their third cup of the season in May by beating Alaves 5-4 in the UEFA Cup final?

9. Which Olympic Champion made a winning start to his professional career by beating Michael Middleton in one round?

10. In which Canadian city were the 2001 World Athletics Championships held?

11. Who beat his brother into second place of the Formula One Canadian Grand Prix?

12. Who scored the 500th Rugby League try of his career by scoring for Salford in 2001?

13. Stephanie Cook ended her career at the World Championships having won Olympic gold in which sport?

14. Arizona Diamondbacks won which major title in November?

15. Australian Darren Lehmann scored over 1400 runs to help which county to their first County Championship since 1968?

16. For which country did Rob Henderson score a hat trick of tries in the Six Nations against Italy?

17. Which South African golfer won the first Major of his career by claiming victory at the US Open in 2001?

18. In which country did Valentino Rossi win a Moto GP race at the Phillip Island Circuit?

19. In 2001 the Ravens won their first Superbowl by beating the New York Giants, which city are they based in?

20. Which Australian won six World Championship swimming gold medals at the 2001 games?

Game 55

On this episode of A Question of Sport are...

Trevor Brooking (Football)
First appeared on the show as a guest in 1980

Tom Daley (Diving)
First appeared on the show as a guest in 2009

Padraig Harrington (Golf)
First appeared on the show as a guest in 2000

Daley Thompson (Decathlon)
First appeared on the show as a guest in 1979

Rugby Union has provided
the show with more regular
captains than any other sport,
four in total. There have been
two jockeys, two cricketers, two
footballers, a snooker player
and a boxer.

Round 1 – Opening Rally

1. Name the 12 cricketers that played for England in their victorious Ashes series in 2005.

Round 2 – One Minute Round

1. For which country did Tommy Bowe score a try in the 2011 Six Nations Championships?

2. In which sport could a night watchman score a triple nelson?

3. In which European city did Usain Bolt win World Championship gold in 2009?

4. Which sporting event is this an anagram of? CRY PRUDE

5. Who defeated Andy Murray in the 2011 Australian Open Singles final?

6. With which sport would you associate the St Kilda Saints, the Essendon Bombers and the Geelong Cats?

7. Which Football League team play their home games at St Mary's Stadium?

These sports stars all share their surnames with Irish counties.

8. Dominic _____ (Cricket)

9. Rinty _____ (Boxing)

10. Paul _____ (Golf)

Round 3 – Mystery Guest

1. I made my international debut at the age of 19 in 1994 (4 points)

    I scored 37 tries for my country before retiring from international duty in 2002 (3 points)

    Despite weighing around 19 stone I could still run the 100m in under 11 seconds, a frightening prospect for my opponents (2 points)

    In the two Rugby Union World Cups I played in I scored a total of 15 tries (1 point)

2. I turned professional in 1984 and within a year I had made headlines around the world (4 points)

    As a 17 year old I won two tournaments in England in the space of a month (3 points)

    I won six Grand Slam Singles throughout my career (2 points)

    In 1992 I won an Olympic gold partnering my compatriot Michael Stich (1 point)

Round 4 – Home or Away

1. *Trevor Brooking.* Who in 2008 became the first player in over 30 years to score in the semi-final and final of the FA Cup in the same season doing so for Portsmouth?

2. *Tom Daley.* Who partnered Pete Waterfield to Olympic silver at the 2004 Games in Athens?

3. *Padraig Harrington.* Whose putt secured the Ryder Cup for Europe in 1985 and in 2002 returned to captain the winning team?

4. *Daley Thompson.* Who became the first British decathlete in 20 years to win a Commonwealth gold medal when he won in Melbourne in 2006?

Round 5 – Captain's Away

1. What was unusual about Rafael Lovera's professional boxing debut in 1975?

2. Henry Cooper, Nigel Mansell and Damon Hill are the only people to have won which award twice in the 20th century?

3. Name the two snooker players who won the World Championships between 2000 and 2010 whose surnames begin with a vowel?

4. Which of these three swimming world records set in 2009 was swam in the quickest time?
   a) Men's 50m Backstroke
   b) Men's 50m Breaststroke
   c) Men's 50m Butterfly

Round 6 – What Happened Next

1. Colchester United are playing Southend United in League One, to keep the crowd entertained during half-time the mascots decide to have a race, what happened next?
   a) Larry the Lion doesn't look where he's going and runs straight into the post.

b) Mr Bull and Sammy the Shrimp tangle with each other as they're going round the goal and they end up having a punch up.

c) As the Colchester substitutes practice on the pitch, a stray ball hits Funky Monkey and his head comes off.

2. Marion Rolland from France is just about to start her downhill run at the Winter Olympics, what happened next?

   a) Rolland's over enthusiastic coach falls through the starting gate and slides down the slope.

   b) As she comes out of the starting gate and attempts to gain speed, Rolland falls over in the first five seconds.

   c) Rolland is forced to delay her start as a moose is loose on the slope.

Round 7 – On the Buzzer

All the answers to this buzzer round begin with the letter L. In the case of a person it's the surname that must start with that letter.

1. Which European won the US Masters on two occasions and captained Europe in the Ryder Cup in 2004?

2. Which English team were beaten 2-0 by Bayern Munich in the 1975 European Cup final?

3. Which fast bowler took his 300th Test wicket to become only the 4th Australian to reach the landmark?

4. Which European won the US Open Men's Singles final in 1985, 1986 and 1987?

5. In which European city do Benfica play their home games in the Estadio da Luz?

6. Which English team won the Heineken Cup in 2001 and 2002 to become the first side to retain the trophy?

7. In which event did Britain's Mary Rand become a world record holder in 1964?

8. Which Austrian won the 1984 Formula One World Championship with McLaren having won his first two World Titles with Ferrari?

9. On which French racecourse is the Prix de l'Arc de Triomphe run?

10. In 2010 which basketball team won the NBA Championship finals by beating the Boston Celtics?

11. Which Scotsman won the Open Championship in 1999 by beating Justin Leonard and Jean Van de Velde in a playoff?

12. Which British athlete won Olympic gold in 2000 with a score of 6584 points?

13. Which England forward scored 100 goals in the Premier League for Southampton?

14. In 2007 which fly half won his 100th cap for the Australian Rugby Union team?

15. Which American boxer was beaten in a Welterweight World Title fight by Roberto Duran in 1980 and then beat him at Super Middleweight level 9 years later?

16. Which Rugby League team won their 11th Challenge Cup with victory in 1999?

17. Which side were captained by Matthew Hoggard at the start of the 2011 County Championship?

18. Which Englishman's first snooker ranking victory came at the Grand Prix in 1998 against Marco Fu?

19. Which Australian won 11 Grand Slam Singles Titles in the 1960s?

20. Which Major League Baseball team won their first World Series title whilst based in Brooklyn and their 5th in a different state?

Game 56

On this episode of A Question of Sport are...

Chris Waddle (Football)
First appeared on the show as a guest in 1986

Geoffrey Boycott (Cricket)
First appeared on the show as a guest in 1987

Gail Emms (Badminton)
First appeared on the show as a guest in 2004

Greg Norman (Golf)
First appeared on the show as a guest in 1986

Round 1 – Opening Rally

1. Name the first ten Englishmen to appear in a World Championship Snooker final at the Crucible.

Round 2 – One Minute Round

1. Which American city's NHL Ice Hockey team are called the Coyotes?

2. For which team have cricketers Wasim Akram, Shivnarine Chanderpaul and Muttiah Muralitharan all played in the County Championship?

3. Which country won the most medals at the 2008 Summer Olympic Games?

4. Which major sporting event is this an anagram of? MAGIC EMPLOYS

5. What nationality are golfers Stuart Appleby and Richard Green?

6. Which 'Golden Boy' American won the Lightweight Boxing gold medal at the 1992 Olympics?

7. Which Football League team play their home games at Roots Hall?

These sports stars all share parts of their names with items of clothing you can wear round your shoulders.

8. _____ Connor (Cricket)

9. Kenny _____ (Football)

10. Geoff _____ (Athletics)

Round 3 – Mystery Guest

1. I was born in 1942 and came to the fore by winning Olympic gold (4 points)

   I changed my name in 1964 and retired when I was nearly 40 after losing in the Bahamas (3 points)

   I was noted for my fleetness of foot and quick wit during my career (2 points)

   I was involved in both the 'Thriller in Manilla' and the 'Rumble in the Jungle' (1 point)

2. I was born in July 1977 and in my early years could be found herding cattle (4 points)

   I learned the ropes in a prestigious school, Dale College and became the first ethnically black player to play for my country (3 points)

   I made my 100th Test appearance for my country in a game against England in 2009 (2 points)

   I became only the third player to take 300 Test wickets for South Africa (1 point)

Round 4 – Home or Away

1. *Chris Waddle.* Which 2011 Premier League chairman became the Republic of Ireland's record international goal scorer 10 years earlier?

2. *Geoffrey Boycott.* Which Englishman made a pair of ducks on his Test debut in 1975 before recording his highest Test score of 333 fifteen years later?

3. *Gail Emms.* In 2010 which England player won Commonwealth Silver medals in both the Men's Doubles and the Mixed Doubles?

4. *Greg Norman.* Which golfer won his first Major as a 22 year old in 1962 and his last 24 years later?

Round 5 – Captain's Away

1. In which sport did Nicola Minnichiello and Gillian Cooke become Britain's first World Champions since 1965?

2. In which American city would you find major sports teams the Lions, the Tigers, and the Redwings?

3. Name the two Test teams that play against each other for the Wisden Trophy in cricket?

4. Which of these teams did not compete in the 2010 Speedway Elite League?
    a) Belle Vue Aces
    b) Poole Pirates
    c) Birkenhead Broncos

Round 6 – What Happened Next

1. Zimbabwe and the West Indies are playing a One Day International cricket match Kemar Roach is about to bowl at Zimbabwe, what happened next?
    a) Batsman Sibanda pulls the ball, and the square leg umpire can't get out the way and catches the ball.
    b) Roach bowls a beamer that goes over both the batsman and wicketkeepers heads for a one bounce four.
    c) As Sibanda tries to defend a yorker, his bat snaps in half and he is bowled.

2. The Canadian Ice Hockey team are on the attack against Germany at the Winter Olympics, Shea Weber has just released a shot on goal, what happened next?
    a) The lights go out midway through Weber's goal-bound shot and the goal is disallowed.
    b) Shea Weber shoots so hard that the puck flies through the netting and the teams play on, not knowing it was a goal.
    c) Weber shoots wide and as Canada try to retrieve the ball, two players smash through the protective boards.

Round 7 – On the Buzzer

This buzzer round is all about the northern hemisphere.

1. Who opened the scoring in the 2005 Champions League final for AC Milan in the first minute against Liverpool?

2. In the Ashes series in 2010/11 which Englishman scored 766 runs at an average of over 127?

3. Which European country did England beat 14-9 in the semi-

final to reach the 2007 Rugby Union World Cup final?

4. In the women's sprint events at the 2008 Summer Olympics which country won five of the six athletics medals?

5. What nationality is the five times Tour de France winner Eddy Merckx?

6. Which American was known as the Brown Bomber and held the World Heavyweight Title for over 11 years?

7. Which Danish golfer was part of Europe's Ryder Cup winning teams in 1997 and 2002?

8. Which country's horse racing 'derby' is held at Capannelle?

9. Which country does the 2011 Australian Open Women's Singles finalist Li Na represent?

10. In which sport did the Everton Tigers beat the Glasgow Rocks in a Championship Playoff final in 2010?

11. Which Arsenal player was sent off in the 2006 Champions League final against Barcelona?

12. For the first time two players from which European country contested the 2006 World Darts Championship final?

13. Which country's Formula One Grand Prix is held at the Marina Bay Street Circuit?

14. Which country has won the most Judo gold medals at the Summer Olympics?

15. Who in 2010 for England against Bangladesh scored only the seventh Test match double century to be recorded at Lord's?

16. Which Scotsman in 2010 became only the second player to record 100 century breaks at the Crucible?

17. Which country has won the most Olympic Games swimming gold medals?

18. Which Austrian won his third Formula One World Title in 1984?

19. In which sport did Italian Alberto Tomba win Winter Olympic gold medals in both 1988 and 1992?

20. Which football club successfully defended the European Cup in 1990 beating Benfica 1-0?

Game 57

On this episode of A Question of Sport are...

Glenn McGrath (Cricket)
First appeared on the show as a guest in 2000

Marvin Hagler (Boxing)
First appeared on the show as a guest in 2001

Tessa Sanderson (Heptathlon)
First appeared on the show as a guest in 1979

David Coulthard (Motor racing)
First appeared on the show as a guest in 1995

Gareth Edwards has been appearing on *A Question of Sport* for the longest period of time. He featured in the first series in 1970 and made an appearance on the show 38 years later in 2008.

Round 1 – Opening Rally

1. Name the 12 teams that played in the top four tiers of English football in the 2010/2011 season whose names begin with the letter S?

Round 2 – One Minute Round

1. Who beat Hunter Mahan in the final singles match of the 2010 Ryder Cup to win the tournament for Europe?

2. Which Football League team play their home games at Meadow Lane?

3. Which tennis Grand Slam tournament have American brothers Bob and Mike Bryan won on five occasions between 2006 and 2011?

4. Who became the coach of the Indian cricket team in 2011?

5. What type of sporting hurdle is this an anagram of? WARM UP JET

6. In which sport did Switzerland's Simon Ammann win two gold medals at the 2010 Winter Olympics?

7. Which French jockey won the Prix de l'Arc de Triomphe three times in the 1990s?

These sports stars all share their surnames with appliances you can cook with.

8. Betty _____ (Tennis)

9. Denis _____ (Darts)

10. Jack _____ (Cricket)

Round 3 – Mystery Guest

1. I was born in Leicester in 1960 and it was in that city that I started my professional career (4 points)

   I played at club level in England, Spain and Japan (3 points)

   I was substituted for England in my final appearance for my country still one goal short of equalling Bobby Charlton's goal scoring record (2 points)

   Since retiring you can see me on television hosting the programme that I used to be seen scoring goals on (1 point)

2. I reached my 40th birthday in 2010 and in the early 90s I moved to America to attend the University of Arizona (4 points)

   I won the first of my 10 Majors in 1995 and represented Europe on 8 occasions in the Solheim Cup (3 points)

   In 2003 I was invited to take part in the Bank of America Colonial golf tournament to become the first woman in over 50 years to play in a PGA event (2 points)

   I am one of the most famous sports stars in my homeland of Sweden (1 point)

Round 4 – Home or Away

1. *Glenn McGrath.* Which player set a post-war Australian Ashes record when he scored 839 runs in a six Test series in 1989?

2. *Marvin Hagler.* Which World Heavyweight Champion successfully defended his title 20 times between 1978 and 1985?

3. *Tessa Sanderson.* Which British athlete won Commonwealth men's javelin medals on four successive occasions without winning gold between 1986 and 1998?

4. *David Coulthard.* Which Italian driver won the 2004 Monaco Grand Prix to give him his first Formula One win in 117 attempts?

Round 5 – Captain's Away

1. In 2002 how were golfers Ernie Els, Stuart Appleby, Thomas Levet and Steve Elkington specifically linked at the Open Championship?

2. In which American city would you find major sports teams the Bears, the Bulls, and the Blackhawks?

3. Name the two Japanese cities that have hosted the Winter Olympic Games?

4. Which of these disciplines is not included in the Men's Olympic gymnastic competition?
    a) Rings
    b) Pommel Horse
    c) Balance Beam

Round 6 – Great Sporting Moments

1. England and Australia couldn't be separated after 80 minutes of play, with the scores level at 17-17 Matt Dawson launched a final offensive drive up field in the pouring rain. The ball came back to the kicker who sent the drop goal between the posts to give England victory. Who scored the Rugby Union World Cup winning points for England in 2003?

2. Deep into extra time the semi-final was decided when the winger latched onto Patrick Vieira's misplaced pass, ran down the left hand side sweeping past Martin Keown and Lee Dixon before rifling the ball into David Seaman's goal. Who scored this FA Cup semi-final winner?

Round 7 – On the Buzzer

This buzzer round is all about 1991.

1. Which country defeated England at Twickenham in the Rugby Union World Cup final?

2. Which golfer triumphed at Augusta to win his only US Masters Title and received the Green Jacket from an Englishman?

3. With Yannick Noah as the non-playing captain which country won tennis' Davis Cup?

4. Which 42 year old former World Heavyweight Champion returned to the ring and challenged again for the World Title?

5. In which field event did Mike Powell break a 24 year old world record at the World Championships?

6. Boris Becker lost to which fellow German in the Men's Singles final at Wimbledon?

7. Two goals from Mark Hughes helped Manchester United beat which side to win the European Cup Winners' Cup final?

8. Whose 10th World Darts final saw him lose 6-0 to Dennis Priestley?

9. In which motor sport did American Wayne Rainey successfully defend a World Championship?

10. Which winger became the first Great Britain player to score five tries in a Rugby League International?

11. Which opening batsman scored his first Ashes century for England against Australia in Sydney?

12. Which bi-annual competition was won by the USA at Kiawah Island?

13. Which team did Tottenham Hotspur beat in the FA Cup final at Wembley?

14. Which centre captained England to the Five Nations Grand Slam?

15. Which snooker player beat Jimmy White to win his only World Championship at the Crucible?

16. Which British tennis player partnered Jeremy Bates to the Australian Open Mixed Doubles Title?

17. Which Spaniard won the first of his five successive Tour de France victories in 1991?

18. Which former *Question of Sport* captain became the first jockey to ride successive 1000 guineas winners in nearly 60 years?

19. Which Scottish athlete won the 10,000m at the World Championships in Tokyo?

20. Famously wearing the number 23 shirt which basketball player won the first of his NBA Championships in 1991?

Game 58

On this episode of A Question of Sport are...

Allan Donald (Cricket)
First appeared on the show as a guest in 2000

Tony Jacklin (Golf)
First appeared on the show as a guest in 1983

Mark Williams (Snooker)
First appeared on the show as a guest in 2000

Brad Fittler (Rugby League)
First appeared on the show as a guest in 2001

Round 1 – Opening Rally

1. Other than Super Heavyweight name the 10 boxing weights that featured in the 2008 Summer Olympic Games.

Round 2 – One Minute Round

1. Which Scotsman captained Europe to Ryder Cup victory in 2002?

2. Which English football team won the BBC Sports Personality Team of the Year Award in 1999?

3. For which county did Ally Brown score a world record one-day score of 268 against Glamorgan in 2002?

4. In which sport did Britain's David Florence win a silver medal at the Olympics in 2008?

5. Which team play their Rugby Union Premiership home games at Kingsholm Stadium?

6. Which American city's NHL Ice Hockey team are called the Capitals?

7. Which fast bowler's name is this an anagram of? WHAT CURLY ONES

These sports stars all share their surnames with types of nuts.

8. Richard _____ (Cricket)

9. Alan _____ (Football)

10. Louise _____ (Athletics)

Round 3 – Mystery Guest

1. I was born in Aberdeen in 1940 (4 points)

   I am the only Scottish footballer to win the European Footballer of the Year Award (3 points)

   I played at club level in England and in Italy but it was in Manchester that I had my greatest success (2 points)

   In the last match of my club career I relegated my former employers by scoring a back-heel (1 point)

2. I was born in Coventry in 1963 and I started playing my chosen sport at the age of 7 (4 points)

   I am considered the best British player in my sport of all time (3 points)

   I won my first Major in 1987 when I claimed victory at the US Open (2 points)

   I have won the Ladies European Tour Order of Merit a record seven times between 1985 and 2006 (1 point)

Round 4 – Home or Away

1. *Allan Donald.* Who against New Zealand in March 2004 became the first South African to play in 100 Tests?

2. *Tony Jacklin.* In 2007 who won his 7th World Matchplay Title at Wentworth, 13 years after winning his first?

3. *Mark Williams.* Which Irishman reached three World Championship finals between 1997 and 2003, winning on one occasion?

4. *Brad Fittler.* Who were the New Zealand brothers who both scored tries in Wigan's 1988 Challenge Cup victory over Halifax?

Round 5 – Captain's Away

1. Name the two countries that compete for the Bledisloe Cup in Rugby Union?

2. In 1994, Phillip DeFreitas, Darren Gough and Devon Malcolm helped Shane Warne perform which Ashes feat for the first time in 90 years?

3. In which American city would you find major sports teams the 76ers, the Flyers, and the Eagles?

4. Which of these disciplines is not included in the Women's Olympic gymnastic competition?
    a) Vault
    b) Balance Beam
    c) Horizontal Bar

Round 6 – What Happened Next

1. The Buffalo Bills are playing the Tennessee Titans, and AJ Trapasso is about to punt the ball down field, what happened next?
    a) Trapasso slips as he is about to punt the ball and he kicks the ball over his own head allowing Buffalo's Bryan Scott to run in for a touchdown.

b) Trapasso's punt hits Buffalo defender Bryan Scott as he tries to charge it down and the ball ricochets to Lavelle Hawkins who runs in a touchdown.

c) Trapasso fakes the kick, sending the entire defence the wrong way, allowing him to run in an unbelievable touchdown.

2. Burton Albion manager Paul Peschisolido is being interviewed after a League Two game on the side of the pitch, what happened next?

a) The Burton players are running backwards during their warm down and clatter straight into their manager.

b) Burton's sprinkler system automatically comes on and soaks the manager.

c) A stray ball is kicked towards Pescisolido who ducks it but it knocks over the sports reporter interviewing him.

Round 7 – On the Buzzer

This buzzer round is all about London.

1. Which side were the only Rugby League team based in London to play in the 2011 Super League?

2. Who scored for Crystal Palace and then Arsenal in FA Cup finals during the 1990s?

3. Which Surrey batsman scored over 8000 Test runs for England?

4. In 2007 which famous race started in London and ended by the Champs Élysées in Paris?

5. Goran Ivanisevic beat Todd Martin to win the Masters Title at which London venue in December 2010?

6. In 2010 which London team did Leicester Tigers beat to win Rugby Union's Guinness Premiership playoff final at Twickenham?

7. Which Tooting born snooker player reached his sixth World Championship final in 1994?

8. At which football stadium did Henry Cooper knock down Muhammad Ali in a World Title fight in 1966?

9. Which Russian athlete broke the Women's Pole Vault world record at Crystal Palace in London in 2005?

10. Which famous race is held every year on the River Thames and starts by Putney Bridge?

11. Born in Hackney in 1957 who beat Bobby George to win his first World Darts Title in 1980?

12. Which famous race was won by Emmanuel Mutai by in a record time in 2011?

13. Who took 5 for 92 against Australia in 2009 in his last England Test match at Lord's?

14. Which team were the first London club to do the League and FA Cup double?

15. Which cricket ground will host the Archery events at the 2012 Summer Olympics?

16. Which basketball team beat the Toronto Raptors in London in the first regular season NBA game to be played in Europe?

17. At which London venue did Phil Taylor win his 15th World Darts Championship in 2010?

18. Ding Junhui beat Liang Wenbo to win which snooker event at London's Wembley Arena in January 2011?

19. In 2007 which London club won the first FA Cup final to be held at the New Wembley?

20. Who did the New York Giants beat at Wembley in 2007 in the first NFL game to be held outside of North America?

Game 59

On this episode of A Question of Sport are...

Peter Beardsley (Football)
First appeared on the show as a guest in 1987

Sean Long (Rugby League)
First appeared on the show as a guest in 2004

Eddie Irvine (Motor racing)
First appeared on the show as a guest in 2001

Adrian Moorhouse (Swimmer)
First appeared on the show as a guest in 1985

Fred Trueman, Brendan Foster, Bobby Moore and Bobby Charlton all appeared as captains on the show in the 1970s. They each sat in the chair on more than one occasion but none captained for an entire series.

Round 1 – Opening Rally

1. James Anderson became the 13th man to take 200 Test wickets for England, who are the 12 players who achieved the feat before him.

Round 2 – One Minute Round

1. In which sport did Rory McLeod, Martin Gould and Ricky Walden compete in the 2011 World championships?

2. Which cricket county is this an anagram of? MORAL GANG

3. Which Football League team play their home games at Boundary Park?

4. Which Swedish tennis player won both the Junior Boys' Championship and the Men's Singles Championship at Wimbledon in the 1970s?

5. Which country won the 2007 Twenty20 Cricket World Cup in South Africa?

6. Which British boxer won the Middleweight gold medal at the 2008 Olympics?

7. Which Englishman was one of the captain's three picks at the 2010 Ryder Cup?

These sports stars all share their surnames with things you might find in a hospital.

8. Hugh _____ (Cycling)

9. Seymour _____ (Cricket)

10. Tony _____ (Rugby Union)

Round 3 – Mystery Guest

1. I was born in Kansas City in 1974 and as a youngster enjoyed playing both American Football and competing in Track and Field (4 points)

   I won three successive World Championship gold medals and an Olympic Title in the 100m between 1997 and 2001 (3 points)

   I broke the world record in 1999 with a time of 9.79 seconds (2 points)

   I ran the anchor leg for the USA as Mark Lewis-Francis held me off to win Olympic gold for Great Britain in 2004 (1 point)

2. In 1989 I won the British Four Man Bobsleigh Championship (4 points)

   That came after I won my first Olympic gold medal in 1984 (3 points)

   I famously said after I won Olympic gold in 1996 that if I went near a rowing boat again people could shoot me (2 points)

   In 2000 I won the BBC Sports Personality of the Year Award in recognition for my Olympic achievements (1 point)

Round 4 – Home or Away

1. *Peter Beardsley.* Who made his Scotland debut in 1995, 17 years after his father scored in the 1978 World Cup against the Netherlands?

2. *Sean Long.* Who in 1999 became the first player to score four tries in a Challenge Cup final?

3. *Eddie Irvine.* Who in 2007 became the third Finnish driver to win the Formula One World Championship?

4. *Adrian Moorhouse.* In 2004 which swimmer won a bronze medal in the Olympic 200m butterfly for Britain?

Round 5 – Captain's Away

1. What type of ball did Adam Gilchrist keep in his glove to help his high grip on the way to scoring 149 in the 2007 World Cup final?

2. In which American city would you find major sports teams the Hawks, the Thrashers, and the Falcons?

3. Name the two players who played Test cricket for England between 2000 and 2010 whose surnames begin with the letter O?

4. Which of these sports has not been included in the Summer Olympic Games?
    a) Billiards
    b) Croquet
    c) Tug of War

Round 6 – What Happened Next

1. DC United are taking on Columbus Crew in a Major League Soccer game in the USA, Colombus Crew are on the attack, what happened next?
    a) DC United goalkeeper Bill Hamid completely miskicks his clearance and Guillermos Schelotto puts the ball into an empty net.
    b) Hamid hoofs the ball clear and it lands on his manager Ben Olsen's head as he is preparing to make a substitution.
    c) A dog has run on to the pitch from behind the goal and heads the ball before Hamid can clear.

2. Japanese baseball sides Hiroshima Carp and the Yokahama BayStars are in action, the pitcher is just about to release the ball, what happened next?
    a) Two of the outfielders both attempt to take the catch but end up colliding with each other, but one of them still pulls off the catch.
    b) One of the fielders prevents a home run by acrobatically scaling the back wall and taking an incredible catch.
    c) The ball is hit over the wall and into the crowd where it lands in a spectator's lap spilling his popcorn everywhere.

Round 7 – On the Buzzer

This buzzer round is all about records.

1. Which English football team went through the 2003/2004 Premier League season unbeaten?

2. Who against England in 2004 became the first cricketer to score 400 runs in a Test innings?

3. In April 2001 which American golfer held all four Major titles at the same time?

4. For which country did John Leslie score a try in a Five Nations game within 9 seconds of the start of the game?

5. Who in 2010 became the first player to record two 9 dart finishes in the same game?

6. Who between 1985 and 2004 scored a record 208 touchdowns in his American Football career with amongst others the San Francisco 49ers?

7. In 1973 Dwight Stones became the first person to break the high jump world record using which technique?

8. Which Welsh kicker scored 1049 points in 87 internationals to become the then world record points scorer in Rugby Union?

9. In 1984 which pair achieved the highest score in Olympic Ice Skating history?

10. Which 52 year old jockey rode his 30th English Classic winner in 1992 on Rodrigo de Triano?

11. Which Major League Baseball team won a record 27th World Series Title by beating the Philadelphia Phillies in 2009?

12. Who in 2009 scored the quickest goal ever recorded in an FA Cup final?

13. In 2007 which team became the first constructor to win 200 Formula One Grand Prix races?

14. Who in 2005 at 7'2" and 320lbs became the biggest ever World Heavyweight Champion?

15. Which American sprinter set the Women's 100m world record in 1988 which still stood at the start of the 2011 season?

16. Which Wigan half back played in a record 9 Challenge Cup winning sides between 1985 and 1995?

17. In which sport did Kareem Abdul-Jabbar score a record 38,387 points between 1969 and 1989?

18. Which Australian scored a record 974 runs in an Ashes series?

19. Which player became the first in Premier League history to score four goals after coming on as a substitute in 1999?

20. In 2001 Roman Sebrle became the first man to record 9000 points in which Olympic event?

Game 60

On this episode of A Question of Sport are...

Michael Atherton (Cricket)
First appeared on the show as a guest in 1991

Andrew Johns (Rugby League)
First appeared on the show as a guest in 2004

Mary Peters (Track athletics)
First appeared on the show as a guest in 1974

Martin Brundle (Motor racing)
First appeared on the show as a guest in 1988

By the end of the 40th series Laura Davies had appeared on the show 18 times as a studio guest, making her the most 'capped' sports woman in the history of the show.

Round 1 – Opening Rally

1. Name the ten teams to have won the English League Cup between 1992 and 2011.

Round 2 – One Minute Round

1. In which city would you be watching football if you were at Windsor Park?

2. Who was named as Europe's Ryder Cup captain for the 2012 competition?

3. What colour jersey does the overall leader of the Tour de France wear?

4. Which English football stadium is this an anagram of? FINE LAD

5. Which British woman partnered Andy Murray in the final of the 2010 Hopman Cup?

6. In which sport did American Shaun White win a Winter Olympic gold in 2010?

7. Which Rugby League team play their Super League home games at the Galpharm Stadium?

These sports stars all share their surnames with things you might find in a classroom.

8. Dave _____ (Baseball)

9. Brian _____ (Tennis)

10. Tony _____ (Football)

Round 3 – Mystery Guest

1. Like my twin brother I played internationally (4 points)

   I was born in 1965 and became captain of my country in 1989 (3 points)

   I won the World Cup in 1987 and 1999 (2 points)

   I scored over 10,000 Test runs for Australia and took nearly 100 wickets too (1 point)

2. I was born in London but was raised in Yorkshire where at the age of 12 I joined the Hallamshire Harriers (4 points)

   I was coached by my father and studied Economics and Social History at Loughborough University (3 points)

   After my sporting career ended I entered politics and was influential in bringing the Olympics to London in 2012 (2 points)

   During my career I had many great tussles with fellow British rivals Steve Ovett and Steve Cram (1 point)

Round 4 – Home or Away

1. *Michael Atherton.* In 2003 which country became the first non-Test playing nation to reach the World Cup semi-finals where they lost to India?

2. *Andrew Johns.* Who in 2009 became Australia's most capped Rugby League player and a year later became their record try scorer?

3. *Mary Peters.* In which event did Judy Oakes set a British record in 1988 which was still standing at the start of the 2011 season?

4. *Martin Brundle.* Who at the Melbourne Grand Prix in 2011 became the first Russian driver to record a podium finish in Formula One?

Round 5 – Captain's Away

1. Who played in 8 successive US Open Singles finals but never won a Wimbledon Singles Title?

2. How did cricketer Gary Pratt play a part in winning the 2005 Ashes for England despite never gaining a Test cap?

3. Name the two NHL Ice Hockey teams that begin with the letter D?

4. Which of these sports has not been included in the Summer Olympic Games?
   a) Cricket
   b) Polo
   c) Shinty

Round 6 – What Happened Next

1. Josh Scanlan is competing in the USBC Team Bowling Trials, he's just about to release the ball, what happened next?

a) He doesn't let go of the ball and slides down the lane with it.

b) He bowls the ball down the wrong lane but still gets a strike.

c) He lets go of the ball too late and it ends up landing behind him.

2. Halfway through a greyhound race at the Shepperton course, what happened next?

a) The floodlights go out and when they come back on the dog handlers can only find 3 of the dogs.

b) A real hare runs on to the track and 'Ginny Lou' decides to chase that instead of the mechanical hare.

c) The mechanical hare jams and stops suddenly causing all big pile-up with all the dogs.

Round 7 – On the Buzzer

This buzzer round is all about the year 2005.

1. Which opening batsman became only the 4th West Indian to score a Test triple century?

2. Which British golfer finished runner up to Tiger Woods at the 2005 Open Championship?

3. Which team beat Manchester United on penalties to win the FA Cup final?

4. Who won 7 races in the season to become the youngest ever Formula One World Champion?

5. Who became the first Australian in 17 years to reach the Men's Australian Open Singles final?

6. Which country won the Grand Slam for the first time in 27

years by winning the 2005 Six Nations?

7. Which American runner won the Men's 400m at the World Championships in 2005?

8. Which British woman won the European Three Day Eventing Title on Toytown?

9. Which Bradford Bulls winger scored a Super League record six tries in a game against Hull?

10. Which British gymnast won her second World Championship medal, two years after winning her first?

11. Who captained England as they regained the Ashes for the first time in 16 years?

12. Who at the age of 17 years and 294 days became Britain's youngest ever Davis Cup player?

13. Who became the first golfer from New Zealand to win a Major since Bob Charles by winning the 2005 US Open?

14. Which club beat AC Milan to win the Champions League?

15. Which Jamaican set a new 100m world record in a time of 9.77 seconds?

16. Which jockey won the Grand National for the second time in the decade with victory on Hedgehunter?

17. Which British Olympic medallist beat David Bailey to win his debut professional boxing bout?

18. Which English qualifier beat Matthew Stevens 18-6 to become Snooker's World Champion?

19. Which Major League Baseball team who play their home games in Illinois won their first World Series Title since 1917?

20. Which Australian fast bowler's 500th Test wicket victim was England's Marcus Trescothick?

The Answers

GAME 1

Round One – Opening Rally
1. Luke Donald
2. Ross Fisher
3. Peter Hanson
4. Padraig Harrington
5. Miguel Angel Jimenez
6. Martin Kaymer
7. Graeme McDowell
8. Rory McIlroy
9. Edoardo Molinari
10. Francesco Molinari
11. Ian Poulter
12. Lee Westwood

Round Two – One Minute Round
1. Ms Dhoni
2. Modern Pentathlon
3. Boxing Day
4. Decathlon
5. Durham
6. Sumo Wrestling
7. Wayne Mardle
8. Pond
9. Kriek
10. Brooke

Round Three – Mystery Guest
1. Fernando Alonso
2. Steffi Graf

Round Four – Home or Away
1. David Beckham
2. Clive Woodward

3. Robert Key
4. Maria Mutola

Round Five – Captain's Away
1. Golf
2. Tour de France
3. Singapore and Spain
4. B

Round Six – What Happened Next
1. B
2. B

Round Seven – On the Buzzer
1. George Gregan
2. Tim Cahill
3. Melbourne Cup
4. Wayne Grady
5. Eddie Charlton
6. Alan Jones
7. Melbourne
8. Speedway
9. Michael Clarke
10. Darts
11. Michael Doohan
12. New Zealand
13. Aussie Rules
14. Cathy Freeman
15. Harry Kewell
16. Cycling
17. Novak Djokovic
18. Pole Vault
19. Ian Thorpe
20. Surfing

GAME 2

Round One – Opening Rally
1. Wasim Akram
2. Curtly Ambrose
3. Kapil Dev
4. Richard Hadlee
5. Anil Kumble
6. Glenn McGrath
7. Muttiah Muralitharan
8. Shaun Pollock
9. Courtney Walsh

10. Shane Warne

Round Two – One Minute Round
1. Italy
2. American Football
3. Ruby Walsh
4. Filippo Inzaghi
5. Swimming
6. Scrum Half
7. Sue Barker
8. Taylor
9. Milla
10. Sailor

Round Three – Mystery Guest
1. Colin Jackson
2. Lleyton Hewitt

Round Four – Home or Away
1. Gerard Pique
2. Simon Shaw
3. Germany
4. Carolina Kluft

Round Five – Captain's Away
1. Henley Regatta
2. Australia
3. Warrington Wolves and Wigan Warriors
4. B

Round Six – Great Sporting Moments
1. Don Fox
2. Derek Redmond

Round Seven – On the Buzzer
1. Monday
2. Glamorgan
3. Allen Johnson
4. Middlesbrough
5. Heavyweight
6. Jacques Villeneuve
7. Squash
8. Ryder Cup
9. Pat Rafter
10. Peter O'Sullevan
11. Swimming
12. Ronnie O'Sullivan

13. St Helens
14. 800m
15. Brive
16. Graham Gooch
17. Martina Hingis
18. Borussia Dortmund
19. Tiger Woods
20. Javier Sotomayer

GAME 3

Round One – Opening Rally
1. Peter Beardsley
2. Terry Butcher
3. Paul Gascoigne
4. Gary Lineker
5. Paul Parker
6. Stuart Pearce
7. David Platt
8. Chris Waddle
9. Des Walker
10. Mark Wright

Round Two – One Minute Round
1. Seve Ballesteros
2. Triple Jump
3. Ayr
4. Gail Emms
5. Sheffield
6. Hearts of Midlothian
7. Oxford
8. Gardener
9. Michael Judge
10. Alastair Cook

Round Three – Mystery Guest
1. Dan Marino
2. John McEnroe

Round Four – Home or Away
1. Trevor Steven
2. Bryan Habana
3. Laura Robson
4. Tom Watson

Round Five – Captain's Away
1. Volleyball

2. London Marathon Wheelchair Race
3. Jim Watt and Ken Buchanan
4. C

Round Six – What Happened Next
1. B
2. C

Round Seven – On the Buzzer
1. Paul Azinger
2. Australia
3. Argentina
4. Aston Villa
5. Ascot
6. Martin Adams
7. Brian Ashton
8. Atlanta
9. James Anderson
10. Aussie Rules Football
11. Amen Corner
12. Austrian
13. Alpine Skiing
14. Mario Andretti
15. Amberleigh House
16. Ben Ainslie
17. Archery
18. Athens
19. Henry Akinwande
20. Chemmy Alcott

GAME 4

Round One – Opening Rally
1. Jenson Button
2. Jim Clark
3. Lewis Hamilton
4. Mike Hawthorn
5. Damon Hill
6. Graham Hill
7. James Hunt
8. Nigel Mansell
9. Jackie Stewart
10. John Surtees

Round Two – One Minute Round
1. Real Madrid
2. Tour de France

3. South Korea
4. Tennis
5. Aston Villa
6. Heptathlon
7. Seattle
8. Barber
9. Baker
10. Butcher

Round Three – Mystery Guest
1. Jose Maria Olazabal
2. Richard Dunwoody

Round Four – Home or Away
1. Nicky Shorey
2. Yngling
3. Rocky Marciano
4. Jana Rawlinson (Pittman)

Round Five – Captain's Away
1. Zimbabwe
2. Marathon
3. Kauto Star and Kicking King
4. C

Round Six – Great Sporting Moments
1. Bob Champion
2. Carl Lewis

Round Seven – On the Buzzer
1. Andrei Arshavin
2. Cardiff
3. Paul O'Connell
4. Yong-Eun Yang
5. Kauto Star
6. Mark Webber
7. Andy Roddick
8. Long Jump
9. Carl Froch
10. Lee Briers
11. Swimming
12. Sea the Stars
13. Rio de Janeiro
14. Ice Dancing
15. Lee Westwood
16. Jonathan Trott
17. Ireland

18. Cycling
19. Samuel Eto'o
20. Phillips Idowu

GAME 5

Round One – Opening Rally
1. Australia
2. China
3. France
4. Germany
5. Great Britain
6. Italy
7. Japan
8. Russia
9. South Korea
10. USA

Round Two – One Minute Round
1. England
2. Football
3. Martina Hingis
4. Eric Cantona
5. Featherweight
6. Castleford Tigers
7. Seven
8. Viollet
9. Rose
10. Lillee

Round Three – Mystery Guest
1. Fabio Capello
2. Sachin Tendulkar

Round Four – Home or Away
1. Bode Miller
2. Steve Finn
3. Serbia
4. Josh Lewsey

Round Five – Captain's Away
1. Chelsea
2. Wrestling
3. Dennis Taylor and Ken Doherty
4. A

Round Six – What Happened Next

1. A
2. B

Round Seven – On the Buzzer
1. Real Madrid
2. Marcus Trescothick
3. Frank Bruno
4. Silverstone
5. Swimming
6. Royal Ascot
7. Watford
8. Sandwich
9. London Irish
10. Crystal Palace
11. Queen's Club
12. Basketball
13. Masters
14. Hampshire
15. London Broncos
16. Henley
17. Bobby George
18. Bath
19. Jermain Defoe
20. Dean Macey

GAME 6

Round One – Opening Rally
1. AC Milan
2. Barcelona
3. Bayern Munich
4. Borussia Dortmund
5. Inter Milan
6. Juventus
7. Liverpool
8. Manchester United
9. Real Madrid
10. Porto

Round Two – One Minute Round
1. Aberdeen
2. Cincinnati
3. Portugal
4. Michael Clarke
5. Yorkshire
6. Equestrian
7. Ice Hockey

8. Nightingale
9. Eagles
10. Crowe

Round Three – Mystery Guest
1. Daniel Vettori
2. Ronnie O'Sullivan

Round Four – Home or Away
1. Dirk Kuyt
2. Aravinda Da Silva
3. Valentino Rossi
4. Best Mate

Round Five – Captain's Away
1. Jules Rimet (World Cup)
2. Three
3. Serbia and Spain
4. C

Round Six – What Happened Next
1. A
2. A

Round Seven – On the Buzzer
1. Luis Felipe Scolari
2. Australia
3. 110m Hurdles
4. Muhammad Ali
5. Barry Sheene
6. Rugby League
7. Juan Manuel Fangio
8. Phil Vickery
9. China
10. Triple Jump
11. Ray Reardon
12. Cycling
13. Zara Phillips
14. Wales
15. Helsinki
16. Mario Andretti
17. Darts
18. Uruguay
19. Lindsay Vonn
20. Judd Trump

GAME 7

Round One – Opening Rally
1. Bradford
2. Castleford
3. Halifax
4. Huddersfield
5. Leeds
6. St Helens
7. Wakefield
8. Warrington
9. Widnes
10. Wigan

Round Two – One Minute Round
1. West Indies
2. Minnesota
3. Mark Williams
4. Double Fault
5. Canoeing
6. Exeter
7. Ascot
8. Kitchen
9. Parlour
10. Hall

Round Three – Mystery Guest
1. Diego Maradona
2. Shane Warne

Round Four – Home or Away
1. Raul
2. Ronan O'Gara
3. Dominic Cork
4. Sonia O'Sullivan

Round Five – Captain's Away
1. 23
2. Pat Jennings
3. Damon Hill and Mika Hakkinen
4. C

Round Six – What Happened Next
1. B
2. B

Round Seven – On the Buzzer
1. Terry Venables
2. 5000m

A QUESTION OF SPORT ~ THE ANSWERS

3. David Gower
4. Barry McGuigan
5. Hull
6. Michael Kiernan
7. Everton
8. Steve Cram
9. Boris Becker
10. Sunil Gavaskar
11. Norway
12. Michel Platini
13. Sandy Lyle
14. Katarina Witt
15. Tour de France
16. Jonathan Davies
17. Steve Cauthen
18. Lee Trevino
19. Dennis Taylor
20. Alain Prost

GAME 8

Round One – Opening Rally
1. Denmark
2. France
3. Germany
4. Greece
5. Italy
6. Netherlands
7. Portugal
8. Serbia
9. Slovakia
10. Slovenia
11. Spain
12. Switzerland

Round Two – One Minute Round
1. Ian Rush
2. South Africa
3. Touring Cars
4. Murrayfield
5. Pittsburgh
6. Stefan Edberg
7. Solheim Cup
8. Cash
9. Sterling
10. Pounds

Round Three – Mystery Guest
1. Ronaldo
2. Bjorn Borg

Round Four – Home or Away
1. David Davies
2. Ryan Sidebottom
3. Ethiopian
4. Joe Frazier

Round Five – Captain's Away
1. Ricardo Carvalho
2. 43
3. Nigel Mansell and Liz McColgan
4. C

Round Six – Great Sporting Moments
1. Race was declared void
2. Seve Ballesteros

Round Seven – On the Buzzer
1. Steve Redgrave
2. Middlesex
3. Swimming
4. Tottenham Hotspur
5. 1500m
6. David Haye
7. Lee Westwood
8. Netball
9. Clinton Woods
10. Epsom
11. Bradford Northern
12. Rowing
13. Dave Beasant
14. Geoffrey Boycott
15. Basketball
16. Chris Ashton
17. Jeremy Bates
18. Cycling
19. Peter Ebdon
20. Scott Parker

GAME 9

Round One – Opening Rally
1. Athens
2. Atlanta

3. Barcelona
4. Beijing
5. Los Angeles
6. Montreal
7. Moscow
8. Munich
9. Seoul
10. Sydney

Round Two – One Minute Round
1. Backstroke
2. Argentina
3. Colombian
4. Scrum Half
5. Crystal Palace
6. West Indies
7. Villeneuves (Gilles and Jacques)
8. Redwine
9. Ginn
10. Brandy

Round Three – Mystery Guest
1. Ian Botham
2. Jonny Wilkinson

Round Four – Home or Away
1. Kevin Nolan
2. Adrian Moorhouse
3. Matthew Stevens
4. Manny Pacquiao

Round Five – Captain's Away
1. Nottinghamshire
2. Luke Donald
3. Aberdeen and Dundee United
4. B

Round Six – What Happened Next
1. B
2. A

Round Seven – On the Buzzer
1. Patrick Vieira
2. Scotland
3. Kevin Sinfield
4. MS Dhoni
5. American Football

6. Cycling
7. Angelo Dundee
8. Seve Ballesteros
9. Nottinghamshire
10. Donald McCain
11. Fabio Cannavaro
12. France
13. Wigan Warriors
14. Peter Schmeichel
15. Tony Jacklin
16. Paul Nicholls
17. New England Patriots
18. Sally Gunnell
19. Paul O'Connell
20. Christian Horner

GAME 10

Round One – Opening Rally
1. Argentina
2. England
3. France
4. Germany
5. Italy
6. Mexico
7. South Korea and Japan
8. South Africa
9. Spain
10. USA

Round Two – One Minute Round
1. Miami
2. Audley Harrison
3. Ryan Giggs
4. Turnberry
5. Robin Cousins
6. South African
7. University Boat Race
8. Cappuccino
9. Coke
10. Perrier

Round Three – Mystery Guest
1. Bryan Habana
2. Sharron Davies

Round Four – Home or Away

1. Sergei Bubka
2. Svetlana Khorkina
3. Dean Headley
4. Lleyton Hewitt

Round Five – Captain's Away
1. Beaten twice in the FA Cup in the same season
2. Ricky Ponting
3. Argentina and Australia
4. A

Round Six – Great Sporting Moments
1. Alan Sunderland
2. Jonathan Edwards

Round Seven – On the Buzzer
1. Andy Fordham
2. Boxing
3. Mark Lewis-Francis
4. Greece
5. Michelle Wie
6. Rowing
7. Shane Warne
8. Kelly Sotherton
9. Gareth Thomas
10. Phil Mickelson
11. Ginger McCain
12. Cycling
13. Athens
14. New Zealand
15. 1500m Freestyle
16. Troon
17. Tunisia
18. Maria Sharapova
19. Bradley Wiggins
20. Boston Red Sox

GAME 11

Round One – Opening Rally
1. Austria
2. Canada
3. China
4. France
5. Germany
6. Norway
7. Russia

8.   South Korea
9.   Sweden
10. USA

Round Two – One Minute Round
1.   Norwich City
2.   Cassius Clay
3.   Germany
4.   Baseball
5.   Netherlands
6.   Australia
7.   Mark Todd
8.   Castle
9.   Knight
10. Bishop

Round Three – Mystery Guest
1.   Tom Watson
2.   Victoria Pendleton

Round Four – Home or Away
1.   Teddy Sheringham
2.   Rubens Barrichello
3.   Danny Crates
4.   Dinara Safina

Round Five – Captain's Away
1.   Cricket
2.   Rowing
3.   Athens and Atlanta
4.   B

Round Six – What Happened Next
1.   B
2.   B

Round Seven – On the Buzzer
1.   Shaun Edwards
2.   Jenny Pitman
3.   Colin McCrae
4.   South Africa
5.   Blackburn Rovers
6.   Frank Bruno
7.   Jonathan Edwards
8.   Rob Andrew
9.   Steffi Graf
10. Baseball

11. David Coulthard
12. Allan Donald
13. Everton
14. Corey Pavin
15. West Indies
16. Johnny Herbert
17. Stephen Hendry
18. Sergio Garcia
19. Andrew Cole
20. Chicago Bulls

GAME 12

Round One – Opening Rally
1. 100 metres
2. 110 metres hurdles
3. 400 metres
4. 1500 metres
5. Discus
6. High Jump
7. Javelin
8. Long Jump
9. Pole Vault
10. Shot Put

Round Two – One Minute Round
1. Aberdeen
2. Weightlifting
3. High Jump
4. Mike Hussey
5. Synchronised Swimming
6. Leeds
7. Rafael Nadal
8. Onions
9. Pepper
10. Leek

Round Three – Mystery Guest
1. Tanni Grey Thompson
2. Joe Calzaghe

Round Four – Home or Away
1. Marco Van Basten
2. Graeme McDowell
3. James Hook
4. Steffi Graf

Round Five – Captain's Away
1. Nadia Comaneci
2. Cross Country Skiing and Rifle Shooting
3. Glamorgan and Gloucestershire
4. A

Round Six – Great Sporting Moments
1. Roger Bannister
2. Nick Faldo

Round Seven – On the Buzzer
1. Pittsburgh Steelers
2. St Louis
3. Tyson Gay
4. Tiger Woods
5. Gymnastics
6. Seattle
7. Tim Howard
8. Miami Heat
9. Formula One
10. Jimmy Connors
11. Kentucky Derby
12. Clint Dempsey
13. Salt Lake City
14. Ben Crenshaw
15. Baseball
16. Andy Roddick
17. Detroit Redwings
18. Michael Johnson
19. Lance Armstrong
20. Indianapolis 500

GAME 13

Round One – Opening Rally
1. Derbyshire
2. Gloucestershire
3. Hampshire
4. Lancashire
5. Leicestershire
6. Northamptonshire
7. Nottinghamshire
8. Warwickshire
9. Worcestershire
10. Yorkshire

Round Two – One Minute Round

1. 15
2. Obafemi Martins
3. Ice Hockey
4. Jason Gillespie
5. Equestrian
6. Northampton Saints
7. Toro Rosso
8. Hart
9. Hand
10. Hipp

Round Three – Mystery Guest
1. Chris Boardman
2. Ricky Ponting

Round Four – Home or Away
1. Zinedine Zidane
2. Willie John McBride
3. Pam Shriver
4. Roy Jones Jr

Round Five – Captain's Away
1. USA
2. Mike Gatting
3. Canada and China
4. B

Round Six – What Happened Next
1. B
2. B

Round Seven – On the Buzzer
1. Charl Schwarztel
2. Sarajevo
3. Sheffield Wednesday
4. Maria Sharapova
5. San Francisco 49ers
6. San Antonio Spurs
7. Solheim Cup
8. Speedway
9. South Africa
10. Sri Lanka
11. Matthew Stevens
12. Sevilla
13. St Helens
14. Sweden
15. Saracens

16. Tessa Sanderson
17. Singapore
18. Somerset
19. Spain
20. Speed Skating

GAME 14

Round One – Opening Rally
1. David Boon
2. Allan Border
3. Ian Healy
4. Justin Langer
5. Glenn McGrath
6. Ricky Ponting
7. Mark Taylor
8. Shane Warne
9. Mark Waugh
10. Steve Waugh

Round Two – One Minute Round
1. Rocket
2. Rangers
3. Andrew Flintoff
4. Germany
5. Sue Barker
6. Houston
7. Serbian
8. Denmark
9. Ireland
10. Jordan

Round Three – Mystery Guest
1. Stephen Hendry
2. Paolo Maldini

Round Four – Home or Away
1. France
2. Matt Biondi
3. Martin Kaymer
4. Amelie Mauresmo

Round Five – Captain's Away
1. Essex
2. Helsinki
3. Germany and Greece
4. C

Round Six – Great Sporting Moments
1. Sam Torrance
2. Jerzy Dudek

Round Seven – On the Buzzer
1. Peter Schmeichel
2. Linford Christie
3. Lester Piggott
4. Spain
5. Dream Team
6. Imran Khan
7. Sally Gunnell
8. Essex
9. Oscar De La Hoya
10. England
11. Old Trafford
12. Nigel Mansell
13. John McEnroe
14. Chris Boardman
15. Duke McKenzie
16. Zimbabwe
17. Albertville
18. Sunderland
19. Party Politics
20. Jimmy White

GAME 15

Round One – Opening Rally
1. Linford Christie
2. Sebastian Coe
3. Jonathan Edwards
4. Sally Gunnell
5. Kelly Holmes
6. Denise Lewis
7. Steve Ovett
8. Tessa Sanderson
9. Daley Thompson
10. Allan Wells

Round Two – One Minute Round
1. Sheffield United
2. Kentucky Derby
3. Jason Robinson
4. Nottinghamshire
5. Red
6. Speedway

7. Melbourne
8. Paris
9. London
10. Dublin

Round Three – Mystery Guest
1. Nigel Mansell
2. Phil Mickelson

Round Four – Home or Away
1. George Graham
2. Shelley Rudman
3. Pat Rafter
4. Raphael Ibanez

Round Five – Captain's Away
1. Hamilton (Todd and Lewis)
2. Jose Mourinho
3. Green Bay Packers and Pittsburgh Steelers
4. A

Round Six – What Happened Next
1. A
2. B

Round Seven – On the Buzzer
1. France
2. Lord's
3. New Zealand
4. French Open
5. Darren Campbell
6. Carl Froch
7. Interlagos
8. Lionel Messi
9. Ernie Els
10. Wigan Warriors
11. India
12. Ginger McCain
13. Michael Vaughan
14. Swimming
15. Tour de France
16. Canada
17. Felipe Massa
18. Paula Radcliffe
19. Wembley
20. Benfica

GAME 16

Round One – Opening Rally
1. Arsenal
2. Aston Villa
3. Chelsea
4. Everton
5. Fulham
6. Ipswich Town
7. Liverpool
8. Manchester United
9. Middlesbrough
10. Tottenham Hotspur

Round Two – One Minute Round
1. Pakistan
2. Princess Anne
3. Virgin Racing
4. Australian
5. Martin Johnson
6. 1979
7. Rochdale
8. Panther
9. Tiger
10. Lyon

Round Three – Mystery Guest
1. George Best
2. Steve Davis

Round Four – Home or Away
1. Gail Devers
2. Tilakaratne Dilshan
3. Joe Bugner
4. Jason Robinson

Round Five – Captain's Away
1. Gianfranco Zola
2. European Touring Car
3. Martin Kaymer and Bernhard Langer
4. C

Round Six – Great Sporting Moments
1. Steve Ovett
2. James Buster Douglas

Round Seven – On the Buzzer

1. Lawrie Sanchez
2. High Jump
3. Eddie 'The Eagle' Edwards
4. Florence Griffith Joyner
5. Diving
6. West Indies
7. Seoul
8. England
9. Steffi Graf
10. Alan Shearer
11. Royal Lytham and St Annes
12. Wigan
13. Swimming
14. Michael Spinks
15. Netherlands
16. Joaquim Cruz
17. Motor Cycling
18. Swiss
19. Sandy Lyle
20. Sean Kerly

GAME 17

Round One – Opening Rally

1. Bath
2. Bristol
3. Sale
4. Saracens
5. London Irish
6. London Wasps
7. Harlequins
8. Leicester Tigers
9. Orrell
10. Gloucester
11. Northampton Saints
12. Newcastle Falcons

Round Two – One Minute Round

1. New York Knicks
2. Catalans Dragons
3. Les Ferdinand
4. Rough Quest
5. Caroline Wozniacki
6. Ian Botham
7. Football (soccer)
8. King

9. Prince
10. Queen

Round Three – Mystery Guest
1. Michael Johnson
2. Greg Rusedski

Round Four – Home or Away
1. Gary Lineker
2. Vijay Singh
3. Jahangir Khan
4. Allan Border

Round Five – Captain's Away
1. Richard Krajicek
2. Jamaica
3. Michael Schumacher and Kimi Raikkonen
4. B

Round Six – What Happened Next
1. C
2. A

Round Seven – On the Buzzer
1. Denmark
2. Doncaster
3. David Duval
4. Nikolay Davydenko
5. Ken Doherty
6. Desert Orchid
7. Kapil Dev
8. Dallas Cowboys
9. Natasha Danvers
10. James Degale
11. Derby County
12. Discus
13. Allan Donald
14. Detroit Redwings
15. John Daly
16. Darts
17. Dynamo Kiev
18. Diving
19. Gail Devers
20. Delhi

GAME 18

Round One – Opening Rally
1. Alan Ball
2. Bobby Charlton
3. Jack Charlton
4. George Cohen
5. Roger Hunt
6. Geoff Hurst
7. Bobby Moore
8. Martin Peters
9. Nobby Stiles
10. Ray Wilson

Round Two – One Minute Round
1. Italy
2. Basketball
3. Austrian
4. Newcastle Falcons
5. Los Angeles
6. Figure Skating
7. Bangladesh
8. Kent
9. Devon
10. Cheshire

Round Three – Mystery Guest
1. Valentino Rossi
2. Yelena Isinbayeva

Round Four – Home or Away
1. Frankie Fredericks
2. Mike Brearley
3. Annika Sorenstam
4. Kevin Sinfield

Round Five – Captain's Away
1. Martina Navratilova
2. Steve McManaman
3. Salford City Reds and St Helens
4. A

Round Six – Great Sporting Moments
1. Robbie Keane
2. Carl Lewis

Round Seven – On the Buzzer

1. Darren Gough
2. Dean Macey
3. Evander Holyfield
4. Richard Dunwoody
5. Ryan Giggs
6. South Africa
7. Paul Lawrie
8. Lance Armstrong
9. Scotland
10. Lindsay Davenport
11. Swimming
12. Carl Fogarty
13. Colin Montgomerie
14. Muhammad Ali
15. Bayern Munich
16. Eunice Barber
17. Robbie and Henry Paul
18. Yevgeny Kafelnikov
19. Eddie Irvine
20. Ruud Gullit

GAME 19

Round One – Opening Rally

1. Tomas Berdych
2. Roger Federer
3. Lleyton Hewitt
4. Goran Ivanisevic
5. Rafael Nadal
6. David Nalbandian
7. Mark Philippoussis
8. Patrick Rafter
9. Andy Roddick
10. Pete Sampras

Round Two – One Minute Round

1. Snooker
2. Vijay Singh
3. Watford
4. Detroit Red Wings
5. Snooker referees
6. Manchester
7. Leicester Tigers
8. Cherry
9. Strawberry
10. Pears

Round Three – Mystery Guest
1. Oscar De La Hoya
2. Jason Robinson

Round Four – Home or Away
1. Henrik Larsson
2. William Fox-Pitt
3. Sergio Garcia
4. Johnny Murtagh

Round Five – Captain's Away
1. Bob Willis
2. Spain
3. Dallas Cowboys and Houston Texans
4. C

Round Six – What Happened Next
1. B
2. A

Round Seven – On the Buzzer
1. Blackburn Rovers
2. Ross Taylor
3. Michael Campbell
4. Italy
5. Formula One
6. Peter Snell
7. Auckland
8. David Kirk
9. Chris Lewis
10. Rowing
11. Doug Howlett
12. Cycling
13. America's Cup
14. Catalans Dragons
15. Netball
16. Brendon McCullum
17. Mark Todd
18. Triathlon
19. Montreal
20. Richard Hadlee

GAME 20

Round One – Opening Rally
1. Anaheim Angels
2. Arizona Diamondbacks

3. Atlanta Braves
4. Boston Red Sox
5. Chicago White Sox
6. Florida Marlins
7. New York Yankees
8. Philadelphia Phillies
9. San Francisco Giants
10. St Louis Cardinals

Round Two – One Minute Round
1. Bird's Nest
2. Warwickshire
3. Juventus
4. Hills (Graham and Damon)
5. West Ham United
6. USPGA Championship
7. Skeleton Bob
8. Salmon
9. Pollock
10. Perch

Round Three – Mystery Guest
1. Gavin Henson
2. Mark Spitz

Round Four – Home or Away
1. Chris Woods
2. Katarina Witt
3. Gustavo Kuerten
4. Canada

Round Five – Captain's Away
1. Ayr
2. Women's Rugby World Cup
3. Sebastian Vettel and Jacques Villeneuve
4. C

Round Six – What Happened Next
1. A
2. B

Round Seven – On the Buzzer
1. Daley Thompson
2. Liverpool
3. Edinburgh
4. Chris Broad
5. Gavin and Scott Hastings

6. Joe Johnson
7. Greg Lemond
8. Richard Dunwoody
9. Chris Evert
10. Greg Norman
11. Argentina
12. Lloyd Honeyghan
13. Ian Botham
14. Jack Nicklaus
15. Australia
16. Shooting
17. Wales
18. Steve Redgrave
19. Nelson Piquet
20. Swimming

GAME 21

Round One – Opening Rally
1. Atletico Madrid
2. Barcelona
3. Deportivo La Coruna
4. Espanyol
5. Mallorca
6. Real Betis
7. Real Madrid
8. Real Zaragoza
9. Sevilla
10. Valencia

Round Two – One Minute Round
1. Ivan Lendl
2. Vinnie Jones
3. Alec Stewart
4. Ian Woosnam
5. Australia
6. Ice Hockey
7. McLaren
8. Green
9. Black
10. Brown

Round Three – Mystery Guest
1. David Campese
2. Laurent Blanc

Round Four – Home or Away

1. Anil Kumble
2. Greg and Jonathan Searle
3. Jody Scheckter
4. Don't Push It

Round Five – Captain's Away
1. Justin Leonard
2. Pool (Anagram Of Polo)
3. Aston Villa and Chelsea
4. A

Round Six – What Happened Next
1. A
2. C

Round Seven – On the Buzzer
1. Blackpool
2. Buffalo Bills
3. Chris Boardman
4. Bradford Bulls
5. Bjorn Borg
6. Boston Celtics
7. Bulgaria
8. Ato Boldon
9. Bangladesh
10. Barcelona
11. Brazil
12. Badminton
13. Steve Beaton
14. Seve Ballesteros
15. Bobbyjo
16. Bath
17. Donald Bradman
18. Boston Red Sox
19. Riddick Bowe
20. Nigel Bond

GAME 22

Round One – Opening Rally
1. Ken Doherty
2. Graeme Dott
3. Peter Ebdon
4. Stephen Hendry
5. John Higgins
6. Shaun Murphy
7. Ronnie O'Sullivan

8. John Parrott
9. Neil Robertson
10. Mark Williams

Round Two – One Minute Round
1. Justin Rose
2. June
3. Bradford Bulls
4. Ille Nastase
5. Commonwealth Games
6. Football World Cup
7. Tourist Trophy
8. Park
9. Forrest
10. Wood

Round Three – Mystery Guest
1. Ian Thorpe
2. Martina Hingis

Round Four – Home or Away
1. Mark Hughes
2. Bradley Wiggins
3. Matthew Hayden
4. Mark Calcavecchia

Round Five – Captain's Away
1. Steve Smith
2. Warrington Wolves
3. Andre Agassi and Stefan Edberg
4. C

Round Six – Great Sporting Moments
1. Carlos Alberto
2. Gianfranco Zola

Round Seven – On the Buzzer
1. Alan Shearer
2. Pete Sampras
3. Australia
4. Darts
5. Horse racing
6. Miami Dolphins
7. Courtney Walsh
8. Vijay Singh
9. Northampton Saints
10. Kevin Keegan

11. Boxing
12. Rubens Barrichello
13. Mary Pierce
14. Cycling
15. Kelly Holmes
16. Sailing
17. Matt Dawson
18. USA
19. Lee Westwood
20. France

GAME 23

Round One – Opening Rally
1. Argentina
2. Australia
3. Canada
4. Fiji
5. Japan
6. Namibia
7. New Zealand
8. Samoa
9. Tonga
10. USA

Round Two – One Minute Round
1. Two
2. Pep Guardiola
3. West Indies
4. Italian
5. Eagle
6. Yorkshire
7. Tony McCoy
8. Hook
9. Rod
10. Maggert

Round Three – Mystery Guest
1. Colin Montgomerie
2. Phil Taylor

Round Four – Home or Away
1. Viv Anderson
2. Kath Grainger
3. Billie Jean King
4. Ellery Hanley

Round Five – Captain's Away
1. Stuart Broad
2. Golf
3. Leicester City and Liverpool
4. B

Round Six – Great Sporting Moments
1. Gareth Southgate
2. Cathy Freeman

Round Seven – On the Buzzer
1. Argentina
2. Mike Weir
3. Carl Lewis
4. Portsmouth
5. Javelin
6. Jenny Pitman
7. Australia
8. Monty Panesar
9. Miami Heat
10. Snooker
11. Rebecca Romero
12. Judo
13. Jacques Villeneuve
14. Jonah Lomu
15. Darts
16. Durham
17. Green Bay Packers
18. US Masters
19. Canoeing
20. Celtic

GAME 24

Round One – Opening Rally
1. Cardiff City
2. Carlisle United
3. Charlton Athletic
4. Chelsea
5. Cheltenham Town
6. Chesterfield
7. Colchester United
8. Coventry City
9. Crewe Alexandra
10. Crystal Palace

Round Two – One Minute Round

1. Newmarket
2. American Football
3. 400m
4. Widnes
5. Pentathlon
6. Luis Figo
7. Bath
8. Carr
9. Lawrie
10. Train

Round Three – Mystery Guest
1. Frankie Dettori
2. Tom Daley

Round Four – Home or Away
1. Everton
2. Mike Phillips
3. Long jump
4. Neil Robertson

Round Five – Captain's Away
1. Sailing
2. Marat Safin
3. Ernie Els and Louis Oosthuizen
4. C

Round Six – Great Sporting Moments
1. Borussia Monchengladbach
2. Roberto Di Matteo

Round Seven – On the Buzzer
1. South Africa
2. Mark Philippoussis
3. Steven Pienaar
4. US Open
5. New Zealand
6. Scrum Half
7. Brazilian
8. Melbourne
9. Diego Forlan
10. Australia
11. Shane Watson
12. Argentina
13. Zimbabwe
14. Tennis
15. Angel Cabrera

16. Paraguay
17. Brisbane
18. Namibian
19. Rowing
20. South Africa

GAME 25

Round One – Opening Rally
1.   Fernando Alonso
2.   Rubens Barrichello
3.   Jenson Button
4.   Giancarlo Fisichella
5.   Lewis Hamilton
6.   Heikki Kovalainen
7.   Robert Kubica
8.   Felipe Massa
9.   Kimi Raikkonen
10. Michael Schumacher
11. Sebastian Vettel
12. Mark Webber

Round Two – One Minute Round
1.   Harlequins RL
2.   Italy
3.   New York Knicks
4.   Rugby League
5.   Osaka
6.   Carlisle United
7.   Old Course at St Andrews
8.   Montana
9.   Georgia
10. Washington

Round Three – Mystery Guest
1.   Ian Woosnam
2.   Wayne Gretzky

Round Four – Home or Away
1.   Fabrizio Ravanelli
2.   David Wilkie
3.   Juan Martin del Potro
4.   Kostya Tszyu

Round Five – Captain's Away
1.   John Regis
2.   Alex Tudor

3. Richard Dunwoody and Carl Llewellyn
4. C

Round Six – Great Sporting Moments
1. Nayim
2. George Foreman

Round Seven – On the Buzzer
1. Rory McIlroy
2. Desert Orchid
3. Frank Bruno
4. Peter Scudamore
5. Michael Chang
6. Barcelona
7. Gavin Hastings
8. High jump
9. Allan Border
10. Worcestershire
11. Jocky Wilson
12. Steve Davis
13. Breaststroke
14. Arantxa Sanchez Vicario
15. Jose Maria Olazabal
16. Michael Thomas
17. Widnes
18. Equestrian
19. Tour de France
20. San Francisco 49ers

GAME 26

Round One – Opening Rally
1. Michael Atherton
2. Mark Butcher
3. Alastair Cook
4. Andrew Flintoff
5. Graham Gooch
6. Nasser Hussain
7. Allan Lamb
8. Kevin Pietersen
9. Alec Stewart
10. Andrew Strauss
11. Marcus Trescothick
12. Michael Vaughan

Round Two – One Minute Round
1. Memphis

2.   Cycling
3.   Huddersfield Giants
4.   Graeme Dott
5.   Charlton Athletic
6.   Badminton
7.   Hampshire
8.   Basil
9.   Sage
10. Ginger

Round Three – Mystery Guest
1.   Ivan Lendl
2.   Olga Korbut

Round Four – Home or Away
1.   Ipswich Town
2.   Neil Jenkins
3.   10km Open Water
4.   Bernard Gallacher

Round Five – Captain's Away
1.   Badminton
2.   Darts
3.   Nelson Piquet and Alain Prost
4.   A

Round Six – What Happened Next
1.   C
2.   C

Round Seven – On the Buzzer
1.   Swimming
2.   Aberdeen
3.   Jackie Stewart
4.   Turnberry
5.   Boxing
6.   John Higgins
7.   Allan Wells
8.   Murrayfield
9.   Ayr
10. Jamie Murray
11. Curling
12. Gavin Hamilton
13. Calcutta Cup
14. Edinburgh
15. Joe Jordan
16. Bowls

17. Jocky Wilson
18. Dan Parks
19. Paul Di Resta
20. Sandy Lyle

GAME 27

Round One – Opening Rally
1. Angel Cabrera
2. Trevor Immelman
3. Zach Johnson
4. Phil Mickelson
5. Jose Maria Olazabal
6. Mark O'Meara
7. Charl Schwarztel
8. Vijay Singh
9. Mike Weir
10. Tiger Woods

Round Two – One Minute Round
1. 1500m
2. Cricket
3. Roger Federer
4. Grand National
5. Force India
6. Peterborough United
7. Malaysia
8. Ford
9. Bush
10. Clinton

Round Three – Mystery Guest
1. Dennis Taylor
2. Lothar Matthaus

Round Four – Home or Away
1. Deco
2. Inge De Brujn
3. Ruby Walsh
4. Alain Prost

Round Five – Captain's Away
1. Field Hockey
2. Golf
3. Arizona Cardinals and Atlanta Falcons
4. A

Round Six – What Happened Next
1. A
2. A

Round Seven – On the Buzzer
1. Manchester
2. Ronaldo
3. Ernie Els
4. Hampden Park
5. Paula Radcliffe
6. Rugby Sevens
7. Lleyton Hewitt
8. Great Britain
9. Shaquille O'Neal
10. Beth Tweddle
11. Nasser Hussain
12. Prix de l'Arc de Triomphe
13. Jason Leonard
14. France
15. Sean Long
16. Swedish
17. Peter Ebdon
18. Canada
19. Kim Collins
20. Surrey

GAME 28

Round One – Opening Rally
1. Aberdeen
2. Celtic
3. Dundee
4. Dundee United
5. Hearts
6. Hibernian
7. Kilmarnock
8. Motherwell
9. Rangers
10. Third Lanark

Round Two – One Minute Round
1. Warwickshire
2. Golf
3. Tranmere Rovers
4. France
5. Snooker
6. Millennium Stadium

7. Long Jump
8. Anderson
9. Hunt
10. Degale

Round Three – Mystery Guest
1. Wasim Akram
2. Lennox Lewis

Round Four – Home or Away
1. Emile Heskey
2. John Smit
3. Christophe Lemaitre
4. Andy Farrell

Round Five – Captain's Away
1. Indianapolis 500
2. 300
3. Chepstow and Ludlow
4. A

Round Six – Great Sporting Moments
1. Joe Frazier
2. Some People Are On The Pitch, They Think It's All Over... It Is Now

Round Seven – On the Buzzer
1. Paul Rideout
2. Pat Rafter
3. Ryder Cup
4. Jason Robinson
5. Viv Richards
6. Rome
7. Royal Lytham and St Annes
8. Roma
9. Keke Rosberg
10. Hasim Rahman
11. Rajasthan Royals
12. Russia
13. Rough Quest
14. Paula Radcliffe
15. Rowing
16. Romanian
17. Rebecca Romero
18. Valentino Rossi
19. Rangers
20. John Regis

GAME 29

Round One – Opening Rally
1. Auckland
2. Brisbane
3. Christchurch
4. Delhi
5. Edinburgh
6. Edmonton
7. Kuala Lumpur
8. Manchester
9. Melbourne
10. Victoria

Round Two – One Minute Round
1. South African
2. Football
3. Cricket
4. Lester Piggott
5. Joe Frazier
6. China
7. Snooker
8. Blair
9. Thatcher
10. Brown

Round Three – Mystery Guest
1. Franz Klammer
2. Nick Faldo

Round Four – Home or Away
1. Theo Walcott
2. France
3. Windsurfing
4. John Part

Round Five – Captain's Away
1. Pam Shriver
2. Marathon
3. Kevin Pietersen and Matt Prior
4. B

Round Six – Great Sporting Moments
1. Bayern Munich
2. Steve Redgrave

Round Seven – On the Buzzer
1. Ice Hockey
2. New Zealand
3. Pat Cash
4. Richard Hadlee
5. Edwin Moses
6. John Lowe
7. Jose Rivero
8. Nigel Mansell
9. Thomas Hearns
10. Coventry City
11. Australia
12. Wayne Gretzky
13. Champion Hurdle
14. Carl Lewis
15. Fatima Whitbread
16. Figure Skating
17. Laura Davies
18. Clive Allen
19. Minnesota
20. France

GAME 30

Round One – Opening Rally
1. England
2. France
3. Germany
4. Italy
5. Netherlands
6. Portugal
7. Romania
8. Scotland
9. Spain
10. Yugoslavia

Round Two – One Minute Round
1. Michel Platini
2. Hull Kr
3. Houston
4. Salt Lake City
5. 3000m
6. Mercedes
7. Bowls
8. Valentine
9. Christmas
10. Easter

Round Three – Mystery Guest
1.   Ernie Els
2.   Lester Piggott

Round Four – Home or Away
1.   Switzerland
2.   Leon Pryce
3.   Roger Black
4.   Mark Selby

Round Five – Captain's Away
1.   Four
2.   New Zealand
3.   Brive and Toulouse
4.   B

Round Six – What Happened Next
1.   B
2.   B

Round Seven – On the Buzzer
1.   Kemar Roach
2.   St Helens
3.   Cheltenham Gold Cup
4.   Chicago Bulls
5.   Jimmy White
6.   K Club
7.   Canada
8.   Carl Lewis
9.   Mark Cueto
10. Gonzalo Higuain
11. Robbie Fowler
12. Swimming
13. Fernando Alonso
14. France
15. Andy Roddick
16. Ben Ainslie
17. Rugby Union
18. Warrington Wolves
19. Jan Zelezny
20. Ryan Sidebottom

GAME 31

Round One – Opening Rally
1.   Baseball
2.   Basketball

3. Beach Volleyball
4. Field Hockey
5. Handball
6. Softball
7. Table Tennis
8. Tennis
9. Volleyball
10. Water Polo

Round Two – One Minute Round
1. Golf
2. West Indies
3. Australian Open
4. Preston North End
5. Netherlands
6. Arkle
7. Arizona
8. Chip
9. Egg
10. Bacon

Round Three – Mystery Guest
1. Michael Schumacher
2. Arantxa Sanchez Vicario

Round Four – Home or Away
1. Gus Poyet
2. Serge Blanco
3. Natasha Danvers
4. Nikolay Valuev

Round Five – Captain's Away
1. Taekwondo
2. Iran
3. Miami Dolphins and Minnesota Vikings
4. C

Round Six – Great Sporting Moments
1. Diego Maradona
2. Red Rum

Round Seven – On the Buzzer
1. It was declared void
2. Donington Park
3. Javelin
4. Michael Atherton
5. Bernhard Langer

6. Jim Courier
7. Stuttgart
8. Evander Holyfield
9. Underwoods
10. Brian Clough
11. Cycling
12. Colin Jackson
13. Middlesex
14. Monaco Grand Prix
15. Jana Novotna
16. Swimming
17. Sheffield Wednesday
18. Tom Watson
19. Jason Robinson
20. Toronto Blue Jays

GAME 32

Round One – Opening Rally
1. Cyprus
2. England
3. Gibraltar
4. Guernsey
5. Isle Of Man
6. Jersey
7. Malta
8. Northern Ireland
9. Scotland
10. Wales

Round Two – One Minute Round
1. Scotland
2. Barcelona
3. Rugby League
4. Reverse Swing
5. Winter Olympic Games
6. Augusta National
7. Boxing
8. Stich
9. Vaughan
10. Owen

Round Three – Mystery Guest
1. Michael Jordan
2. Seve Ballesteros

Round Four – Home or Away

1. Dennis Wise
2. Ryan Jones
3. New Zealand
4. Carl Fogarty

Round Five – Captain's Away
1. Badminton
2. Thomas Bjorn
3. Jack Brabham and Alan Jones
4. A

Round Six – What Happened Next
1. A
2. A

Round Seven – On the Buzzer
1. Gareth Thomas
2. Turin
3. Table Tennis
4. Daley Thompson
5. Toronto Raptors
6. Toro Rosso
7. Turnberry
8. Triple jump
9. Tottenham Hotspur
10. Mike Tindall
11. Sachin Tendulkar
12. Tokyo
13. Carlos Tevez
14. Roscoe Tanner
15. Triathlon
16. David Toms
17. Ten Pin Bowling
18. Tampa Bay Buccaneers
19. Jermain Taylor
20. Trinidad and Tobago

GAME 33

Round One – Opening Rally
1. Barnsley
2. Birmingham City
3. Blackburn Rovers
4. Blackpool
5. Bolton Wanderers
6. Bradford City
7. Brighton and Hove Albion

8. Bristol City
9. Burnley
10. Bury

Round Two – One Minute Round
1. Will Carling
2. Manchester United
3. Tennis
4. Commonwealth Games
5. Hibernian
6. US Masters
7. Gold
8. Nicol
9. Steele
10. Silva

Round Three – Mystery Guest
1. Ronan O'Gara
2. Michael Phelps

Round Four – Home or Away
1. Wesley Sneijder
2. Michelle Kwan
3. Sanath Jayasuriya
4. Phil Mickelson

Round Five – Captain's Away
1. Baseball
2. David James
3. Matthew Stevens and Mark Williams
4. C

Round Six – What Happened Next
1. C
2. A

Round Seven – On the Buzzer
1. Rough Quest
2. Dickie Bird
3. Rallying
4. Newcastle United
5. Roger Black
6. Greg Norman
7. Ascot
8. Wigan
9. Gareth Southgate
10. Cliff Richard

11. Darts
12. Bath
13. Ben Ainslie
14. Basketball
15. Lancashire
16. Andy Farrell
17. American Football
18. Sri Lanka
19. Haile Gebrselassie
20. Tom Lehman

GAME 34

Round One – Opening Rally
1. Ferrari
2. Force India
3. Hispania racing team
4. Lotus
5. McLaren
6. Mercedes
7. Red Bull
8. Renault
9. Sauber
10. Toro Rosso
11. Virgin Racing
12. Williams

Round Two – One Minute Round
1. Shane Warne
2. Portsmouth
3. Brazil
4. Peter Scudamore
5. Alpine Skiing
6. Swedish
7. Lennox Lewis
8. Wright
9. Poulter
10. Bell

Round Three – Mystery Guest
1. Ayrton Senna
2. Ellen MacArthur

Round Four – Home or Away
1. Lothar Matthaus
2. Leicester Tigers
3. Graeme Smith

4.   Sweden

Round Five – Captain's Away
1.   Gymnastics
2.   Phillips Idowu
3.   Everton and Exeter City
4.   B

Round Six – Great Sporting Moments
1.   Michael Thomas
2.   Robin Cousins

Round Seven – On the Buzzer
1.   Turkey
2.   Lord's
3.   Epsom
4.   Athens
5.   Sydney
6.   Augusta
7.   Queens Park Rangers
8.   British Show Jumping Derby
9.   Texas
10.   St Helens
11.   Boston Red Sox
12.   Jayne Torvill and Christopher Dean
13.   Melbourne
14.   Paris
15.   Berlin
16.   Prix de l'Arc de Triomphe
17.   Madison Square Garden
18.   Queen's Club
19.   Victoria
20.   Turin

GAME 35

Round One – Opening Rally
1.   Australia
2.   Croatia
3.   Czech Republic
4.   France
5.   Germany
6.   Russia
7.   Serbia
8.   Spain
9.   Sweden
10.   USA

Round Two – One Minute Round
1. Ipswich Town
2. Grand National
3. Arthur Ashe
4. Barcelona
5. Middlesex
6. Australian
7. 35
8. June
9. May
10. Januarie

Round Three – Mystery Guest
1. Tony McCoy
2. Chris Gayle

Round Four – Home or Away
1. Paul Lambert
2. Scotland
3. Jim Laker
4. Virginia Leng

Round Five – Captain's Away
1. Bob Beamon
2. Franz Beckenbauer
3. Graeme McDowell and Rory McIlroy
4. A

Round Six – What Happened Next
1. B
2. A

Round Seven – On the Buzzer
1. Martina Navratilova
2. Steve Backley
3. Crystal Palace
4. Graham Gooch
5. Scotland
6. Graham Taylor
7. Stefan Edberg
8. Merlene Ottey
9. Nick Faldo
10. Grand National
11. Swimming
12. Stanley Cup
13. Stephen Hendry
14. Wigan

15. Ayrton Senna
16. Mike Tyson
17. Badminton
18. Phil Taylor
19. Basketball
20. Joe Montana

GAME 36

Round One – Opening Rally
1. AC Milan
2. Bologna
3. Cagliari
4. Fiorentina
5. Inter Milan
6. Juventus
7. Lazio
8. Napoli
9. Roma
10. Sampdoria
11. Torino
12. Verona

Round Two – One Minute Round
1. Italy
2. Troon
3. Graeme Swann
4. Brazil
5. Cricket
6. Gymnastics
7. Tottenham Hotspur
8. Villa
9. Gower
10. Duval

Round Three – Mystery Guest
1. Fred Perry
2. Paula Radcliffe

Round Four – Home or Away
1. Kevin Prince Boateng
2. JPR Williams
3. Lennox Lewis
4. Niki Lauda

Round Five – Captain's Away
1. Handled the ball

2. Ian Woosnam
3. Bayern Munich and Borussia Dortmund
4. A

Round Six – What Happened Next
1. A
2. B

Round Seven – On the Buzzer
1. Fernando Alonso
2. Green Bay Packers
3. Nick Faldo
4. Joe Calzaghe
5. Ice Dancing
6. Valentino Rossi
7. Chelsea
8. Snooker
9. Kauto Star
10. West Indies
11. France
12. Serena Williams
13. New York Yankees
14. Wigan
15. Andrew Strauss
16. Darts
17. Wasps
18. La Lakers
19. Liu Xiang
20. Matthew Pinsent

GAME 37

Round One – Opening Rally
1. Baltimore Ravens
2. Denver Broncos
3. Green Bay Packers
4. Indianapolis Colts
5. New England Patriots
6. New Orleans Saints
7. New York Giants
8. Pittsburgh Steelers
9. St. Louis Rams
10. Tampa Bay Buccaneers

Round Two – One Minute Round
1. Darts
2. Fred Couples

3. Rugby League
4. France
5. Rowing
6. Portugal
7. Cricket
8. Motor Cycling
9. Skiing
10. Cycling

Round Three – Mystery Guest
1. Iuean Evans
2. Mark Boucher

Round Four – Home or Away
1. Thierry Henry
2. Jason Kenny
3. Nijinsky
4. Greg Norman

Round Five – Captain's Away
1. Judd Trump
2. Five
3. Northampton Saints and Newcastle Falcons
4. C

Round Six – Great Sporting Moments
1. Steve Morrow was dropped by his teammates and broke his shoulder
2. Jean Van de Velde

Round Seven – On the Buzzer
1. Grand National
2. Gary Speed
3. Geoff Ogilvy
4. Junior Witter
5. Jenson Button
6. Munster
7. Nikolay Davydenko
8. Skeleton Bob
9. Ricky Ponting
10. Lisa Dobriskey
11. Melbourne
12. Zinedine Zidane
13. St Helens
14. Graeme Dott
15. Chris Paterson
16. Mark Ramprakash
17. New Zealand

18.   Kobe Bryant
19.   Miroslav Klose
20.   Mark Cavendish

GAME 38

Round One – Opening Rally
1.   Michael Ball
2.   Nick Barmby
3.   Gareth Barry
4.   Joey Barton
5.   James Beattie
6.   David Beckham
7.   Darren Bent
8.   David Bentley
9.   Lee Bowyer
10.   Wayne Bridge
11.   Wes Brown
12.   Nicky Butt

Round Two – One Minute Round
1.   Lincoln City
2.   Canada
3.   Netball
4.   Argentina
5.   Cover Point
6.   Mark Woodforde
7.   New Zealand
8.   Gerrard
9.   Harmison
10.   Collins

Round Three – Mystery Guest
1.   Viv Richards
2.   George Foreman

Round Four – Home or Away
1.   Darren Campbell
2.   Brian O'Driscoll
3.   1980
4.   Kim Clijsters

Round Five – Captain's Away
1.   Green
2.   Laura Davies
3.   Oldham Athletic and Oxford United
4.   C

Round Six – Great Sporting Moments
1. Alan Kennedy
2. Maradona scored with the Hand of God

Round Seven – On the Buzzer
1. Blackpool
2. Carl Fogarty
3. Rugby League
4. Leeds
5. Boxing
6. UK Championship
7. Steve Smith
8. Aintree
9. Durham
10. Kevin Davies
11. Dickie Bird
12. Gateshead
13. St Leger
14. Newcastle Falcons
15. Warrington
16. Hoylake
17. Swimming
18. Andy Carroll
19. Sheffield
20. Darts

GAME 39

Round One – Opening Rally
1. Seve Ballesteros
2. Nick Faldo
3. Padraig Harrington
4. Martin Kaymer
5. Bernhard Langer
6. Paul Lawrie
7. Sandy Lyle
8. Graeme McDowell
9. Jose Maria Olazabal
10. Ian Woosnam

Round Two – One Minute Round
1. Football
2. Glamorgan
3. Celtic Park
4. Swedish
5. Red Rum
6. Basketball

7. George Foreman
8. Blizzard
9. Hale
10. Snow

Round Three – Mystery Guest
1. Jayne Torvill
2. Matt Giteau

Round Four – Home or Away
1. Steve Heighway
2. Jason Leonard
3. Andy Roddick
4. Yelena Isinbayeva

Round Five – Captain's Away
1. Two
2. Efan Ekoku
3. Warwickshire and Worcestershire
4. A

Round Six – Great Sporting Moments
1. Fernando Torres
2. Mark Lewis-Francis

Round Seven – On the Buzzer
1. Raymond Van Barneveld
2. Cheltenham
3. France
4. Pippa Funnell
5. Ricky Ponting
6. Paula Radcliffe
7. Rowing
8. Jim Furyk
9. Ronaldo
10. Juan Pablo Montoya
11. Belgium
12. Shot Put
13. Martina Navratilova
14. Barry Geraghty
15. Swimming
16. Andre Agassi
17. Fernando Alonso
18. Jonny Wilkinson
19. Celtic
20. Ken Doherty

GAME 40

Round One – Opening Rally
1. Australia
2. Bangladesh
3. Canada
4. India
5. Kenya
6. Netherlands
7. New Zealand
8. Pakistan
9. South Africa
10. Sri Lanka
11. West Indies
12. Zimbabwe

Round Two – One Minute Round
1. Canada
2. Virginia Wade
3. Wales
4. Ice Hockey
5. Plymouth Argyle
6. USPGA Championship
7. Tilakaratne Dilshan
8. Scudamore
9. Ebdon
10. Schmeichel

Round Three – Mystery Guest
1. Gareth Edwards
2. Richard Hadlee

Round Four – Home or Away
1. Henning Berg
2. Rory Underwood
3. Mark Cavendish
4. New Zealand

Round Five – Captain's Away
1. Marcus North
2. 2016 Summer Olympics
3. Robert Karlsson and Henrik Stenson
4. B

Round Six – What Happened Next
1. A
2. B

A QUESTION OF SPORT ~ THE ANSWERS

Round Seven – On the Buzzer
1. Monaco
2. Malaysia
3. Phil Mickelson
4. Miami Dolphins
5. Shaun Murphy
6. Andy Murray
7. Munster
8. Middlesbrough
9. Floyd Mayweather Jr
10. Miinnehoma
11. Marathon
12. Ellen MacArthur
13. Middlesex
14. Jose Mourinho
15. Rory McIlroy
16. Montreal
17. Richie McCaw
18. Amelie Mauresmo
19. Glenn McGrath
20. Adrian Moorhouse

GAME 41

Round One – Opening Rally
1. Scott Carson
2. Tim Flowers
3. Robert Green
4. Joe Hart
5. David James
6. Nigel Martyn
7. Paul Robinson
8. David Seaman
9. Peter Shilton
10. Chris Woods

Round Two – One Minute Round
1. England
2. Somerset
3. Australia
4. Sam Torrance
5. Carl Froch
6. Wales
7. Miguel Angel Jimenez
8. Gymnastics
9. Figure Skating
10. Motor Cycling

Round Three – Mystery Guest
1. Richie McCaw
2. Ben Ainslie

Round Four – Home or Away
1. Andrew Mehrtens
2. Nicole Cooke
3. Graeme Hick
4. Ecuador

Round Five – Captain's Away
1. Liverpool
2. Darts
3. Phillip Price and Ian Woosnam
4. A

Round Six – Great Sporting Moments
1. Geoff Hurst
2. Dave Beasant

Round Seven – On the Buzzer
1. Stephen Hendry
2. Jamie Murray
3. Raymond Van Barneveld
4. Swimming
5. Frankie Dettori
6. Tom Daley
7. Christine Ohuruogu
8. Gymnastics
9. Didier Drogba
10. Justine Henin
11. Matt Prior
12. Rallying
13. Percy Montgomery
14. Tyson Gay
15. San Antonio Spurs
16. Sergio Garcia
17. Lewis Hamilton
18. Ding Junhui
19. Liverpool
20. Monty Panesar

GAME 42

Round One – Opening Rally
1. Lindsay Davenport
2. Steffi Graf

3. Martina Hingis
4. Conchita Martinez
5. Amelie Mauresmo
6. Martina Navratilova
7. Jana Novotna
8. Maria Sharapova
9. Serena Williams
10. Venus Williams

Round Two – One Minute Round
1. Burnley
2. Sochi
3. Ice Hockey
4. Zimbabwe
5. Slam Dunk
6. Li Na
7. Melbourne Cup
8. Northeast
9. North
10. South

Round Three – Mystery Guest
1. Martin Johnson
2. Jack Nicklaus

Round Four – Home or Away
1. Frank Rijkaard
2. Peter Siddle
3. St Kitts and Nevis
4. Terry Griffiths

Round Five – Captain's Away
1. Peter Fleming
2. Canada
3. Sergio Garcia and Miguel Angel Jimenez
4. C

Round Six – What Happened Next
1. B
2. C

Round Seven – On the Buzzer
1. Pat Jennings
2. Middlesex
3. Brian O'Driscoll
4. Boxing
5. The Curragh

6. Sonia O'Sullivan
7. Ken Doherty
8. Padraig Harrington
9. Martin O'Neill
10. Gaelic Football
11. Pentathlon
12. Tour de France
13. Barry McGuigan
14. Keith Wood
15. Kevin Moran
16. Irish Grand National
17. Kevin O'Brien
18. Paul McGinley
19. Steve Staunton
20. Ulster

GAME 43

Round One – Opening Rally
1. Argentina
2. Brazil
3. Czechoslovakia
4. England
5. France
6. Germany
7. Hungary
8. Italy
9. Netherlands
10. Spain
11. Sweden
12. Uruguay

Round Two – One Minute Round
1. Colorado
2. Field Hockey
3. Adam Gilchrist
4. Helsinki
5. Albatross
6. Canterbury Crusaders
7. Middlesbrough
8. Hamilton
9. Edinburgh
10. Victoria

Round Three – Mystery Guest
1. James Toseland
2. Roger Federer

Round Four – Home or Away
1. Italy
2. Netherlands
3. Allyson Felix
4. Retief Goosen

Round Five – Captain's Away
1. Tim Cahill
2. Triple Jump
3. Sale Sharks and Saracens
4. B

Round Six – What Happened Next
1. A
2. B

Round Seven – On the Buzzer
1. Chicago
2. Cheltenham Gold Cup
3. Coventry City
4. Jim Courier
5. Christchurch
6. Colin Charvis
7. Alastair Cook
8. Canada
9. Ali Carter
10. Czech Republic
11. Angel Cabrera
12. Chepstow
13. China
14. Curling
15. Catalans Dragons
16. Calgary
17. Henry Cooper
18. James Cracknell
19. Cyprus
20. Chile

GAME 44

Round One – Opening Rally
1. Linford Christie
2. Sebastian Coe
3. Steve Cram
4. Jonathan Edwards
5. Kelly Holmes
6. Liz McColgan

7. Steve Ovett
8. Paula Radcliffe
9. Daley Thompson
10. Fatima Whitbread

Round Two – One Minute Round
1. Bradford City
2. Wigan
3. Ireland
4. Real Madrid
5. Darts
6. Brazil
7. Whirlwind
8. Funk
9. Sole
10. Rapp

Round Three – Mystery Guest
1. Johan Cruyff
2. Floyd Mayweather Jr

Round Four – Home or Away
1. Wales
2. Australia
3. Asafa Powell
4. South Africa

Round Five – Captain's Away
1. Boxing
2. All born abroad
3. Ajax and Psv Eindhoven
4. B

Round Six – Great Sporting Moments
1. Mary Decker
2. Michael Owen

Round Seven – On the Buzzer
1. Boxing
2. Winter Olympics
3. Brian Lara
4. Jose Maria Olazabal
5. Tour de France
6. Roberto Baggio
7. Baseball
8. 400m
9. Wigan

10. Warwickshire
11. Yvonne Murray
12. Darts
13. Chris Sutton
14. Sergei Bubka
15. Ernie Els
16. Willie Carson
17. Carl Fogarty
18. Spain
19. Mark Foster
20. New York Rangers

GAME 45

Round One – Opening Rally
1. Austria
2. Canada
3. France
4. Germany
5. Italy
6. Japan
7. Norway
8. Switzerland
9. USA
10. Yugoslavia

Round Two – One Minute Round
1. Charl Schwartzel
2. France
3. Sugar Ray Leonard
4. Champions League
5. Hampshire
6. Rallying
7. American
8. Cycling
9. Swimming
10. Boxing

Round Three – Mystery Guest
1. Jessica Ennis
2. Andy Murray

Round Four – Home or Away
1. Cliff Thorburn
2. Chantal Petitclerc
3. Martin Crowe
4. Buffalo Bills

Round Five – Captain's Away
1. Croquet
2. Jose Mourinho
3. London and Los Angeles
4. C

Round Six – What Happened Next
1. B
2. C

Round Seven – On the Buzzer
1. Wayne Rooney
2. Gloucester
3. Numbersixvalverde
4. Lewis Hamilton
5. Molinari brothers
6. Andrew Strauss
7. Celtic Crusaders
8. Judd Trump
9. Rugby Union
10. Millwall
11. Paula Radcliffe
12. Open Championship
13. USA
14. Force India
15. Australia
16. Keith Deller
17. Beach Volleyball
18. Jimmy Greaves
19. Boris Becker
20. Michael Clarke

GAME 46

Round One – Opening Rally
1. Australia
2. Canada
3. England
4. India
5. Kenya
6. Malaysia
7. New Zealand
8. Nigeria
9. Scotland
10. Singapore
11. South Africa
12. Wales

Round Two – One Minute Round
1. Golf
2. Nottinghamshire
3. Jane Sixsmith
4. Football
5. Argentina
6. Exeter Chiefs
7. Aberdeen
8. Judge
9. Durie
10. Wigg

Round Three – Mystery Guest
1. Kelly Holmes
2. Alain Prost

Round Four – Home or Away
1. Newcastle United
2. Sale Sharks
3. Peter Ebdon
4. Maurice Greene

Round Five – Captain's Away
1. Ian Botham
2. Table Tennis
3. Miami Heat and Orlando Magic
4. C

Round Six – Great Sporting Moments
1. Aston Villa
2. Ricky Villa

Round Seven – On the Buzzer
1. Ian Rush
2. George North
3. Light Heavyweight
4. Swimming
5. Mark Williams
6. Weightlifting
7. Celtic Crusaders
8. Portsmouth
9. Ice Hockey
10. Lynn Davies
11. Enzo Maccarinelli
12. Ryan Jones
13. Show jumping
14. 1958

15. Mark Hughes
16. Ray Reardon
17. 400m Hurdles
18. Gareth Thomas
19. Robert Croft
20. Darts

GAME 47

Round One – Opening Rally
1. Andre Agassi
2. Boris Becker
3. Bjorn Borg
4. Jimmy Connors
5. Jim Courier
6. Stefan Edberg
7. Ivan Lendl
8. John McEnroe
9. Ille Nastase
10. John Newcombe
11. Pete Sampras
12. Mats Wilander

Round Two – One Minute Round
1. Liverpool
2. Wladimir Klitschko
3. French
4. Bangladesh
5. Netball
6. Heineken Cup
7. Boston
8. Viola
9. Horne
10. Organ

Round Three – Mystery Guest
1. Robin Cousins
2. Cathy Freeman

Round Four – Home or Away
1. Toulouse
2. Michael Phelps
3. Colin Jackson
4. Jonathan Trott

Round Five – Captain's Away
1. Wrestling

2. Roger Federer
3. AC Milan and Inter Milan
4. A

Round Six – What Happened Next
1. C
2. A

Round Seven – On the Buzzer
1. Martin Adams
2. Canada
3. Curling
4. Delhi
5. Diego Forlan
6. Andres Iniesta
7. Australia
8. Muttiah Muralitharan
9. Chris Paterson
10. Christian Malcolm
11. Rory McIlroy
12. New Orleans Saints
13. Andy Murray
14. Weightlifting
15. Warrington Wolves
16. Abu Dhabi
17. Tony McCoy
18. San Francisco Giants
19. France
20. Lee Westwood

GAME 48

Round One – Opening Rally
1. Andrew Cole
2. Les Ferdinand
3. Robbie Fowler
4. Jimmy Floyd Hasselbaink
5. Thierry Henry
6. Frank Lampard
7. Michael Owen
8. Alan Shearer
9. Teddy Sheringham
10. Dwight Yorke

Round Two – One Minute Round
1. Valencia
2. Neil Robertson

3. Lebron James
4. Gymnastics
5. England
6. Badminton
7. King Of The Mountains
8. Mustard
9. Honey
10. Pepper

Round Three – Mystery Guest
1. Carl Lewis
2. Virginia Wade

Round Four – Home or Away
1. Roger Kingdom
2. Mon Mome
3. Joe Johnson
4. Simon Whitlock

Round Five – Captain's Away
1. Glasgow
2. Match abandoned after ten balls (shortest Test)
3. Leicester Tigers and Leinster
4. B

Round Six – Great Sporting Moments
1. Archie Gemmill
2. Trevor Francis

Round Seven – On the Buzzer
1. USA
2. Rowing
3. Canada
4. Field Hockey
5. Munich
6. Shooting
7. Javier Mascherano
8. Romanian
9. Marie-Jose Perec
10. Tennis
11. USA
12. Usain Bolt
13. Chariots of Fire
14. Mexico City
15. Boxing
16. 50 kilometres
17. Chris Hoy

18. Canoeing
19. Jackie Joyner-Kersee
20. Paris

GAME 49

Round One – Opening Rally
1. Allan Border
2. Shivnarine Chanderpaul
3. Rahul Dravid
4. Sunil Gavaskar
5. Mahela Jayawardene
6. Jacques Kallis
7. Brian Lara
8. Ricky Ponting
9. Sachin Tendulkar
10. Steve Waugh

Round Two – One Minute Round
1. Blackpool
2. Frankie Dettori
3. Triathlon
4. Corey Pavin
5. Nina Carberry
6. Sailing
7. Bahrain
8. Rose
9. Berry
10. Thorne

Round Three – Mystery Guest
1. Usain Bolt
2. Lewis Hamilton

Round Four – Home or Away
1. Francis Lee
2. Chris Ashton
3. Jamie Murray
4. Thomas Bjorn

Round Five – Captain's Away
1. Greenidge
2. Curling
3. Philadelphia Phillies and Pittsburgh Pirates
4. C

Round Six – What Happened Next

1. A
2. C

Round Seven – On the Buzzer
1. Graham Bell
2. Mark O'Meara
3. Michael Owen
4. Triple Jump
5. Sheffield Eagles
6. Alec Stewart
7. Newcastle
8. Melbourne Cup
9. Chris Boardman
10. Justin Rose
11. Iwan Thomas
12. Mika Hakinnen
13. Kuala Lumpur
14. Hermann Maier
15. Australia
16. John Higgins
17. Mark Foster
18. Pete Sampras
19. Argentina
20. Graeme Hick

GAME 50

Round One – Opening Rally
1. Birkdale
2. Carnoustie
3. Hoylake
4. Muirhead
5. Portrush
6. Royal Lytham & St Annes
7. Royal St George (Sandwich)
8. Royal Troon
9. St Andrews
10. Turnberry

Round Two – One Minute Round
1. Millennium Stadium
2. Dallas
3. England
4. Edwin Moses
5. Dundee United
6. Steve Davis
7. USA

8. Glass
9. Wells
10. Tapp

Round Three – Mystery Guest
1. François Pienaar
2. Kapil Dev

Round Four – Home or Away
1. Malcolm Marshall
2. Mo Farah
3. Andre Agassi
4. Sam Waley-Cohen

Round Five – Captain's Away
1. Martin Kaymer
2. Champion Jockey
3. Exeter City and Newcastle United
4. A

Round Six – Great Sporting Moments
1. Virginia Wade
2. Eric Cantona

Round Seven – On the Buzzer
1. Alan Shearer
2. 200
3. Miroslav Klose
4. Alastair Cook
5. Jason Leonard
6. McLaren
7. 400m Hurdles
8. Australia
9. Stephen Hendry
10. St Helens
11. Peter Scudamore
12. 170
13. South Africa
14. Valentino Rossi
15. Greg Norman
16. 36
17. Steffi Graf
18. Adam Gilchrist
19. Paul Scholes
20. USA

GAME 51

Round One – Opening Rally
1. Andre Agassi
2. Boris Becker
3. Bjorn Borg
4. Pat Cash
5. Jimmy Connors
6. Stefan Edberg
7. Roger Federer
8. Lleyton Hewitt
9. Goran Ivanisevic
10. Richard Krajicek
11. John McEnroe
12. Rafael Nadal
13. Pete Sampras
14. Michael Stich

Round Two – One Minute Round
1. New Zealand
2. Kilmarnock
3. Motor Racing
4. Trina Gulliver
5. Horse Racing
6. Colin Montgomerie
7. Cycling
8. Rowing
9. Swimming
10. Motor Cycling

Round Three – Mystery Guest
1. Jacques Kallis
2. Chris Hoy

Round Four – Home or Away
1. Muttiah Muralitharan
2. The Belfry
3. Tommy Stack
4. James Degale

Round Five – Captain's Away
1. The Davis Cup
2. James Gardener
3. Calgary and Vancouver
4. A

Round Six – What Happened Next

A QUESTION OF SPORT ~ THE ANSWERS

1. A
2. A

Round Seven – On the Buzzer
1. Rangers
2. Ali Carter
3. Joe Calzaghe
4. Annabel Croft
5. Ian Poulter
6. Jonny Wilkinson
7. Durham
8. Women's 400m
9. David Coulthard
10. Timmy Murphy
11. Cycling
12. New Zealand
13. Fernando Torres
14. Lawrence Dallaglio
15. Poland
16. Ice Hockey
17. Tom Daley
18. Anthony Kim
19. Wales
20. Tour de France

GAME 52

Round One – Opening Rally
1. Athletics
2. Boxing
3. Canoeing
4. Equestrian
5. Gymnastics
6. Modern Pentathlon
7. Rowing
8. Sailing
9. Swimming
10. Taekwondo

Round Two – One Minute Round
1. Philadelphia
2. 1991
3. Kevin Pietersen
4. Rugby Union
5. Clay
6. Triple Jump
7. San Siro

8. Cross
9. Pugh
10. Bell

Round Three – Mystery Guest
1. Martin Offiah
2. Venus Williams

Round Four – Home or Away
1. Mika Hakkinen
2. Terry Alderman
3. Steve Collins
4. David Trezeguet

Round Five – Captain's Away
1. It was neither for or against England
2. Tennis
3. Edinburgh and Edmonton
4. A

Round Six – What Happened Next
1. A
2. B

Round Seven – On the Buzzer
1. Betty Stove
2. France
3. Italian
4. Iker Casillas
5. Raymond Van Barneveld
6. Imola
7. Swimming
8. Switzerland
9. Jean Van de Velde
10. French
11. Bergamasco
12. Conchita Martinez
13. Cycling
14. Germany
15. Carolina Kluft
16. Netherlands
17. Costantino Rocca
18. Robert Kubica
19. Toulouse
20. Real Madrid

GAME 53

Round One – Opening Rally
1. Seve Ballesteros
2. Fred Couples
3. David Duval
4. Ernie Els
5. Nick Faldo
6. Bernhard Langer
7. Tom Lehman
8. Greg Norman
9. Nick Price
10. Vijay Singh
11. Tiger Woods
12. Ian Woosnam

Round Two – One Minute Round
1. England
2. 1997
3. Rugby Union
4. London
5. Wembley
6. Sailing
7. Argentina
8. Motor Cycling
9. Skiing
10. Swimming

Round Three – Mystery Guest
1. Denise Lewis
2. Roy Keane

Round Four – Home or Away
1. Robert Croft
2. Jason Gardener
3. Mikkel Kessler
4. Mario Andretti

Round Five – Captain's Away
1. The race was declared void
2. Yellow and Blue
3. Peter Hanson and Padraig Harrington
4. A

Round Six – Great Sporting Moments
1. John Barnes
2. Gary Sobers

Round Seven – On the Buzzer
1. Portsmouth
2. Pittsburgh Steelers
3. Gary Player
4. Manny Pacquiao
5. Pole Vault
6. Ricky Ponting
7. Michael Phelps
8. Poland
9. Papillon
10. Chris Paterson
11. Paris
12. John Parrott
13. Perpignan
14. Matthew Pinsent
15. Pakistan
16. Philadelphia Phillies
17. Mike Powell
18. Portugal
19. John Part
20. Phoenix Suns

GAME 54

Round One – Opening Rally
1. Algeria
2. Angola
3. Cameroon
4. Egypt
5. Ghana
6. Ivory Coast
7. Morocco
8. Nigeria
9. Senegal
10. South Africa
11. Togo
12. Tunisia

Round Two – One Minute Round
1. Barry McGuigan
2. Gillingham
3. Stewart Cink
4. Wicket Keeper
5. Turin
6. Tennis
7. Kenya
8. Golf

9.   Swimming
10. Motor Cycling

Round Three – Mystery Guest
1.   Matthew Pinsent
2.   Muttiah Muralitharan

Round Four – Home or Away
1.   Chris Gayle
2.   Davis Love III
3.   Toronto Blue Jays
4.   France

Round Five – Captain's Away
5.   Steve Williams
6.   Afghanistan
7.   Steven Gerrard and Robert Green
8.   B

Round Six – What Happened Next
1.   A
2.   C

Round Seven – On the Buzzer
1.   Sven Goran Eriksson
2.   Darts
3.   Ellen MacArthur
4.   Italy
5.   Goran Ivanisevic
6.   Ice Hockey
7.   Ronnie O'Sullivan
8.   Liverpool
9.   Audley Harrison
10. Edmonton
11. Ralf Schumacher
12. Martin Offiah
13. Modern Pentathlon
14. World Series
15. Yorkshire
16. Ireland
17. Retief Goosen
18. Australia
19. Baltimore
20. Ian Thorpe

GAME 55

Round One – Opening Rally
1. Ian Bell
2. Paul Collingwood
3. Andrew Flintoff
4. Ashley Giles
5. Steve Harmison
6. Matthew Hoggard
7. Geraint Jones
8. Simon Jones
9. Kevin Pietersen
10. Andrew Strauss
11. Marcus Trescothick
12. Michael Vaughan

Round Two – One Minute Round
1. Ireland
2. Cricket
3. Berlin
4. Ryder Cup
5. Novak Djokovic
6. Aussie Rules Football
7. Southampton
8. Cork
9. Monaghan
10. Mayo

Round Three – Mystery Guest
1. Jonah Lomu
2. Boris Becker

Round Four – Home or Away
1. Nwankwo Kanu
2. Leon Taylor
3. Sam Torrance
4. Dean Macey

Round Five – Captain's Away
1. It was for a world title
2. BBC Sports Personality of the Year
3. Peter Ebdon and Ronnie O'Sullivan
4. C

Round Six – What Happened Next
1. A
2. B

Round Seven – On the Buzzer
1.   Bernhard Langer
2.   Leeds United
3.   Brett Lee
4.   Ivan Lendl
5.   Lisbon
6.   Leicester Tigers
7.   Long Jump
8.   Niki Lauda
9.   Longchamp
10. Los Angeles Lakers
11. Paul Lawrie
12. Denise Lewis
13. Matt Le Tissier
14. Stephen Larkham
15. Sugar Ray Leonard
16. Leeds Rhinos
17. Leicestershire
18. Stephen Lee
19. Rod Laver
20. Los Angeles Dodgers

GAME 56

Round One – Opening Rally
1.   Nigel Bond
2.   Steve Davis
3.   Peter Ebdon
4.   Joe Johnson
5.   Shaun Murphy
6.   Ronnie O'Sullivan
7.   John Parrott
8.   Mark Selby
9.   John Spencer
10. Jimmy White

Round Two – One Minute Round
1.   Phoenix
2.   Lancashire
3.   USA
4.   Olympic Games
5.   Australian
6.   Oscar de la Hoya
7.   Southend United
8.   Cardigan
9.   Jackett
10. Capes

Round Three – Mystery Guest
1. Muhammad Ali
2. Makhaya Ntini

Round Four – Home or Away
1. Niall Quinn
2. Graham Gooch
3. Nathan Robertson
4. Jack Nicklaus

Round Five – Captain's Away
1. Bobsleigh
2. Detroit
3. England and West Indies
4. C

Round Six – What Happened Next
1. C
2. B

Round Seven – On the Buzzer
1. Paolo Maldini
2. Alastair Cook
3. France
4. Jamaica
5. Belgian
6. Joe Louis
7. Thomas Bjorn
8. Italy
9. China
10. Basketball
11. Jens Lehmann
12. Netherlands
13. Singapore
14. Japan
15. Jonathan Trott
16. John Higgins
17. USA
18. Niki Lauda
19. Skiing
20. AC Milan

GAME 57

Round One – Opening Rally
1. Scunthorpe United
2. Sheffield United

3.   Sheffield Wednesday
4.   Shrewsbury Town
5.   Southampton
6.   Southend United
7.   Stevenage Borough
8.   Stockport County
9.   Stoke City
10. Sunderland
11. Swansea City
12. Swindon Town

Round Two – One Minute Round
1.   Graeme McDowell
2.   Notts County
3.   Australian Open
4.   Duncan Fletcher
5.   Water Jump
6.   Ski Jumping
7.   Olivier Peslier
8.   Stove
9.   Ovens
10. Hobbs

Round Three – Mystery Guest
1.   Gary Lineker
2.   Annika Sorenstam

Round Four – Home or Away
1.   Mark Taylor
2.   Larry Holmes
3.   Mick Hill
4.   Jarno Trulli

Round Five – Captain's Away
1.   Involved in a four way playoff
2.   Chicago
3.   Nagano and Sapporo
4.   C

Round Six – Great Sporting Moments
1.   Jonny Wilkinson
2.   Ryan Giggs

Round Seven – On the Buzzer
1.   Australia
2.   Ian Woosnam
3.   France

4. George Foreman
5. Long jump
6. Michael Stich
7. Barcelona
8. Eric Bristow
9. Motorcycling
10. Martin Offiah
11. Michael Atherton
12. Ryder Cup
13. Nottingham Forest
14. Will Carling
15. John Parrott
16. Jo Durie
17. Miguel Indurain
18. Willie Carson
19. Liz McColgan
20. Michael Jordan

GAME 58

Round One – Opening Rally
1. Bantamweight
2. Featherweight
3. Flyweight
4. Heavyweight
5. Light Flyweight
6. Light Heavyweight
7. Light Welterweight
8. Lightweight
9. Middleweight
10. Welterweight

Round Two – One Minute Round
1. Sam Torrance
2. Manchester United
3. Surrey
4. Canoeing
5. Gloucester
6. Washington
7. Courtney Walsh
8. Almond
9. Brazil
10. Hazel

Round Three – Mystery Guest
1. Denis Law
2. Laura Davies

Round Four – Home or Away
1. Gary Kirsten
2. Ernie Els
3. Ken Doherty
4. Kevin and Tony Iro

Round Five – Captain's Away
1. Australia and New Zealand
2. Taking a hat trick
3. Philadelphia
4. C

Round Six – What Happened Next
1. C
2. B

Round Seven – On the Buzzer
1. Harlequins RL
2. Ian Wright
3. Alec Stewart
4. Tour de France
5. Albert Hall
6. Saracens
7. Jimmy White
8. Highbury
9. Yelena Isinbayeva
10. University Boat Race
11. Eric Bristow
12. London Marathon
13. Andrew Flintoff
14. Tottenham Hotspur
15. Lord's
16. New Jersey Nets
17. Alexandra Palace
18. Masters
19. Chelsea
20. Miami Dolphins

GAME 59

Round One – Opening Rally
1. Alec Bedser
2. Ian Botham
3. Andy Caddick
4. Andrew Flintoff
5. Darren Gough
6. Steve Harmison

7.   Matthew Hoggard
8.   John Snow
9.   Brian Statham
10. Fred Trueman
11. Derek Underwood
12. Bob Willis

Round Two – One Minute Round
1.   Snooker
2.   Glamorgan
3.   Oldham Athletic
4.   Bjorn Borg
5.   India
6.   James Degale
7.   Luke Donald
8.   Porter
9.   Nurse
10. Ward

Round Three – Mystery Guest
1.   Maurice Greene
2.   Steve Redgrave

Round Four – Home or Away
1.   Scot Gemmill
2.   Leroy Rivett
3.   Kimi Raikkonen
4.   Steve Parry

Round Five – Captain's Away
1.   Squash ball
2.   Atlanta
3.   Graham Onions and Jimmy Ormond
4.   A

Round Six – What Happened Next
1.   A
2.   B

Round Seven – On the Buzzer
1.   Arsenal
2.   Brian Lara
3.   Tiger Woods
4.   Scotland
5.   Phil Taylor
6.   Jerry Rice
7.   Fosbury Flop

8.   Neil Jenkins
9.   Jane Torvill and Christopher Dean
10. Lester Piggott
11. New York Yankees
12. Louis Saha
13. Ferrari
14. Nikolay Valuev
15. Florence Griffith-Joyner
16. Shaun Edwards
17. Basketball
18. Donald Bradman
19. Ole Gunnar Solskjaer
20. Decathlon

GAME 60

Round One – Opening Rally
1.   Arsenal
2.   Aston Villa
3.   Birmingham City
4.   Blackburn Rovers
5.   Chelsea
6.   Leicester City
7.   Liverpool
8.   Manchester United
9.   Middlesbrough
10. Tottenham Hotspur

Round Two – One Minute Round
1.   Belfast
2.   Jose Maria Olazabal
3.   Yellow
4.   Anfield
5.   Laura Robson
6.   Snowboarding
7.   Huddersfield Giants
8.   Chalk
9.   Teacher
10. Book

Round Three – Mystery Guest
1.   Steve Waugh
2.   Sebastian Coe

Round Four – Home or Away
1.   Kenya
2.   Darren Lockyer

3. Shot Put
4. Vitaly Petrov

Round Five – Captain's Away
1. Ivan Lendl
2. Sub fielder that ran out Ricky Ponting
3. Dallas Stars and Detroit Redwings
4. C

Round Six – What Happened Next
1. B
2. B

Round Seven – On the Buzzer
1. Chris Gayle
2. Colin Montgomerie
3. Arsenal
4. Fernando Alonso
5. Lleyton Hewitt
6. Wales
7. Jeremy Wariner
8. Zara Phillips
9. Lesley Vainikolo
10. Beth Tweddle
11. Michael Vaughan
12. Andy Murray
13. Michael Campbell
14. Liverpool
15. Asafa Powell
16. Ruby Walsh
17. Amir Khan
18. Shaun Murphy
19. Chicago White Sox
20. Glenn McGrath